ALERT!
PERILOUS
TIMES

ALERT! PERILOUS TIMES

A PREPPER'S GUIDE TO THE LAST DAYS

JAMES A. DURHAM

DESTINY IMAGE® PUBLISHERS, INC.
P.O. Box 310, Shippensburg, PA 17257-0310
"Promoting Inspired Lives."

This book and all other Destiny Image and Destiny Image Fiction books are available at Christian bookstores and distributors worldwide.

For more information on foreign distributors, call 717-532-3040.

Or reach us on the Internet: www.destinyimage.com

ISBN 13: TP 978-0-7684-5830-5

ISBN 13 EBook: 978-0-7684-5831-2

HC ISBN: 978-0-7684-5833-6

LP ISBN: 978-0-7684-5832-9

For Worldwide Distribution.

1 2 3 4 5 6 7 8 9 10 11 /23 22 21 20

But know this, that in the last days perilous times will come: (2 Timothy 3:1)

TABLE OF CONTENTS

ACKNOWLEDGEMENTS

This book came as a gift from the Lord. The primary revelation for this book came more quickly than in any of my previous writings. I believe this book is a prophetic work releasing a word from the Lord about the urgency of preparing for perilous times and learning to stay alert and on watch. I am grateful to Jim Lamb, a member of our Board of Ministry, for releasing a prophetic word he received from the Lord telling me to write this book and to my wife Gloria for confirming it with her own testimony. I am also grateful beyond mere words for Gloria's help in editing this book and checking the accuracy of the scriptural references. I also want to acknowledge my daughter, Michelle, who consistently urged me to continue to write the book.

INTRODUCTION

Over a period of several days, I received a series of related visions. The content of these visions was very clear to me at that time, but I didn't understand what I was to do with these revelations until later. In each of these visions, I was shown people packing for a trip. They didn't appear to be packing for ordinary circumstances. They seemed to be rushed and anxious about their travels. I soon came to realize that each of these families was preparing to move to a safer place during troubling times. In military terminology, they were "bugging out." This may sound odd at first, but they appeared to be both prepared and unprepared at the same time. They had lists of the things they wanted to take and paused to check them over and over. They were making sure they had all they needed. At the same time, I was aware they were very concerned that they might be missing something.

In each vision, these people suddenly remembered an infant child in another room. Filled with embarrassment, they quickly went to the nursery to get their baby. In each family, one of the parents placed the child in a special backpack for carrying an infant. Everything they needed to gather appeared to be complete. Then I heard the Lord say, "Don't forget to take the Holy Spirit with you!" This was part of the unpreparedness of each family. The Holy Spirit was not on the checklist for their "bug out bag." Each family quickly welcomed the Spirit of the Lord, and then moved out in faith with their meager belongings.

This series of visions began with the Lord showing me several openings into Heaven. I call these "open portals." In each of the openings, I saw many dark clouds, which appeared to be moving back and forth in front of each portal. I received this as a prophetic warning about the enemy's attempt to block the Lord's people from seeing and experiencing an Open Heaven when they need it most. As I continued to focus my spiritual eyes on the open portals, I heard the Lord saying, "Do not let worry, fears, or challenges block your view of the Open Heaven." Afterward, as I was reading the Word of God, I suddenly came on the following Scripture:

> *Oh, that You would rend the heavens! That You would come down! That the mountains might shake at Your presence—as fire burns brushwood, as fire causes water to boil—to make Your name known to Your adversaries, that the nations may tremble at Your presence! When You did awesome things for which we did not look, You came down, the mountains shook at Your presence. For since the beginning of the world men have not heard nor perceived by the ear, nor has the eye seen any God besides You, Who acts for the one who waits for Him.*
> (Isaiah 64:1-4)

This passage touched my heart and became my prayer as well. Have you prayed something like this? Have you cried out to the Lord to rip heaven open and come down to you in your hour of need? I know I have prayed this many times. Did the Lord open the heavens for me and come down? Normally my answer to this question would be "Yes!" However, on one occasion I was praying for the Lord to come down and fix the evil circumstances in our world when I clearly heard Him say, "No! I have already done that. Now it is your turn to make things happen." You see, He has already torn the Heavens open and descended into our world to finish a work on our behalf. Look at the passage below and begin to rejoice that He has already answered your prayer and given you the desires of your heart.

> *At that time Jesus came from Nazareth in Galilee and was baptized by John in the Jordan. As Jesus was coming up out of the water, he saw heaven being torn open and the Spirit descending on him like a dove. And a voice came from heaven: "You are my Son, whom I love; with you I am well pleased."* (Mark 1:9-11)

In the visions of the Lord, I continued to look at those open portals into Heaven. The dark clouds were still moving to obscure the openings and block my sight. It was then that I heard the Lord make a series of decrees. "Do not get discouraged! Do not give up! Do not quit! All these things which seem to block your view of the Open Heaven are a deception. Do not believe them. Believe me! Believe my Word! Heaven is always open." I received these decrees and promises as a word from the Lord for you also. Don't let the enemy block your ability to see in the spiritual realm. Do not let dark clouds of hardship, suffering, grief, or persecution obscure your ability to experience the open heavens provided by the Lord. Don't give up when your victory is close at hand.

As I continued to watch these families rushing to gather things they would need, I thought about what the Lord was saying. We may need to move quickly in the last days when seasons of tribulation come upon us, but we must not get into fear. Remember 2 Timothy 1:7, "*For God has not given us a*

spirit of fear, but of power and of love and of a sound mind."
We must not be discouraged or allow ourselves to give up
hope. The Lord is with us in all things and for all time. Trust
in Him and you will not be disappointed.

The final vision in this series began with me seeing a large
plate full of food being placed in my hands. At first, I was
only seeing the plate of food, but as I began to look around
I saw something wonderful. I was filled with joy to see that
we were in a large banquet room in Heaven. Tables were set,
the food was prepared and the guests were arriving for the
great wedding feast of the Lamb. I was filled with joy as I
received this awesome word of encouragement. How about
you? Remember and believe what John wrote in Revelation
19:9, "*Then he said to me, 'Write: Blessed are those who are
called to the marriage supper of the Lamb!' And he said to
me, 'These are the true sayings of God.'*"

Times of tribulation will not be the end of your story if
you are a born again disciple of Jesus Christ. You will not
end with failure or defeat. The victory has already been won.
You are in the winner's circle. You are an overcomer! You are
standing on the promises of Jesus which shall never fail you.
You have everything to live for and you will never die. You
have eternal life. You will join with the saints of all time to
proclaim together your victory in Jesus. Remember how John
described it in the book of Revelation.

> *Then I heard a loud voice saying in heaven,
> "Now salvation, and strength, and the kingdom
> of our God, and the power of His Christ have
> come, for the accuser of our brethren, who
> accused them before our God day and night,
> has been cast down. And they overcame him by
> the blood of the Lamb and by the word of their
> testimony, and they did not love their lives to
> the death.* (Revelation 12:10-11)

As I continued to ponder these things, I received a prophetic word from Jim Lamb, a member of our Board of Ministry. He said that he had a very strong inclination from the Lord that I was supposed to write a spiritual prepper book for the end times. My wife, Gloria, quickly added that she had the same understanding from the Lord. I didn't make an immediate commitment to write this book. That night I woke up slightly after midnight with a terrible headache. I got up and turned on my computer waiting for the headache to subside. In the next two hours I outlined most of this book, which included many of the passages from the Bible used in the following pages. Finally, the headache was gone, and I went back to sleep and dreamed the content of two more chapters, which I added to this text when I awoke from my sleep. Have you awakened from your sleep? Are you hearing the Lord calling you to get ready and stay alert? Is the Lord opening your eyes as if from sleep so that you can understand what Yeshua ha Messiach taught about the coming end of the age?

A few days later, as I pushed my cart through a large discount store, my eyes were drawn to one particular magazine on a shelf full of many others. It was a magazine for "preppers." I didn't read the magazine, but looked closely at the cover. Many pictures were put together in a collage depicting various scenarios of possible future chaos and tribulation. I saw pictures of weapons people would use for self-defense. Various kinds of foods were labeled to indicate their potential use in survival or emergency situations. An article for building a survival shelter was also highlighted on the cover. I looked, but didn't see any reference to spiritual readiness. It occurred to me that there are more than enough books, magazines and articles available in stores and on the internet about physical preparedness, but not enough on spiritual and mental readiness.

One of the things the Lord made clear to me in the visions and revelations mentioned above is that we must prepare in spirit, soul and body. Many people are preparing in the natural and trying to meet all their physical needs in the troubled times to come. This is good, but it doesn't go far enough. I remembered Jesus' instructions to the disciples to have a weapon: *"Then He said to them, 'But now, he who has a money bag, let him take it, and likewise a knapsack; and he who has no sword, let him sell his garment and buy one. For I say to you that this which is written must still be accomplished in Me: 'And He was numbered with the transgressors.' For the things concerning Me have an end.' So they said, 'Lord, look, here are two swords.' And He said to them, 'It is enough.'"* (Luke 22:36-38). I understood the Lord to be saying, it is good to be physically prepared, but don't overdo it. It is time to train and strengthen yourself to develop mental toughness and spiritual resilience.

The last days will be extremely challenging for everyone to include the most committed disciples of Yeshua ha Messiach. To be prepared for the coming days of trouble and tribulation we must become both mentally strong and spiritually capable of maintaining an unshakable resolve to stand with the Lord. In other words, we must be strong in spirit, soul and body in order to have the endurance and resolve to not only survive but to thrive in these coming hard times and threatening situations. Much of what I received from the Lord was about these two aspects of being a spiritual prepper. Are you mentally tough enough to serve the Lord faithfully in the end times? Are you spiritually strong enough to remain faithful even unto death? Each of us needs to make an honest assessment of our readiness, and begin now to train up and prepare for the coming "Day of the Lord." This is what the remainder of this book is about.

CHAPTER ONE
GETTING READY

But know this, that in the last days perilous times will come: For men will be lovers of themselves, lovers of money, boasters, proud, blasphemers, disobedient to parents, unthankful, unholy, unloving, unforgiving, slanderers, without self-control, brutal, despisers of good, traitors, headstrong, haughty, lovers of pleasure rather than lovers of God, having a form of godliness but denying its power. And from such people turn away! (2 Timothy 3:1-5)

One of the lessons I learned in the military is that everyone has a difficult time staying alert when there is no perceived imminent threat. Everyone who has been asked to stand guard during peacetime will understand what I am talking about. There are so many stories about the difficulty soldiers have staying awake and alert when they are unaware of a real threat. Guards at the gates tend to get slack over time, and it is necessary for their leaders to constantly teach and evaluate in order to keep them focused and alert.

After a series of terrorist attacks effecting Americans around the World, security was much more intense on the installation where I was assigned. A large gathering of security specialists from many nations was meeting on our installation to establish a plan to protect our people around the world. At the same time, those of us in ministry were preparing for the Christmas season. I had been selected to play one of the three wise men in the Christmas pageant. A professional makeup artist had been hired to make us look as realistic as possible. The costumes were also carefully chosen for authenticity. That Sunday morning, I was in the pageant on two separate parts of the installation, which meant that I had to exit one gate and enter another to get to the first location and reverse the pattern on the way back.

As I entered the main post on my return trip, a security guard had stopped a family on the way to chapel services and was carefully searching the vehicle and each person in it. I had very little time to get to the next service and wondered how long it would take me to get through considering how I was dressed. The guard finally allowed the family to pass and it was my turn. He simply waved me through without asking any questions. As I gratefully passed the guard knowing I could arrive on time at the chapel, several thoughts went through my mind about passing so easily through the gate when security was so tight. I wondered if we were really prepared. I wondered who would watch over our safety and security. Think about it. Who has your back and is watching over you during these last days.

Staying awake and alert is difficult. This is still a problem today for otherwise faithful disciples who have grown weary waiting for the prophesied "Day of the Lord." Many do not want to hear about it anymore. They have lost their belief that it may happen during their time on watch. How about you? Have you grown weary waiting? Have you lost your zeal to be found ready on the coming Day of the Lord? Have you gotten tired of lessons on Biblical Prophecy, because you haven't seen any of the signs occurring? If you are struggling with staying alert, it is time to listen again to what Jesus is saying to you in Matthew 26:40-41, *"What! Could you not watch with Me one hour? Watch and pray, lest you enter into temptation. The spirit indeed is willing, but the flesh is weak."*

This is the reason the Lord has to keep reminding us that perilous times are coming, and we must stay alert and pray lest we get caught up unprepared in the disastrous events about to unfold. Through the prophets of old He warned of what is to come. As you consider the message delivered by Zephaniah in the passage below, can you feel the urgency once again? Is the Lord waking you up and challenging you to move up to a greater level of awareness? Are you being inspired to be more diligent in your preparations? Unfortunately, most people only wake up for a few moments and then fall asleep again as the disciples did in the garden while Yeshua prayed.

> *The great day of the Lord is near; it is near and hastens quickly. The noise of the day of the Lord is bitter; there the mighty men shall cry out. That day is a day of wrath, a day of trouble and distress, a day of devastation and desolation, a day of darkness and gloominess, a day of clouds and thick darkness, a day of trumpet and alarm against the fortified cities and against the high towers.* (Zephaniah 1:14-16)

When the Lord pressed upon me the need to write this book and awaken His people again, I found myself asleep like those before me as well as those around me. That is my confession. I believe we need to be very honest in this season if we are going to be able to accept the changes the Lord is challenging us to make. Make an honest assessment of your own situation. Don't get defensive or ignore the warning signs in your own spiritual walk with the Lord. This is the time to hear Him say again through the words of the Apostle Paul:

Therefore He says: "Awake, you who sleep, arise from the dead, and Christ will give you light. See then that you walk circumspectly, not as fools but as wise, redeeming the time, because the days are evil. Therefore do not be unwise, but understand what the will of the Lord is. And do not be drunk with wine, in which is dissipation; but be filled with the Spirit, speaking to one another in psalms and hymns and spiritual songs, singing and making melody in your heart to the Lord, giving thanks always for all things to God the Father in the name of our Lord Jesus Christ, submitting to one another in the fear of God." (Ephesians 5:14-21)

What can we do to prepare for the day of the Lord? The prophet Zephaniah received some advice directly from the Lord to answer this question. The season we are in now is first and foremost a time for spiritual preparation. Many people today are focused on physical preparations. Many are promoting things like stocking up on emergency food supplies, building shelters in safe locations and gathering supplies and weapons to support and protect themselves and their loved ones. I am not criticizing any of these actions. I am simply reporting what the Lord placed on my heart. The most important preparations are those which will give us spiritual resilience and tough mindedness along with an understanding of how to operate in the spiritual gift of discernment. Listen to the Word of the Lord given through the prophet Zephaniah:

Before the decree brings forth, before the day passes as the chaff, before the fierce anger of the Lord comes upon you, before the Day of the Lord's anger comes upon you! Seek the Lord, all you humble of the earth who have done His

> *ordinance. Seek righteousness! Seek humility!*
> *It may be you will be hidden on the Day of*
> *the Lord's anger.* (Zephaniah 2:2-3, ONMB)

In this passage, the Lord declared three critically important aspects for developing spiritual and mental readiness. The most important is to *"Seek the Lord."* Without the strength gained through an intimate relationship with the Lord all else is likely to fail. Now is the time to seek Him with all your heart and soul. Now is the time to walk with Him and let Him teach you what you need to know to survive in the perilous time which will soon come upon the earth. In many ways I have become convinced that we are already living in these days. Have you sensed that as well? The times are perilous and the only covering which will adequately protect us is the blood of Yeshua ha Messiach.

The second directive for our spiritual preparedness is to "Seek righteousness!" This is not a very popular topic today, because for some people it conjures up memories of criticisms released by some seemingly "self-righteous" person. Nothing could be further from the true meaning of this directive. Biblical righteousness has to do with developing a right relationship with the Lord. Self-righteousness will block and possibly prevent us from getting right with the Lord. His command to us is to love one another as He has loved us and even be willing to give our life for others.

The key to seeking righteousness is found in the third directive given through Zephaniah: "Seek humility!" Self-righteousness is rooted in pride and self-centeredness. True Biblical righteousness emerges through those who are truly humble before the Lord and who are willing to serve others in obedience to the Lord. Remember the promise in James 4:6, *"But He gives more grace. Therefore He says: 'God resists the proud, but gives grace to the humble.'"* Could you use more grace? Do you long for greater intimacy with the Lord? Now is the time to humbly draw near to Him, because He is ready and willing to draw near to you.

The Lord always leaves us with a message of hope. In the passage above, the prophet gives a glimmer of hope in the concluding part of this passage: "*It may be you will be hidden on the Day of the Lord's anger.*" The Lord wants us to know that these perilous times will come. He wants us to know that He will be there for us. In the midst of the worst of times, we can experience the blessing and favor of the Lord. This message is consistent throughout the scriptures. The New Testament culminates with powerful prophetic messages given to the Apostle John in a direct revelation from the Lord. Are you heeding these warnings?

> *For they are spirits of demons, performing signs, which go out to the kings of the earth and of the whole world, to gather them to the battle of that great day of God Almighty. "Behold, I am coming as a thief. Blessed is he who watches, and keeps his garments, lest he walk naked and they see his shame."* (Revelation 16:14-15)

The perilous times to come will be filled with demonic spirits working to deceive the leaders of this age and draw everyone into cataclysmic warfare and great suffering. The Lord does not want His followers to be deceived as so many will be. Ahead of the manifestation of these things, He is calling us to wake up, understand the times and remain watchful and alert. The calling He placed on me to release the messages of this book were given to help you prepare for these coming events. He gave me a confirmation of this one morning not long after telling me to write this down for you. In the next few paragraphs I will share with you the message I received.

Early one morning I received a confirmation that the Lord is giving me revelation and visions for a new book I am writing, "Alert: Perilous Times: A Prepper's Guide to the Last Days." I am not writing about gathering food, building hidden dwellings or preparing defensive tools as many others have already written these things. I am writing about the spiritual preparations we need to make to be ready for what is coming in what the Bible calls "the last days." Actually, the Lord began to answer my prayer the day before I lifted it up to Him. The Lord's help began with the visions and revelations which came to me yesterday.

I was becoming more and more aware that I needed to get into better physical condition. At the beginning of my worship time, I did some exercises as I sang many of my usual praise and worship songs. Then I put on my large Tallit and Kippah as I got on my knees to pray. I began by praying for Shalom in Jerusalem and all of Israel. Then I prayed the James 4:7 prayer, which I personalized as follows: "Father God I submit to you. All I have and all I ever will have I submit to you. All I am and all I ever will be I submit to you. I resist the Devil and in accordance with your word and in the mighty name of Yeshua ha Messiach he has no choice but to flee and take all his works with Him in Yeshua's Name. Amen and Amen!" After praying the James 4:7 prayer, I went face down and prayed in the Spirit for several minutes. I confessed that I needed help writing this new book, and asked for the Spirit of wisdom and revelation, counsel and might, understanding and the fear of the Lord to come to me and release what I needed to know and understand (see Isaiah 11:2). As I was writing down the things the Lord revealed to me, I looked up this passage from Isaiah and was then led by the Holy Spirit to the next three verses:

> *His delight is in the fear of the Lord, and He shall*
> *not judge by the sight of His eyes, nor decide*
> *by the hearing of His ears; but with righteous-*
> *ness He shall judge the poor, and decide with*

equity for the meek of the earth; He shall strike the earth with the rod of His mouth, and with the breath of His lips He shall slay the wicked. Righteousness shall be the belt of His loins, and faithfulness the belt of His waist. (Isaiah 11:3-5)

Suddenly, I had another open vision in which I was shown an ancient machine using belts and pulleys to do some kind of heavy work. I was fascinated by the machine and thought about the high level of technology given to the people who built this machine in ancient times. Then the Holy Spirit revealed the message to go with this vision. A time is coming when all our technology and tools based on the use of electricity and fossil fuels will come to an end. In that day, we will need to go back to the use of or perhaps re-invent the kinds of machines I was seeing this morning. Our dependency on the power grid to run all our devices will soon prove to be useless. Now is a season to learn as much as we can about the ways our ancestors accomplished difficult tasks and provided food for themselves and their families.

As I pondered these things, I was given another vision. I saw a desolated area where many tools were rusted beyond restoration. I was reminded of Daniel 9:26, *"And after the sixty-two weeks Messiah shall be cut off, but not for Himself; and the people of the prince who is to come shall destroy the city and the sanctuary. The end of it shall be with a flood, and till the end of the war desolations are determined."* In the vision, it appeared that a great fire had swept through the area and melted many tools together so they were no longer usable. I saw piles of computers and smart phones which no longer worked. They were in fairly good condition, but could not be used because there was no power to run them and there was no internet to access for connections. I was led to understand that all these electronic devices will be useless and unavailable for those who live through these times of tribulation. How will people who have built such a dependency on these things survive without them?

I wondered if the things I was shown were only about the natural world or if they also had a meaning in the spiritual realm. The Lord told me that the visions and revelations were for both the present and the future. We will need to cast off many things which have been useful and convenient in our belief systems. Many of the things held dear by the church and many believers today are based on the doctrines of man rather than on the Word of God. None of these things will be of any use in the season to come as the end draws near. Spiritual preppers will plan ahead to learn the ways of the Lord and be totally committed to following Him closely during this coming season. This is the only way to survive and thrive during the perilous times to come. I was reminded of what Paul wrote to his spiritual son, Timothy, about the times we will soon face. Pause and meditate on these things as you study it again.

> *But know this, that in the last days perilous times will come: For men will be lovers of themselves, lovers of money, boasters, proud, blasphemers, disobedient to parents, unthankful, unholy, unloving, unforgiving, slanderers, without self-control, brutal, despisers of good, traitors, headstrong, haughty, lovers of pleasure rather than lovers of God, having a form of godliness but denying its power. And from such people turn away! For of this sort are those who creep into households and make captives of gullible women loaded down with sins, led away by various lusts, always learning and never able to come to the knowledge of the truth. (2 Timothy 3:1-7)*

Are you a spiritual prepper? Are you getting ready for the times of desolation to come? Have you cast off the doctrines of man so you can focus on the Word of God? Are you feeling what I am feeling – that we are drawing perilously close to these days? I encourage you to prepare now for the things to come. Be spiritually ready to serve the Lord faithfully and to walk in divine health during these last days. Be ready in spirit, soul and body. I pray that the Lord will reveal to you all you need to know about the times to come and to understand how He is calling you to serve in this generation. I pray these things in the mighty name of Yeshua ha Messiach! Amen and Amen! If you really want to be ready, listen to the teachings of Yeshua. The four gospels have an exceptionally large amount of His teachings on prepping for the times to come. It is fixed and certain that these times will appear. The question is: Are you ready?

> *Let your waist be girded and your lamps burning; and you yourselves be like men who wait for their master, when he will return from the wedding, that when he comes and knocks they may open to him immediately. Blessed are those servants whom the master, when he comes, will find watching. Assuredly, I say to you that he will gird himself and have them sit down to eat, and will come and serve them. And if he should come in the second watch, or come in the third watch, and find them so, blessed are those servants. But know this, that if the master of the house had known what hour the thief would come, he would have watched and not allowed his house to be broken into. Therefore you also be ready, for the Son of Man is coming at an hour you do not expect."* (Luke 12:35-40)

RECOGNIZE THE URGENCY

Staying alert and watching are two parts of our spiritual journey, which have proven to be very difficult for us. Jesus told His sleepy disciples: "The spirit is willing, but the flesh is weak." This word from the Lord is also for you and me. The truth is: we tend to grow weary watching. We cannot help it as long as we live in the flesh. This is why it is so important for us to build up our mental toughness and spiritual resilience now. Paul challenges us in Galatians 6:9, "*And let us not grow weary while doing good, for in due season we shall reap if we do not lose heart.*" Claim this promise for yourself right now. Those who remain alert and watchful will reap a reward in due season. Amen?

In the military, leaders came up with a way to help soldiers on guard duty stay awake and alert. They designated someone as the sergeant of the guard to make surprise visits on the soldiers. If he/she finds them sleeping on duty, they will be required to pay a heavy price. Fear of these surprise visits has motivated many sleepy soldiers to stay awake and remain alert. There is a message similar to this from the Bible. We are reminded over and over that time is short. We are reminded that the Lord will be coming soon. Those awake and alert will be rewarded. Those who have fallen asleep may have to pay a heavy price for their failure to obey the Lord. Near the end of the Bible we are reminded once more of the season to come.

> *And another angel came out of the temple, crying with a loud voice to Him who sat on the cloud, "Thrust in Your sickle and reap, for the time has come for You to reap, for the harvest of the earth is ripe." So He who sat on the cloud thrust in His sickle on the earth, and the earth was reaped.* (Revelation 14:15-16)

READINESS REQUIRES A PLAN

Prepare yourself and be ready, you and all your companies that are gathered about you; and be a guard for them. After many days you will be visited. (Ezekiel 38:7-8a)

Another lesson I learned in almost 35 years of military service is that success depends on developing detailed plans for every operation. This is a difficult process for many people to learn and a challenge for others to teach. The problem is that the promised benefits have been deferred to a later time, and these promises have been given to a generation desiring instant results. People prefer tasks which yield immediate rewards. Unfortunately it will not be like this during the last days. People who do not rise to this challenge are doomed to constantly experience things they are completely unprepared to handle.

Do you have a plan? More specifically, do you have a plan for dealing with the perilous times coming at the end of the age? Have you considered the challenges, evaluated the risks and calculated the cost? Have you compared your resources, all your friendly forces and your natural and supernatural capabilities with those of the opposing forces? Most people resist this kind of process, however the Lord long ago taught us to do this very thing. Consider what Yeshua said to the multitudes of people who followed Him:

> *Or what king, going to make war against another king, does not sit down first and consider whether he is able with ten thousand to meet him who comes against him with twenty thousand? (Luke 14:31)*

Many believers make the age old mistake of failing to prepare. Some believe everything they need will be provided at the last minute by the Holy Spirit. I admit that this may happen, but one thing I learned during over 50 years of ministry is that the Holy Spirit does not reward laziness. My experience has been that He is so good and faithful to provide after I have done the part assigned to me. He is so good that He often provides "*exceedingly abundantly above all that we ask or think, according to the power that works in us*, (Ephesians 3:20) The Apostle Paul understood the faithfulness of the Lord when he wrote the passage below to the Corinthian church. Notice that he is not telling us to make our plans "*according to the flesh*" (worldly wisdom), but with the wisdom of God released to those who follow Him.

> *Therefore, when I was planning this, did I do it lightly? Or the things I plan, do I plan according to the flesh, that with me there should be Yes, Yes, and No, No? But as God is faithful, our word to you was not Yes and No.* (2 Corinthians 1:17-18)

Here is an additional thought. We are created in the image of God, and as such we should expect to do the same things He does (within limitations of course). One thing the Lord does is to make plans and follow them. The Apostle Paul referred to this attribute of the Lord in the passage below. Everything about our salvation along with His will and purpose are part of a master plan. When we follow His plan, we are destined for success. When we decide not to follow His plan problems soon arise. A part of how we succeed is to make careful and detailed plans for our part of His work. We are most successful when we do this under the guidance of the Holy Spirit.

> *In him we were also chosen, having been pre-destined according to the plan of him who works*

*out everything in conformity with the purpose
of his will, in order that we, who were the first
to hope in Christ, might be for the praise of his
glory.* (Ephesians 1:11-12, NIV)

READINESS REQUIRES TRAINING

The important first step is to have a Spirit led plan in place for dealing with the perilous times coming in the last days, but we need to go further. The military provides another great example. People are trained for their specific role in an operation. A part of this training is to practice your actions over and over until they become second nature. All the skills you will employ in an operation are practiced until they become a matter of muscle memory. If you do not reach this level of readiness, you will have great difficulty making correct choices and doing precise movements at the necessary moment. The Lord made a plan for this and shared it with us.

*And He Himself gave some to be apostles, some
prophets, some evangelists, and some pastors
and teachers, for the equipping of the saints for
the work of ministry, for the edifying of the body
of Christ,* (Ephesians 4:11-12)

In recent months I have been in contact with numerous people who appear to believe we should all be evangelists. They maintain that every action of the church is to win souls for the kingdom. First, I want to say that winning souls is a very important part of our work for the Lord. At the same time, it is important to remember that some additional things need to be done to increase our effectiveness in the harvest. We need to have apostles who study the Word of God and teach others their appropriate roles. We need prophets who hear from the Lord and keep us focused on His mission and purpose. We need pastors who minister to the people and help to restore the injured so they are able to return to their mission fields. We need teachers who work to insure that each laborer in the harvest has the proper understanding of the Lord's work, purpose and plan.

I have found that in each of these five offices of ministry there are individuals who believe their specific office of ministry is the only appropriate way to serve the Lord. People who believe this way are ill informed and in need of more training to stay focused on their part of the mission. The Lord's plan is based on an understanding that all five offices of ministry are needed to achieve the dual purpose Paul revealed to the Ephesian church: *"the equipping of the saints for the work of ministry, for the edifying of the body of Christ,"* In this season as I have been preparing to write this book, the Lord has told me over and over that this is a time for teachers to arise and speak the Lord's truth in love. Too many people are speaking their own understanding of truth with too little love. Consider again what Paul wrote to His spiritual son, Timothy.

> *Have nothing to do with godless myths and old wives' tales; rather, train yourself to be godly. For physical training is of some value, but godliness has value for all things, holding promise for both the present life and the life to come.* (1 Timothy 4:7-8, NIV)

READINESS REQUIRES PRACTICE

There is an old Vaudeville joke which asks the question: "How do you get to Carnegie Hall?" The surprising answer to a question asking for directions is: "Practice, practice, practice." Another old adage is "practice makes perfect." All of these old teachings point to one primary fact. You do not improve and stay sharp at any skill unless you discipline yourself to stay in practice. Are you practicing your plan for dealing with the perilous times ahead? As I searched the scriptures for passages referring to practice, I found that most of them make reference to problems arising because people practice the wrong things.

These Biblical teachings given to a previous generation are also instructive for us. In this instance, we need to evaluate ourselves and find out if we are practicing things contrary to the will and purpose of the Lord. To become ready to properly deal with the challenges of the last days, we need to be free from these practices. I recommend that you do as I did and spend time on a Biblical search for teachings about the need for practicing the right things. As you do this, take note of all those things which displease the Lord; those things which are contrary to His Word. Then make a plan to stop practicing those things.

Next take note of the things we are instructed in the Word of God to practice. Begin now to spend time regularly practicing the good things and the holy things you find during your search. It is not too late to start. Now is a good time to begin. To aid you in your search, I have listed several of the things we need to be practicing right now. Add these things to your plan and strengthen your readiness for the perilous times.

> *In this the children of God and the children of the devil are manifest: Whoever does not practice righteousness is not of God, nor is he who does not love his brother.* (1 John 3:10)

> *Whatever you have learned or received or heard from me, or seen in me—put it into practice. And the God of peace will be with you.* (Philippians 4:9, NIV)

He replied, "My mother and brothers are those who hear God's word and put it into practice." (Luke 8:21, NIV)

Therefore everyone who hears these words of mine and puts them into practice is like a wise man who built his house on the rock. (Matthew 7:24, NIV)

Train up a child in the way he should go, and when he is old he will not depart from it. (Proverbs 22:6)

Have nothing to do with godless myths and old wives' tales; rather, train yourself to be godly. (1 Timothy 4:7, NIV)

He trains my hands for battle; my arms can bend a bow of bronze. (Psalm 18:34, NIV)

I believe we are already living in the early stages of the perilous times Paul warned Timothy to watch for. For too long the church has acted as if we have lots of time to prepare. Some teachers have mistakenly led many people to believe they have plenty of time to get ready. This is a false teaching which will lull the people of God into falling asleep when they need most to be awake. Time is short. Be ready now. I believe the Apostle John is in agreement about the urgency of being ready now. In 1 John 2:18 he tells us that almost two thousand years ago they were in the last hour: "*Little children, it is the last hour; and as you have heard that the Antichrist is coming, even now many antichrists have come, by which we know that it is the last hour.* I often ask myself and others: If it was the "*last hour*" when John wrote this, what is it now? Perhaps we are living in the last five minutes before Messiah returns.

Are you ready? Do you have a plan? Are you practicing your plan? These are important questions for every serious spiritual prepper.

SPEND YOUR TIME WISELY

Don't spend your time calculating the day or hour when these things will occur. You will never be able to figure this out; especially with your natural wisdom and reason. Even Yeshua didn't know the dates and times of these things. In the passage below, study His teaching and make the wise decision to obey His Word. Spend your time in getting ready, staying alert and watching for his sudden appearance. In the past, the great men and women of the Bible were only prepared for perilous times as they obediently followed what the Lord told them to do. Continuously seek the wisdom of the Lord if you plan to be properly prepared for the coming perilous times.

> *But of that day and hour no one knows, not even the angels of heaven, but My Father only. But as the days of Noah were, so also will the coming of the Son of Man be. For as in the days before the flood, they were eating and drinking, marrying and giving in marriage, until the day that Noah entered the ark, and did not know until the flood came and took them all away, so also will the coming of the Son of Man be. Then two men will be in the field: one will be taken and the other left. Two women will be grinding at the mill: one will be taken and the other left. Watch therefore, for you do not know what hour your Lord is coming. But know this, that if the master of the house had known what hour the thief would come, he would have watched and not allowed his house to be broken into. Therefore you also*

be ready, for the Son of Man is coming at an hour you do not expect. (Matthew 24:36-44)

There is good news in the midst of all these warnings about the coming perilous times. The Lord will always protect and defend His own. He made a promise and He will keep it. One instance of this promise is found in Matthew 28:20b: *"and lo, I am with you always, even to the end of the age. Amen (truly);"* You can count on all the promises of Yeshua. You can trust that He will do what He said He will do. One very important thing to do during our time of preparation is to study again His promises, and speak them over and over until they take strong root in our hearts.

DO NOT GET INTO FEAR

Please be aware that Yeshua did not teach these things to give us fear. His teachings were given to assure us that He will make it right for us in the last days. Don't be afraid of what the world will do. Fear (holy awe) the Lord and you don't have to fear man. Take hold of His promises and stand on them. Look again at what He promised in Matthew chapter twenty four. Note especially the promise that His angels will *"gather together His elect from the four winds, from one end of heaven to the other."*

> *Immediately after the tribulation of those days the sun will be darkened, and the moon will not give its light; the stars will fall from heaven, and the powers of the heavens will be shaken. Then the sign of the Son of Man will appear in heaven, and then all the tribes of the earth will mourn, and they will see the Son of Man coming on the clouds of heaven with power and great glory. And He will send His angels with a*

great sound of a trumpet, and they will gather together His elect from the four winds, from one end of heaven to the other. (Matthew 24:29-31)

As he carefully considered the times and seasons, Paul was led to release a charge which applies to all believers. I want to conclude this chapter by releasing this charge to you once again. I believe that every promise and directive of the Bible has been handed down to this age because it is for us. I accept the charge and now it is your turn to decide for yourself. Time is short and you need to redeem the time. Make your decision to follow Yeshua right now and never depart from it. Accept the charge Paul gave to his spiritual son Timothy and make it your own today!

I charge you therefore before God and the Lord Jesus Christ, who will judge the living and the dead at His appearing and His kingdom: Preach the word! Be ready in season and out of season. Convince, rebuke, exhort, with all longsuffering and teaching. For the time will come when they will not endure sound doctrine, but according to their own desires, because they have itching ears, they will heap up for themselves teachers; and they will turn their ears away from the truth, and be turned aside to fables. But you be watchful in all things, endure afflictions, do the work of an evangelist, fulfill your ministry. (2 Timothy 4:1-5)

PART ONE
BUILDING MENTAL TOUGHNESS

But know this, that in the last days perilous times will come: (2 Timothy 3:1)

There is no question about the meaning of this declaration, which Paul made to Timothy. Nothing here should lead us into confusion. We must accept the fact that perilous times are coming. In the early church and in every succeeding generation people have felt they are living in the beginning of these prophesied times. Have you felt the same way? I have, and I am convinced that these perilous times have already begun. It is no longer possible to ignore the warnings because we think this message is about something in the distant future. The real question which we are being forced to answer is whether we are ready or not.

Remember the old children's game of "Hide and Seek." The selected seeker covers his/her eyes and counts while the others hide. When this player gets to the specified number, he/she shouts: "Ready or not, here I come." Are you hearing the Lord declaring this message to our generation? John heard it for his generation as recorded in Revelation 22:20, "*He who testifies to these things says, 'Surely I am coming quickly.' Amen. Even so, come, Lord Jesus!"* In the last half of this verse, John is declaring that he is ready for the Lord to return. How about you? Are you ready? If not, it is critically important to be making preparations now. I urge you to take the apostle's advice in 1 Peter 4:7, (NIV), *"The end of all things is near. Therefore be clear minded and self-controlled so that you can pray."* Thoughtfully consider this warning from the Apostle Peter. If you are not mentally and spiritually ready, it will hinder your ability to pray. Don't be hindered when you will need this most.

One of the main attributes we need for these perilous times is mental toughness. I believe this is what Paul was saying to the church in Ephesians 4:14 *"…we should no longer be children, tossed to and fro and carried about with every wind of doctrine, by the trickery of men, in the cunning craftiness of deceitful plotting,"* To remain anchored in the will and plan of the Lord, we must break free from all forms of deception and false teaching. We must stay in the Word of God and let the Word of God be firmly established in our hearts.

SNOWFLAKE OR FLINTFACE?

In our generation, when we need this soundness of mind most, we find the enemy intensely moving to block it. We are living in an unprecedented time when much of our educational and governmental systems are dedicated to training young people to exhibit mental weakness rather than toughness. A new term which describes the status of many in this generation has emerged: "snowflake." This term is used to describe a tragic form of mental weakness, which seems to be on the increase among our young people, political activists, news media personnel and many liberal politicians.

False teachers in this season celebrate when young people, following their lead, have a mental meltdown when confronted with ideas other than those they have been taught by these deceptive leaders. They rejoice when young adults cannot handle the election of a political candidate other than the one they have been told to support. They rebel, often violently, when they don't get their way in their social or political systems. They are overwhelmed by fear, anxiety and pseudo-stress. Never forget the lesson Paul gave in 2 Timothy 1:7, *"For God has not given us a spirit of fear, but of power and of love and of a sound mind.*

What is the spiritual alternative to being a snowflake? I like to use the description found in Isaiah chapter fifty to describe someone who has mastered the art of mental toughness. This is a person who has chosen to have a face like flint. In the days of Isaiah, flint was one of the hardest know substances. It could be made into knives, spearheads, or tools. You may break it, but it will not bend. Mentally tough people do not bend. They have made a decision to follow the Lord. They have decided that they can trust Him with their honor, their hopes and their lives. Think about it as you read the passage below. Isaiah made this assertion during extremely perilous times as he spoke the Word of God to a generation who did not want to hear it.

> *Because the Sovereign Lord helps me, I will not be disgraced. Therefore have I set my face like flint, and I know I will not be put to shame. He who vindicates me is near. Who then will bring charges against me? Let us face each other! Who is my accuser? Let him confront me!* (Isaiah 50:7-8, NIV)

Have you set your face like flint in total determination to stand with the Lord no matter what you may face? Are you mentally tough like Isaiah was in his generation? In these perilous times we must have total faith in the Lord. We need to rid ourselves of every kind of doubt and uncertainty. Don't become a snowflake. Don't be like the people James described in the passage below.

> *But let him ask in faith, with no doubting, for he who doubts is like a wave of the sea driven and tossed by the wind. For let not that man suppose that he will receive anything from the Lord; he is a double-minded man, unstable in all his ways.* (James 1:6-8)

It is time for the Lord's people to stop being tossed about like waves of the sea when the wind gets strong. It is time for the Lord's people to know the truth and be resolved to stand firmly on the Word of the Lord. Perhaps you need to take a spiritual inventory right now. Do you find yourself being double-minded and unstable in your ways when you are faced with controversy? Do you struggle to believe that the Lord will always be present to guide and protect you? Now is the time to resolve to be like flint rather than like a snowflake. Now is the time to get mentally tough for the Lord. Spend some time thinking about these challenges before moving on to the next chapter. I recommend that you consider the teachings below and understand how they should impact your mental toughness.

> *But we have the mind of Christ.*
> (1 Corinthians 2:16b)

> *Let this mind be in you which was also in Christ Jesus,* (Philippians 2:5)

> *Therefore let us, as many as are mature, have this mind; and if in anything you think otherwise, God will reveal even this to you. Nevertheless,*

to the degree that we have already attained, let us walk by the same rule, let us be of the same mind. (Philippians 3:15-16)

FOUR CRITICALLY IMPORTANT TASKS

There are many tasks associated with developing mental toughness, but for this study I have limited the discussion to four things which the Lord put on my heart for this process. The first and I believe foremost step you must take if you don't want to be a spiritual "snowflake" is learning to avoid taking offense from what others say or do. The second critical step is to develop a plan and practice it. You need a plan which will keep you spiritually alert at all times. Next, avoid all spiritual and social deception by receiving and implementing the spiritual gift of discernment. The final and perhaps most difficult strategy for many people is to avoid getting caught up in all the conspiracy theories circulating in ever greater numbers. In the next four chapters, we will look at how to utilize these skills more effectively.

PRAYER

And this I pray, that your love may abound still more and more in knowledge and all discernment, that you may approve the things that are excellent, that you may be sincere and without offense till the day of Christ, being filled with the fruits of righteousness which are by Jesus Christ, to the glory and praise of God. (Philippians 1:9-11)

CHAPTER TWO
AVOIDING OFFENSE

And then many will be offended, will betray
one another, and will hate one another. Then
many false prophets will rise up and deceive
many. And because lawlessness will abound, the
love of many will grow cold. But he who endures
to the end shall be saved. (Matthew 24:10-13)

As I began to write this chapter, a question kept coming into
my mind. Why begin this teaching about the coming perilous times by dealing with offense? Even though it seemed a
little strange to me, I had a strong feeling this was where the
Holy Spirit was leading me to begin. My thoughts kept going
back to the passage above. I found this teaching of Yeshua
to be both challenging and enlightening. In this simple yet
complex statement, Yeshua points to a sequence of events
which will result in the breakdown of the relationships we
will need most. These are the relationships needed to support
and sustain people as they go through experiences of extreme
duress both emotionally and spiritually. If unbroken, each of
these things has the potential to help unify and strengthen
His followers. According to Yeshua, this destructive sequence
will begin with many people being offended. The atmosphere

created by one or more offended people literally opens a door for all kinds of destructive spiritual forces to manifest, and then to be unleashed on the body of believers. This is the spiritual reason why we begin with this topic.

DON'T FALL INTO THE OFFENSE TRAP

For us to work together in preparing for the "last days," we must be in unity. Offenses tear away at the very fabric of that essential bond. The first century church went through some extremely perilous times. It was their unity which helped to keep them together. In unity, they not only survived but thrived during times of extreme persecution. The Lord added (or multiplied) their numbers daily. This gives us a clear perspective of how the Lord wants us to live in unity and love with all believers. Notice the beautiful way Luke reported on the condition which existed after the disciples received the Holy Spirit.

> *Now the multitude of those who believed were of one heart and one soul; neither did anyone say that any of the things he possessed was his own, but they had all things in common. And with great power the apostles gave witness to the resurrection of the Lord Jesus. And great grace was upon them all.* (Acts 4:32-33)

One sad truth is that offended people can be among the most destructive and hate filled people in the world. Yeshua saw a time in the future when people would behave very much as they do today. He warned His followers in the passage at the beginning of this chapter that bitter and offended people are more likely to betray those close to them. The enemy from within is often capable of doing more damage than the enemy on the outside. Taking our cue from Yeshua's teaching, we understand that offense will initiate a process which follows a specific pattern resulting in a breakdown of the unity, which is so critically important for us to be overcomers.

A group of offended people betraying and hurting one another is the exact opposite of the lifestyle Yeshua prescribed for His followers in John 13:34-35, "*A new commandment I give to you, that you love one another; as I have loved you, that you also love one another. By this all will know that you are My disciples, if you have love for one another.*" He wanted this lifestyle for them and us for at least two powerful reasons. The foremost reason is that love and harmony will help prepare us to be citizens in the Kingdom of God. The second reason is that He wants us to maintain this lifestyle in order to be a powerful witness for the rest of the world. Uncharacteristic love and unity will draw people to Yeshua when their lives are filled with hardship, deprivation, disharmony and strife. If believers look and act just like everyone else during hard circumstances why would anyone want to join them? Love and unity are the main keys to our successful witness to the world. Tragically this can all be broken down if His disciples allow themselves to become offended.

When their love grows cold, people no longer have a desire to support and care for one another. Then the level of their love and caring drastically declines. Many groups of believers who were once close and supportive of one another have allowed overly sensitive and easily offend members to break their bonds of peace, unity and love. You can probably name more than one group you have known which went through this kind of spiritual decline. When this happens you will most likely feel helpless to do anything to break up the destructive pattern. This is why it is so important to take measures ahead of time to insure that the process never begins. Failing this, we need to be able to quickly discern the problem so that we can intervene before it goes too far.

There are more than mere natural forces involved when a group begins to go through this kind of decline. You can count on the fact that a demonic force is operating secretly in the background. Here is an important fact to know if you are going to successfully deal with these challenges. The enemy preys on people who are easily offended. He is constantly on the lookout for people with character defects which make them susceptible to offense. He knows that people who are easily offended are vulnerable to his deceptive practices. One of the principles of warfare is "security." If the enemy can get on the inside, he can do significantly more damage than with an external attack. He is constantly on the prowl to find vulnerable people he can use for his purposes. Take note of Peter's warning in the passage below:

> Be self-controlled and alert. Your enemy the
> devil prowls around like a roaring lion looking
> for someone to devour. Resist him, standing
> firm in the faith, because you know that your
> brothers throughout the world are undergoing
> the same kind of sufferings. And the God of all
> grace, who called you to his eternal glory in
> Christ, after you have suffered a little while, will
> himself restore you and make you strong, firm
> and steadfast. To him be the power for ever and
> ever. Amen. (1 Peter 5:8-11, NIV)

The enemy is looking for someone to devour. Don't let that be you! When you are deeply offended, you will also become vulnerable to the deception of the enemy. If you have wondered why it always feels like major spiritual attacks come through people who appeared at one time to be loving and supportive of you, now you know. Using your natural abilities and worldly wisdom you will not be able to discern the potential of other people to harm you and others in your group of believers. The disciples were unaware until the very end what one among them (with a character defect) was about to do to Yeshua.

> *Then Satan entered Judas, surnamed Iscariot, who was numbered among the twelve. So he went his way and conferred with the chief priests and captains, how he might betray Him to them. And they were glad, and agreed to give him money.* (Luke 22:3-5)

Judas had been offended by the things Yeshua was teachings. He was also offended by some of the actions Yeshua had taken. Satan worked through one of Judas' character defects to harm the Lord. Just as Yeshua had prophesied, he went from being offended to betraying Yeshua and all the other members of his group. People who have progressed this far down the path of offense are often open for and willing to listen, receive and act on false teachings. Judas lost faith in the Messiah and fell victim to the enemy's most often used demonic influence. Will we do the same? We need to search ourselves very carefully to see if there is any defect in our personality which makes us vulnerable to the enemy's deception.

Perhaps you have seen this happen in groups you have been a part of in the past? I am guessing you have. Offense often manifests itself as bitterness. Ask yourself: Is there any root of bitterness in your heart? It is very important for each of us to answer this question as honestly as we can. Sometimes it is easier to see these things in the character and behavior of others. You may have witnessed other people who first became offended and then let themselves be filled with bitterness, envy and strife. As the bitterness goes unresolved, it may eventually be manifested as a deep and abiding hatred. After you learn to see it in others, always turn back in introspection to see if any of this is working in your own mind and spirit. When these things begin to manifest, you must recognize that this is just one step away from the type of violent reactions Yeshua described as "lawlessness."

People who are easily offended by others will always live in spiritual defeat. In addition, they will generally be mentally weak and emotionally fragile. People who have these traits are easily overcome by their emotions. Because they react so negatively after being offended, they open spiritual doors in the group which allow false prophets to rise up and deceive other people. Then lawlessness may begin to abound. In the beginning, these people appear to be on fire with the love of God for one another. Then suddenly they grow cold and demonstrate the opposite of love toward others. In this season, those who stand out as role models in the spiritual realm are the ones who remain faithful until the end. They hold fast to their belief in a reward coming in the end and remain strong through perilous times.

The statement by Yeshua referenced at the beginning of this chapter is a poignant description of many people around the world today and especially in the USA. Almost anything you do will offend some people. I remind you that people who are so easily offended are called "snowflakes" in this generation. Almost any controversy or conflict will cause them to spiral down into defeat. At its worst we are seeing people who have a total meltdown like a snowflake near heat. They are unable to function when they hear ideas which are not exactly like their own.

College campuses carefully select speakers who will not cause controversy or offend these snowflakes so they will not meltdown emotionally and strike out violently. Our right to freedom of speech is usually tossed out in order to appease the snowflakes. Appeasement does not work. The more you willingly give up the more they want. By allowing the rights of others to be lost to appease the vocal and violent minority, we are establishing a culture intolerant of all ideas and expression which differ from one accepted view. As public demonstrations grow more frequent and more violent, we see that we have already entered the age of "lawlessness" which Jesus predicted. Have you noticed that the word demonstration begins with the word "demon?" I'm just saying.

In this season, you must come to grips with one powerful truth: some of the things you say and do will offend large numbers of these highly sensitive and self-centered individuals. This is tragic in terms of its toll on human relationships. It is also tragic on a personal level. Offended people become more and more at odds with the people close to them. This often results in something even more destructive. They tend to become increasing isolated from the very people they need most. The trauma and pain they experience from broken relationships also continues to grow for those who are already so fragile in their emotions. As I reflect on this situation, I am more and more convinced the only thing which can change this situation is another powerful revival that will usher in another "Great Awakening."

OFFENDED BY THE LORD

Today many people are immediately offended by any mention of the Lord. If you use any of His special names publically, you will likely see an immediate negative reaction from some people. Matthew 13:57, "*And they took offense at him. But Jesus said to them, 'Only in his hometown and in his own house is a prophet without honor.'*" Think about this: this passage says they took offense. Clearly you can take offense without any special training or skill. The challenging question is: are you able to let go of offense as soon as it manifests? This is where you need some help. You need help from the Holy Spirit to receive the gift of "*discerning of spirits*" (1 Corinthians 12:10) so that you will clearly understand what you are dealing with as you begin to feel offended. You will also need training and guidance on how to set yourself free from these oppressive attacks. Finally, you need to intentionally practice these spiritual skills until they operate quickly, automatically and effectively.

Yeshua is our example in so many areas of our spiritual walk. This is no exception. Begin to study how Yeshua handled these spiritual issues when they arose. On one occasion when people in His hometown became offended by His teaching, they reacted with extreme anger. Using a passage from the prophet Isaiah, Yeshua gave a simple but profound description of who He was and His purpose for being here at this time. This didn't calm them down, but brought out a violent reaction. Learn a lesson from this. People will at times become offended simply from knowing who you are in the Kingdom of God and what your purpose and destiny are for the Lord. You can offend some people simply by showing up. In the passage below, notice the progression the crowd made from being offended to becoming a lawless mob attempting to destroy the object of their offense.

> *So all those in the synagogue, when they heard these things, were filled with wrath, and rose up and thrust Him out of the city; and they led Him to the brow of the hill on which their city was built, that they might throw Him down over the cliff. Then passing through the midst of them, He went His way.* (Luke 4:28-30)

Notice how Yeshua handled the situation. Rather than getting into a theological debate or a physical fight, He just walked away. When lawlessness breaks out, the situation will not likely be resolved by more information or your personal defense. Don't waste time trying to justify yourself or your actions. When emotional people turn violent, it is time to walk away. You may be able to discuss it another day, but you will not be successful today. It takes great spiritual strength to walk away when you are being attacked by others. It takes awareness, skill and training to make the right choice in these potentially violent moments.

People today are as quick to take offense as the crowd wanting to throw Yeshua off of a high precipice. Some people have been led to believe that it is okay to lash out at anyone who offends them. Today, we actually see many people in influential positions who excuse the violent actions of crowds who can be rightly described as mobs or anarchists. This occurs most often went leaders are offended by the same people or viewpoints which caused the mob to become violent. They are oblivious to the damage they are doing to their culture and the rights and freedoms of others. These are the actions of extremely self-serving and self-centered people ill equipped to be leaders or to hold positions which influence others.

Yeshua warned us about a future time when these things would become the norm rather than the exception. He warned us about what might happen to those who stand with Him in perilous times. We may not be far from the time Yeshua described in Matthew 24:9, *"Then they will deliver you up to tribulation and kill you, and you will be hated by all nations for My name's sake."* As this time approaches, disciples of Yeshua need to be alert and on guard to preserve themselves and protect others in the body of believers. I encourage you to look again at the passage of scripture used at the beginning of this chapter. Study it and prepare yourself so that you can remain alert to what you will likely face in the coming perilous times. To assist you, I am using it again at this point.

> *And then many will be offended, will betray one another, and will hate one another. Then many false prophets will rise up and deceive many. And because lawlessness will abound, the*

love of many will grow cold. But he who endures to the end shall be saved. (Matthew 24:10-13)

DON'T BE OFFENDED BY YESHUA

The first step we need to take is to insure that we do not take offense at Yeshua. Ask the Holy Spirit to keep you alert to what is happening in your own heart and mind during these perilous times. Remember that you are blessed if you are not offended by Yeshua Messiah. Also remember the empowering words of Proverbs 20:27, "*The spirit of a man is the lamp of the LORD, searching all the inner depths of his heart.*" Ask the Lord to shine His light in the inner depths of your heart. You cannot help others when you are caught in the same spiritual trap. Get yourself free and let the Spirit guide you in staying free from offense. Then you will be much more able to help others around you. Take it to the Lord remembering and claiming this promise: "*Therefore if the Son makes you free, you shall be free indeed.*" (John 8:36)

As we prepare for the perilous times which we know are coming, we may wonder if there is any good news from the Lord about this situation. I assure you that there is always good news in every situation regardless of how bad it may look at the time. A part of our challenge is remembering to look for it when we need it most. It is not really hidden. It is only hidden when we take our eyes off of Yeshua. From time to time we need to remind ourselves to look to the Lord and seek the good news, which will give us strength in time of need. The passage below reminds us that the Lord is aware of our every need even before we ask.

> *In the same way, the Spirit helps us in our weakness. We do not know what we ought to pray for, but the Spirit himself intercedes for us with groans that words cannot express. And he who*

searches our hearts knows the mind of the Spirit, because the Spirit intercedes for the saints in accordance with God's will. (Romans 8:26-27)

Even a spiritual powerhouse like the prophet John needed some reassurance from time to time. In prison awaiting his execution, he asked his followers to go to Jesus and ask the questions weighing heavy on him in that moment. He wanted to know if he was right in calling Jesus the "Lamb of God." Had he really accomplished what the Lord had called him to do? Jesus didn't seem to be doing the things he had expected and he want to know if He was really the Messiah. In perilous times, doubts may cloud your mind and raise spiritual question in your own walk with the Lord. At times like this, remember that the Lord has already given the answers in His Word.

Jesus answered and said to them, "Go and tell John the things you have seen and heard: that the blind see, the lame walk, the lepers are cleansed, the deaf hear, the dead are raised, the poor have the gospel preached to them. And blessed is he who is not offended because of Me." (Luke 7:22-23)

The main point for us in this passage is: *"blessed is he who is not offended because of Me."* Don't let your own questions block your faith and prevent you from fulfilling your purpose and destiny. Don't let doubts cloud your mind and hinder you from your spiritual mission. Follow John's example. Take all these things to the Lord and let Him realign your focus. Don't wait and allow yourself to become offended by the Lord. When people fall for this trick of the enemy, they block the Lord's blessing in their own lives and work. Don't wait. Go to Yeshua now.

People can go from praise to offense and from questioning to violence in a very short period of time. Things happen very quickly in the spiritual realm and you may not have time to think it through before you act. This is why it is so important to get ready now and stay ready for the coming times. If they reacted to Jesus this way, you can be certain they will react to you the same way. Think about what Yeshua said in John 15:18 (NIV), *"If the world hates you, keep in mind that it hated me first."* In all things related to the last days, Yeshua is both our primary teacher and example. Always go to His teachings first as you prepare yourself spiritually.

> *And when the Sabbath had come, He began to teach in the synagogue. And many hearing Him were astonished, saying, "Where did this Man get these things? And what wisdom is this which is given to Him, that such mighty works are performed by His hands! Is this not the carpenter, the Son of Mary, and brother of James, Joses, Judas, and Simon? And are not His sisters here with us?" So they were offended at Him.* (Mark 6:2-3)

Think about what these offended people missed. They didn't get to see many miracles, signs, wonders, or healings. They were blocked from understanding who was in their midst. Think about how much you desire to see the Lord and to sit under his leadership and teachings. The dark side here is that many today will still allow offense to block their spiritual vision and limit their ability to receive what the Lord wants to impart to them. Can you imagine the frustration and loss you would feel if you had to look back and realize that you missed one of the greatest moments in human history? For these and many other reasons you need to stay free from offense. If you allow offense to rule your spiritual life, you will always be defeated. Whatever happens, do not miss the time of your visitation. Remember the admonition of Yeshua in the passage below.

> *Now as He drew near, He saw the city and wept over it, saying, "If you had known, even you, especially in this your day, the things that make for your peace! But now they are hidden from your eyes. For days will come upon you when your enemies will build an embankment around you, surround you and close you in on every side, and level you, and your children within you, to the ground; and they will not leave in you one stone upon another, because you did not know the time of your visitation."* (Luke 19:41-44)

DON'T OFFEND OTHERS:

We must not only keep free from the effects of others being offended by us. We must also be on guard so that we do not intentionally offend them. Don't get me wrong. They will be offended. The challenge is to stay free from being responsible for their actions and reactions. It is very difficult to heal a break brought about by an offense. Solomon understood that very clearly when he wrote Proverbs 18:19. "*A brother offended is harder to win than a strong city, and contentions are like the bars of a castle.*"

Solomon had many chances to practice this teaching with his own brothers. Can you imagine having sixty nine brothers who all want to be king in your place? Can you imagine all the ways they tried to maneuver into his office as king? He learned the hard way how difficult it is to heal a relationship broken by offense. This was a lesson he learned well enabling him to deal effectively with many other people besides all those brothers. He was under constant watch by the critical eyes of unintended and often secret enemies. Solomon learned the importance of understanding that you will have to deal with offense, but try not to cause it to happen. I like the way The Mcssage Bible renders Proverbs chapter thirty:

> *If you're dumb enough to call attention to your-self by offending people and making rude ges-tures, don't be surprised if someone bloodies your nose. Churned milk turns into butter; riled emotions turn into fist fights.* (Proverbs 30:32-33, TMSG)

The truth is: people will be offended by you because of their own character defects, but you need to avoid intention-ally causing these offenses. Reacting to and dealing with all these spiritual struggles will occupy too much of your time and spiritual energy. There may be times in your life when you offend someone in a place of power and authority. You need to be ready to handle this. In the passage below you see what can happen even when you are innocent of any wrongdoing.

> *It came to pass after these things that the butler and the baker of the king of Egypt offended their lord, the king of Egypt. And Pharaoh was angry with his two officers, the chief butler and the chief baker. So he put them in custody in the house of the captain of the guard, in the prison, the place where Joseph was con-fined.* (Genesis 40:1-3)

The Lord gave these two unbelievers dreams about the final outcome of the king's offensive reaction which landed them in prison. One received good news and the other received bad news. The one who first bravely stepped forward and sought wisdom from Joseph received good news. In perilous times we are reminded again to take it to the Lord. Joseph was clear that their dreams were given meaning by the Lord and not by a man.

The unexpected outcome was that Joseph was also set free from his unjustified imprisonment by an offended husband. The challenge for Joseph was that he had to remain strong and faithful while he waited for two more years for deliverance. Don't give up if things don't happen immediately. The Lord has a plan and His timing is always perfect. The Lord had more in mind than merely bringing Joseph out of prison. He had in mind the saving of the lives of an entire nation and many others who were living close to Egypt. The Lord had in mind bringing Israel's whole family to Egypt to prepare them for their Kingdom destiny.

The Lord has your situation in mind and He also has in mind all those who need help through your ministry. Don't give up while waiting to be set free from your spiritual imprisonment. Submit to the Lord and accept His timing. He has something much more glorious in mind for you than escaping prison bars. Stay strong and be of good courage. Avoid being offended by others as you avoid causing offense. Wait upon the Lord. He has something more in mind for you than you may know and understand in this moment. Trust Him to do what is best.

Always remember Yeshua's lessons on dealing with offense. When people are deeply offended they may resort to violent behavior. When I was young, I foolishly believed that I could live free from offense by doing whatever was necessary to please people. You already know this doesn't work, but I had to learn this lesson the hard way. Many people will react unexpectedly because they choose to see everything through the filters of the enemy's deception. Their hearts are filled more with hate than love. Their plans and actions are centered on their own needs without any regard for others. You simply cannot please all people. Try to please the Lord instead by listening to His teaching, receiving His help and obeying His commands.

> *Then He said to the disciples, "It is impossible that no offenses should come, but woe to him through whom they do come! It would be better for him if a millstone were hung around his neck, and he were thrown into the sea, than that he should offend one of these little ones. Take heed to yourselves. If your brother sins against you, rebuke him; and if he repents, forgive him. And if he sins against you seven times in a day, and seven times in a day returns to you, saying, 'I repent,' you shall forgive him." (Luke 17:1-4)*

When Yeshua was on this earth doing His ministry, religious people were always trying to trick Him into saying or doing something contrary to the Torah. When He dealt effectively with their critical attacks, they became even more offended. Learn a lesson from what He faced. In the midst of it all, try to avoid reacting to your critics by taking offense at what they say and do. On one occasion, Yeshua had a very creative way of dealing with one of their religious traps. He gave Peter a supernatural method of paying the Temple tax and avoided offending the religious leaders.

> *Nevertheless, lest we offend them, go to the sea, cast in a hook, and take the fish that comes up first. And when you have opened its mouth, you will find a piece of money; take that and give it to them for Me and you. (Matthew 17:27)*

The teachings of Yeshua about avoiding offense went far beyond dealing with those who attacked Him. He was concerned for the spiritual welfare of others; especially the children. In those days, children were to be seen but not heard. They were expected to stay out of the way of the important things the adults were doing. When children were brought to Yeshua, the disciples were unhappy about the interruption. Yeshua had to make a correction. He let them know how important the children are and challenged all of us to avoid offending them. Listen to what He is saying to you in Luke 17:2, *"It would be better for him if a millstone were hung around his neck, and he were thrown into the sea, than that he should offend one of these little ones."*

People who choose to offend and bring hurt to others are in danger of judgment from the Lord. This judgment may not come quickly, but understand that it is coming. Like children, some adults continue to indulge their own needs while neglecting others. Some of these people are even angered at the sight of a homeless person or a beggar. When they are offended, they may react with anger and violence. Those who practice these things should take note of Yeshua's warning in the passage below.

> *The Son of Man will send out His angels, and they will gather out of His kingdom all things that offend, and those who practice lawlessness, and will cast them into the furnace of fire. There will be wailing and gnashing of teeth.* (Matthew 13:41-42)

Not only is judgment coming upon those who cause offense, but rescue and freedom are being provided for the victims of others. The apostles were under constant attack by offended religious leaders as well as those who rejected their witness. Most of the disciples were killed and others severely persecuted because they stood for Jesus. I often study the Word to see how they responded so I can learn how to better deal with my own experiences. A great example is given in the passage below. They were falsely accused and viciously attacked by an offended mob. They were arrested and beaten. Then they were locked in stocks at the local jail. How did they respond?

> *But at midnight Paul and Silas were praying and singing hymns to God, and the prisoners were listening to them. Suddenly there was a great earthquake, so that the foundations of the prison were shaken; and immediately all the doors were opened and everyone's chains were loosed.* (Acts 16:25-26)

Because Paul and Silas were faithful to the Lord and avoided letting offense lead them into the mistake of an angry response, a great salvation came to the jailer and his family. Imagine the impact their behavior had on the other prisoners. They were quietly listening to the praise and worship as the Holy Spirit moved in their hearts. The Lord can set you free from your circumstances. He can supernaturally bring you out of imprisonment. Don't let offense block the Lord's deliverance. Don't let offense block the path to winning souls for the Lord. Get free and stay free from all offense. My best advice about offense is – don't give it and don't receive it! Do whatever it takes to help others avoid offense. Remember Paul's teaching in Romans 14:21, "*It is good neither to eat meat nor drink wine nor do anything by which your brother stumbles or is offended or is made weak.*"

Many people today are making a terrible mistake and do not know it. At universities around the world a vicious pattern of antisemitism is at work. Many people believe they are doing the right thing by attacking Israel and supporting the Palestinians. Jewish people around the world are being attacked and killed simply because they are the children of Israel. A foolish doctrine called "replacement theology" has spread across the academic world. This is founded on the false notion that God has replaced the Children of Israel as His chosen people. This is not Biblically correct. It is not supported in either the Old or New Testaments. The Lord warned about the outcome of this behavior in Jeremiah 2:3. *"Israel was holiness to the Lord, the firstfruits of His increase. All that devour him will offend; disaster will come upon them, says the Lord."*

It has become unpopular to talk about what pleases or displeases the Lord. Many people believe they are above and beyond the commandments of the Lord. For these people a time of judgment is coming. Yeshua was born Jewish and announced that He came to save the lost children of Israel. All of the apostles were Jewish. Paul taught that in evangelism we should always go to the Jews first and then to the Gentiles. Replacement theology is based on the teachings of man and not those of the Lord. If you want to be ready for the perilous times to come you must get free from this terrible doctrine, which is leading to so much abuse of the Lord's people. I encourage you to study the passage below and seek to avoid every practice which is an abomination to the Lord.

> *These six things the Lord hates, Yes, seven are an abomination to Him: A proud look, a lying tongue, Hands that shed innocent blood, a heart that devises wicked plans, feet that are swift in running to evil, a false witness who speaks lies, and one who sows discord among brethren.* (Proverbs 6:16-19)

CHAPTER THREE
STAYING ALERT

Stay alert; be in prayer so you don't wander into temptation without even knowing you're in danger. There is a part of you that is eager, ready for anything in God. But there's another part that's as lazy as an old dog sleeping by the fire. (Matthew 26:41, TMSG)

Early one morning during my worship time, in a series of visions, the Lord showed me some things which are out of balance. I saw things in the nations and in homes which are not level or steady. I began to understand that some things, some nations and some people are in for a fall and will soon come crashing down. Then I began to see people being caught in infidelity. Some of these people were well known because they are celebrities, church leaders, or political leaders. Others were unknown, but they had something in common with the others. Their hidden sins will soon be exposed. I asked the Lord if this was about something in the natural or something spiritual, and the Lord said both. Then He said "I cannot bless those who are unfaithful in their relationships with Me and their spouses." Infidelity will be the most common but not the only cause of the downfall of many in this season. The Lord described this approaching time as a season of judgment.

Then I saw the immorality of some of these people being publically exposed. Instead of becoming humble and repenting, they became aggressive. They boldly defended their behavior based on ideas and philosophies which are contrary to the Word of God and the social norms of the majority of people. Their attempts to justify their behavior made them look worse and increased the spiritual, emotional and social dangers to their souls as they were falling away. They didn't understand the real danger is that they have chosen to step outside of the Lord's blessing and favor. When they are publically exposed, they will not have a defender or advocate, and their fall will be great.

There is a strong need for repentance and getting back into a right relationship with the Lord as well as with other people. To some of you I am supposed to say, "You are in great danger because you have stepped out from under your cover of protection. Don't try to mix your faith in the Lord with other belief systems. Do not embrace socially accepted but immoral lifestyles. The patience of the Lord is at an end. Repent now and get back into a right relationship with your first love." Remember what the Lord said to the church in Ephesus in Revelation 2:4-5, *"Nevertheless I have this against you, that you have left your first love. Remember therefore from where you have fallen; repent and do the first works, or else I will come to you quickly and remove your lampstand from its place—unless you repent."*

For those who think they have plenty of time to repent and return to the Lord, pay attention to the Lord's teaching in Matthew 24:42, (TMSG), *"So stay awake, alert. You have no idea what day your Master will show up."* Is the Lord speaking this warning to you today? Is your heart being led into a season of repentance? Do you hear the Holy Spirit calling you to return to the family of the Lord? The good news is there is still time, however there isn't much of it. Remember what John wrote in his first letter to the church, which he called his *"little children."*

> *Little children, it is the last hour; and as you have heard that the Antichrist is coming, even now many antichrists have come, by which we know that it is the last hour.* (1 John 2:18)

When John called them *"little children"* it was not an insult or an accusation about their spiritual maturity. It was a term of endearment, which indicated that they were teachable. Remember what Yeshua said in Matthew 18:3-4, *"Assuredly, I say to you, unless you are converted and become as little children, you will by no means enter the kingdom of heaven. Therefore whoever humbles himself as this little child is the greatest in the kingdom of heaven."* In this statement, Yeshua was challenging those listening to Him to remain humble and teachable. Are you listening to Him? Are you still teachable? Can you hear this voice speaking to you as a follower of Yeshua ha Messiach? Can you receive all His warnings about the shortness of time before the Lord returns?

Have you ever wondered how much time is left? If you are reading this book I know you have. Think about it. I ask you to think about it again: if it was the last hour when John wrote this almost two thousand years ago, what time is it now? Perhaps we are in the last five minutes or maybe even less. If you get a sense of what this means for you and for me, perhaps you are feeling some urgency right now to get ready and stay alert. Perhaps the Lord is calling you into a season of repentance so that you will be fully equipped for the next season of great grace. Perhaps you will also become fully ready for the return of the Lord.

Since you do not know exactly when it will happen, you must remain alert at all times. This is incredibly difficult for most of us. After years of experience and training in the military I know most people cannot stay focused and alert for very long. It takes a lot of energy to do your job and keep a sharp focus on security. When you try to do this, it feels like your internal batteries are draining quickly. In this area, people are a little bit like flashlights. Without noticing it until the last moment, their internal battery power is about to suddenly run out. The eyes close, the light goes off and people fall asleep when they most need to be awake and watching. Listen to Paul's advice in the passage below:

> *Don't burn out; keep yourselves fueled and aflame. Be alert servants of the Master, cheerfully expectant. Don't quit in hard times; pray all the harder.* (Romans 12:11-12, TSMG)

Yeshua's disciples experienced this after He told them to watch and pray with Him. This was to be His last night as a living person on the Earth and He wanted His closest followers to stand watch with Him. Over and over, He came back to them and found them asleep on watch. His response to their lack of alertness is recorded in Luke 22:45-46, *"When he rose from prayer and went back to the disciples, he found them asleep, exhausted from sorrow. 'Why are you sleeping?' he asked them. 'Get up and pray so that you will not fall into temptation.'"* In this passage, Yeshua points to the real danger facing us now. If you don't remain alert and pray, you may fall into temptation yourself. Perhaps you don't believe this can happen to you, but remember it happened to all the disciples who were self-assured they were ready to stand with Him even to death. It didn't work out as they expected.

Tempted to protect their own welfare, they deserted and denied Yeshua. Here is the point. No matter how many times we affirm that we will stand with Him in perilous times we may fail as they failed if we don't take all the steps necessary to prepare. Because of the frailty of the flesh, it is necessary for us to constantly remind ourselves about the shortness of time without getting caught up in trying to establish the exact day and hour. We speak of the shortness of time to keep ourselves on the alert. We say it so that we can encourage ourselves and others to stay on watch and avoid temptation. Listen to the advice of Yeshua in the passage below:

> *Watch therefore, for you do not know when the master of the house is coming—in the evening, at midnight, at the crowing of the rooster, or in the morning—lest, coming suddenly, he find you sleeping. And what I say to you, I say to all: Watch*! (Mark 13:35-37)

Have you noticed how quickly we can go from a high point in our spiritual walk with the Lord to our lowest point? Peter experienced this shortly after one of his spiritual high points when he was the first to recognized and publicly proclaim that Yeshua was the Messiah – the son of the living God. He felt so lifted up by Yeshua's praise that he believed he was authorized to tell the Lord what to do and prevent Him from dying on the cross. He fell so fast his head was probably spinning. He went from receiving the Lord's praise: "*blessed are you*" to being severely admonished with the words: "*get behind me Satan*." It all happened in the twinkling of an eye. I know what you are thinking: That couldn't happen to me! Don't be so certain. If we don't stay alert, it can happen to any of us.

A DIFFICULT CHALLENGE

No one said it would be easy. Those who have served in the military know that staying alert never comes naturally for us. Soldiers must constantly practice the skills necessary to remain militarily alert. When writing to His spiritual son,

Paul compares believers to "good soldiers." Are you a good soldier for the Lord? If so, it is time to heed Paul's advice in 2 Timothy 2:3, *"Endure hardship with us like a good soldier of Christ Jesus."* Good soldiers don't give up because the task is difficult. They don't run from the sounds of battle. They run toward the battle prepared to fight the good fight of faith. When the going gets tough, they put more effort into it to achieve a positive outcome.

Good soldiers don't get caught up in the concerns and worries over the things of the flesh. They remember what Paul wrote to Timothy: *"No one serving as a soldier gets involved in civilian affairs—he wants to please his commanding officer."* We have to live in this world until the Lord releases us to be with Him. Because of this we have to attend to certain physical needs. This isn't the issue. The issue is getting caught up in these things to the degree that you lose your ability to remain awake and alert to the things of the spiritual realm.

When believers get caught up in the concerns of the world, they lose their focus on the Lord and get slack about watching for His return. If they persist in this behavior, they will eventually allow themselves to become vulnerable to the work of the enemy. Many have grown weary of watching and waiting in our generation, but we must always remember that we have an enemy and he is waiting for an opportunity to do his evil work on us. Yeshua taught us to remain aware of the enemy's plan and purpose for our lives: *"The thief does not come except to steal, and to kill, and to destroy."* (John 10:10) Don't run from an awareness of the enemy's evil purpose for your life. If you become spiritually alert to the work of the enemy and his devious plans to harm you, it will help you to remain on watch. Listen to what Peter is saying to you in the passage below and heed his warning. It happened to him and he knows the price he had to pay.

Be self-controlled and alert. Your enemy the devil prowls around like a roaring lion looking for someone to devour. Resist him, standing firm in the faith, because you know that your brothers throughout the world are undergoing the same kind of sufferings. (1 Peter 5:8, NIV)

STOP BEING SURPRISED

But you, brothers, are not in darkness so that this day should surprise you like a thief. You are all sons of the light and sons of the day. We do not belong to the night or to the darkness. So then, let us not be like others, who are asleep, but let us be alert and self–controlled. (1 Thessalonians 5:4-6, NIV)

It is not enough to suit up with the appropriate spiritual armor. It is good to be covered by the spiritual protection the Lord has provided, but more is needed. After you cover yourself with the Lord's protection it is time to take a stand for Him and remain alert until He comes. You can see this working in the Ephesian church. After making them aware of the armor provided by the Lord, Paul advised the Ephesian church to always be alert and pray. Not only pray for yourself, but pray for all the "saints" (all believers).

In the military, soldiers stand guard to protect their entire unit. They take turns being on watch in order to share this burden, responsibility and privilege. We need to learn these lessons once more in the church today. Soldiers are trained and clearly understand their mission. They must remain alert while some of the others get some rest and sleep. It is the same in the spiritual realm. Are you standing watch over others? Are you covering them with your prayers and guarding the spiritual gates while they rest? Consider Paul's advice to the church in Ephesus.

> *In addition to all this, take up the shield of faith, with which you can extinguish all the flaming arrows of the evil one. Take the helmet of salvation and the sword of the Spirit, which is the word of God. And pray in the Spirit on all occasions with all kinds of prayers and requests. With this in mind, be alert and always keep on praying for all the saints.* (Ephesians 6:16-18, NIV)

When you don't know the day or the hour, it is important to be alert all the time. If we knew when He plans to return, many would take it easy and rest until slightly before that hour. During the period leading up to that moment, people would leave themselves and their fellow believers at the mercy of an enemy who has no mercy. This is one of the main reasons why it is so important for our spiritual protection that we remain unaware of the exact time of His return. It keeps us on our toes. It inspires us to wake up and be ready right now. Yeshua was very clear about this.

> *No one knows about that day or hour, not even the angels in heaven, nor the Son, but only the Father. Be on guard! Be alert! You do not know when that time will come.* (Mark 13:32-33, NIV)

The capacity of most believers to be surprised in the spiritual realm has always amazed me. As I continued to study the Word of God, I wondered how this could be since He warned us so many times in a variety of ways and through many different sources. Over and over the Lord has cautioned us to remain awake and alert. I have been doing the same thing for you in this book. If it seems repetitive, I am pleased. You must always be aware that you have an enemy and you also know that perilous times are coming. So I ask the question again: When will we stop being surprised by enemy attacks and the coming of trials, temptations and tribulation?

> *Dear friends, do not be surprised at the painful trial you are suffering, as though something strange were happening to you. But rejoice that you participate in the sufferings of Christ, so that you may be overjoyed when his glory is revealed. If you are insulted because of the name of Christ, you are blessed, for the Spirit of glory and of God rests on you.* (1 Peter 4:12-14, NIV)

It takes years of practice and powerful spiritual gifts to enable you to rejoice when you are given the opportunity to suffer. I don't know a nice way to say this so I will just make it plain. Somehow, the majority of believers retain such a great capacity to be unaware of the work of the enemy. The Lord had me write a book about this: "A Warriors Guide to the Seven Spirits of God, Part 1." One of the main purposes for writing this book was to help people rise above the temptation to lose their focus, and to help them stop being surprised by enemy attacks. This is what the enemy does and this is who he is. So how can his attacks keep surprising us? I also had another reason for writing the Warrior's Guide. It was to help people understand both the purpose for and the blessings, which come to them as they endure pain, suffering and hardship for the Lord.

> *However, if you suffer as a Christian, do not be ashamed, but praise God that you bear that name. For it is time for judgment to begin with the family of God; and if it begins with us, what will the outcome be for those who do not obey*

the gospel of God? And, "If it is hard for the righteous to be saved, what will become of the ungodly and the sinner?" So then, those who suffer according to God's will should commit themselves to their faithful Creator and continue to do good. (1 Peter 4:16-19, NIV)

UNDERSTANDING THE TIMES AND KNOWING WHAT TO DO

I have always appreciated the description of spiritual wisdom given in 1 Chronicles 12:32, "...*of the sons of Issachar who had understanding of the times, to know what Israel ought to do,*" Do you have this kind of wisdom? Do you understand the spiritual times we are living in right now? Do you know through divine revelation what the Body of Christ should be doing in this season? Are you prepared for His imminent return? If you know that you lack the wisdom you need, do you know where to get it? It is not hidden. It is not a mystery too great for our mortal minds to understand. The Lord has revealed it to us in order to help us get ready and to stay alert in this season.

> *If any of you lacks wisdom, let him ask of God, who gives to all liberally and without reproach, and it will be given to him. But let him ask in faith, with no doubting, for he who doubts is like a wave of the sea driven and tossed by the wind. For let not that man suppose that he will receive anything from the Lord; he is a double-minded man, unstable in all his ways.* (James 1:5-8)

The Lord is our source and He is extremely generous to those who follow Him. He wants you to have everything you need to be prepared and ready for the greatest season in human history – the return of Yeshua ha Messiach. This is the time to build up your trust in the Lord. This is the time to cry out for wisdom. When He returns, it will be too late to prepare. It will be too late for unprepared people to be found doing the things that please Him. Now is the appointed time. We must make a plan and stand watch waiting patiently during our generation. I want to please the Lord when He returns by been found doing the things which honor and bless Him. How about you?

DON'T WASTE WHAT THE LORD HAS GIVEN

I want to suggest that the Lord has already given us everything we need. Sometimes people behave as if they are waiting for the Lord to provide something more or to show them more clearly what is needed. You must always remember Yeshua's words on the cross: "*It is finished!*" He has already given all we need. We cannot fall back on the excuse that He needed to do more or provide more. It never works to blame the Lord for our shortcomings, failures, or sins. I believe this spiritual reality was behind one of His most well-known parables.

> *So he who had received five talents came and brought five other talents, saying, "Lord, you delivered to me five talents; look, I have gained five more talents besides them." His lord said to him, "Well done, good and faithful servant; you were faithful over a few things, I will make you ruler over many things. Enter into the joy of your lord." He also who had received two talents came and said, "Lord, you delivered to me two talents; look, I have gained two more talents besides them." His lord said to him, "Well done, good and faithful servant; you have been faithful over a few things, I will make you*

*ruler over many things. Enter into the joy of
your lord."* (Matthew 25:20-23)

I have a vivid memory from my youth about this parable. I
can remember hearing a pastor using this parable as the basis
for his Sunday Sermon. To make it more understandable to
the people, he suggested that the talent was one silver coin.
This would have been approximately one day's wage at that
time. In my young mind this seemed to minimize the failure
of the man who only received one coin. What could he possibly do with one coin? As a result of thinking this way, I had
difficulty understanding the harsh reaction of the master upon
his return. The problem with my assessment was that a talent
was approximately 75 pounds of silver or gold. You can actually do quite a bit with 75 pounds of silver; not to mention 75
pounds of gold. Think about the size of a talent as you read
the passage below:

> *Then he who had received the one talent came
> and said, 'Lord, I knew you to be a hard man,
> reaping where you have not sown, and gath-
> ering where you have not scattered seed. And
> I was afraid, and went and hid your talent in
> the ground. Look, there you have what is yours.'*
> *"But his lord answered and said to him, 'You
> wicked and lazy servant, you knew that I reap
> where I have not sown, and gather where I have
> not scattered seed. So you ought to have depos-
> ited my money with the bankers, and at my
> coming I would have received back my own with
> interest. So take the talent from him, and give it
> to him who has ten talents. 'For to everyone
> who has, more will be given, and he will have
> abundance; but from him who does not have,
> even what he has will be taken away. And cast*

*the unprofitable servant into the outer darkness.
There will be weeping and gnashing of teeth.'*
(Matthew 25:24-30)

How much has the Lord given you to responsibly and effectively manage until His return? I want to suggest that it is much more than you have believed it to be in the past. Most people tend to minimize what they were given in order to maximize their lack of responsibility for their limited returns on investment. When you consider the power and potential given in one of the spiritual gifts mentioned by Paul in 1 Corinthians chapter twelve, you realize that you cannot even begin to estimate how much good can be done for the Kingdom of God with any one of these gifts. As you read the passage below one more time, pause and think about the power and potential released in each of these amazing gifts.

> *But the manifestation of the Spirit is given
> to each one for the profit of all: for to one is
> given the word of wisdom through the Spirit,
> to another the word of knowledge through
> the same Spirit, to another faith by the same
> Spirit, to another gifts of healings by the same
> Spirit, to another the working of miracles to
> another prophecy, to another discerning of
> spirits, to another different kinds of tongues, to
> another the interpretation of tongues. But one
> and the same Spirit works all these things, dis-
> tributing to each one individually as He wills.*
> (1 Corinthians 12:7-11)

The Lord has given you riches beyond what you would ever ask or think. He has given you the powerful gifts of the Spirit, which can daily manifest in healings, miracles, signs and wonders. Similar to the gifts Moses received, you have everything you need to get the attention of rulers and nations. All these are given for the same reason. According to God, Moses received them: "*...so they will know that I am the Lord.*" You have every gift you need to evangelize the world for Yeshua. Consider the magnitude of what Paul is describing for the church in Ephesus.

> *Blessed be the God and Father of our Lord Jesus Christ, who has blessed us with every spiritual blessing in the heavenly places in Christ, just as He chose us in Him before the foundation of the world, that we should be holy and without blame before Him in love, having predestined us to adoption as sons by Jesus Christ to Himself, according to the good pleasure of His will, to the praise of the glory of His grace, by which He made us accepted in the Beloved.* (Ephesians 1:3-6)

You didn't merely receive a tiny little blessing so that you would be able to barely get by from day to day. You have received "*every spiritual blessing in the heavenly places in Christ.*" You have received more than enough for everything the Lord has purposed in your life and ministry. You have received grace to meet every need and favor to open every door of opportunity. The key is to receive it by faith without any doubts. Another important key is to avoid double-mindedness at all costs. Stand firm and resolute in faith as you wait faithfully for the Lord.

MAKE A PLAN AND WORK IT

During one of my overseas assignments, I was in the Officer's Club sitting with the Commander during a unit party. Many of the officers had already had far too much to drink and were behaving in ways which embarrassed the commander. He leaned over close to me and said, "I am going to call an alert at 4:00 a.m., because I want them to see how excessive drinking impairs their ability to perform their duties. You don't need to come in for this one." Not being a drinker paid off for me that night because I was allowed to sleep a few hours longer than the rest of the team.

At the time when this happened, certain units had been designated as having rapid response status. This meant they were on call at all times and could be called up to deploy is a very short period of time; normally two hours. When I was assigned to one of these units, I was only allowed to be on leave during very limited periods of the year. Everyone in the unit had to be accessible 24 hours a day every day we were on watch. If you were assigned outside the country, your unit was automatically given this status. The word "alert" referred to the command to report to your unit with your "A-Bag" within a specified time. The "A-Bag" was a large canvas duffle bag containing all the clothing and hygiene items you would need during the first 3-7 days of a deployment. This bag had to be packed and accessible at all times.

Because my first stateside unit was designated for rapid deployment, my military experience began with numerous early morning alert calls. These calls normally came between 2:00 a.m. and 4:00 a.m. The possibility of a deployment was very real and these calls were extremely serious in nature. This was made very clear as we were briefed about a time when our unit was called up a few months earlier and the situation was real and the mission was classified. The unit deployed early one morning and did not return for several months. The families were not told the location of those who deployed because of the extreme sensitivity of the mission. A part of being alert and ready was to have plans in place to take care of your family in your absence. You also had to prepare your family members for your sudden departure and the potential long wait they might face before they found out where you would be located and when you might return.

This was the type of "Alert" the commander spoke of late at night as the drunken party continued in the Officers Club. You have probably guessed how this event played out. It was a stark awakening for the officers and staff members in the unit. I believe the commander asked me not to attend the gathering because of the colorful language he intended to use with the group; language he didn't want to use in front of the unit chaplain. The next day, the entire staff was emotionally shaken and poorly prepared to handle the work issues of the day. It was a powerful learning experience no one wanted to repeat.

Are you ready if our Lord and commander calls an "Alert" tonight? Will you be sober and able to respond appropriately to the needs of the moment? Do you have a spiritual "A-Bag" packed and ready for deployment? If the Lord returns today, will He be pleased with your readiness? Will He find you ready in spirit, soul and body to take on the challenges of your spiritual mission in the Kingdom of God? The Lord has repeatedly sounded the call to be alert, ready and watching when He returns. Will you pass the test Yeshua gave in Luke 18:8b, *"However, when the Son of Man comes, will he find faith on the earth?"*

Military units have plans for almost every possible contingency. Here is an example that may surprise you. When I was assigned in the Atlanta, Georgia area in the 1990s, we practiced former president Jimmy Carter's funeral every year. At this writing, he is still alive, but all military units must be ready at all times in order to provide appropriate honors for dignitaries. They must behave in an exceptionally professional manner with very little time to prepare. Are you ready to honor the Lord and behave in something like a professional spiritual manner when the Lord suddenly returns? Like the military, responsible disciples should have a plan and practice it regularly.

As with the other key components of readiness, it is essential to have a plan for almost every contingency and work it regularly in order to succeed in a way pleasing to our Commander-In-Chief. The necessary strengths, skills and traits do not happen unintentionally or work well by accident. They are gifts from the Lord given through the work of the Holy Spirit in our midst. Receive them and be faithful to obediently use them as you are directed by the Holy Spirit.

> *Therefore, since we are surrounded by such a great cloud of witnesses, let us throw off everything that hinders and the sin that so easily entangles, and let us run with perseverance the race marked out for us. Let us fix our eyes on Jesus, the author and perfecter of our faith, who for the joy set before him endured the cross, scorning its shame, and sat down at the right hand of the throne of God. Consider him who endured such opposition from sinful men, so that you will not grow weary and lose heart. In your struggle against sin, you have not yet resisted to the point of shedding your blood.* (Hebrews 12:1-4, NIV)

CHAPTER FOUR
DISCERNING DECEPTION

*However, we speak wisdom among those who
are mature, yet not the wisdom of this age,
nor of the rulers of this age, who are coming
to nothing. But we speak the wisdom of God
in a mystery, the hidden wisdom which God
ordained before the ages for our glory, which
none of the rulers of this age knew; for had they
known, they would not have crucified the Lord
of glory.* (1 Corinthians 2:6-8)

The wisdom of God enlightens us in two very important
yet seemingly opposite ways. First, it sheds light on the
things we ought to do in order to serve God well. At first this
action appears to be the most positive approach because it
speaks of adding things, which will improve our relationships.
The second role of God's light is to illuminate the things we
should not do if it is our heart's desire to please Him. To many
people this seems to be negative because it suggests they stop
doing things which please themselves. On the other hand it is
positive because it rids you of the things which hinder your
relationship with the Lord. It is actually positive because it
removes the very things which have been blocking the flow of

the Lord's favor. The thing which looks most negative actually releases the most positive force available to you in this world.

This chapter is about one of the things in that latter category, which needs to be illuminated by the light of God in these last days. It is about one of those things we should not do. We must not allow ourselves to be deceived by the wisdom of the world or by the clever plots of the enemy who is trying to rule this world one heart at a time. Deception is the most dangerous phenomena in these last days. You will never be able to understand what is happening in the spiritual realm if your mind is ruled by the deep darkness of the enemy's deception. Therefore one of the greatest challenges for this generation is learning how to avoid being caught up in deception.

The fact is you are going to need help if you are to successfully avoid deception. One of the main problems with deception is that you don't know you have it. You cannot know what you don't know. Blocking your ability to see in the spiritual realm is the key element of spiritual deception. You need for the Spirit of the Lord to enlighten your mind and give you spiritual discernment so you can remain free from the darkness of this world. The answers we need have always been a mystery beyond the understanding of the rulers and scholars of any given age. This reality will never change. Those considered to have the wisdom of the world have proven over and over that they are unable to see and hear the truth of God. They are unable to understand what is happening in the spiritual realm. Listen to David's diagnosis of the darkness in his generation: *"The fool says in his heart, 'There is no God.' They are corrupt, their deeds are vile; there is no one who does good."* (Psalm 14:1, NIV)

This situation hasn't changed much in the last few thousand years. Our generation is as foolish as those living in David's time. The only real change is that the foolishness and corruption in the world has gotten worse. Most have merely chosen to ignore the problem in hopes that it will go away.

This has never worked in the past and will not work now or in the future. To compound the problem for those living by worldly wisdom, they don't understand that they have a problem. How pervasive is this problem? Let's look again at David's diagnosis. In the passage below, David gives us a sad and tragic answer to that question:

> *The Lord looks down from heaven on the sons of men to see if there are any who understand, any who seek God. All have turned aside, they have together become corrupt; there is no one who does good, not even one.* (Psalm 14:2-3, NIV)

In the perilous times of these last days the darkness has gotten worse and will continue to do so over time. Believe it or not, a day is coming when the Lord will add his darkness to that of the enemy. This darkness will be so intense that it will literally be felt as physical pain. The Apostle John received a revelation about this and recorded it for us in Revelation 16:10, "*Then the fifth angel poured out his bowl on the throne of the beast, and his kingdom became full of darkness; and they gnawed their tongues because of the pain.*" A reasonable and enlightened generation should be able to discern what should be done, but this will not happen in the last days. Those who need the light of God most will be the very ones who refuse to see it or to accept the reality of what it illuminates.

In the last days, the wise men and women of this world will be like those in Egypt during Moses' generation. They challenged the signs of the Lord released by Moses by using their wisdom and magical arts to make their situation worse. When Moses' staff became a snake, they made more snakes. When they were overwhelmed by frogs, they used their occult skills to produce more frogs. When the river turned into blood, they made the water on the land turn into blood. When Moses gave a powerful revelation of the power of the creator God to the Egyptians, they rejected him rather than repenting and getting right in His eyes. It will be like that in the perilous times, which are already coming upon us. Listen carefully to John's warning in Revelation 16:11, *"They blasphemed the God of heaven because of their pains and their sores, and did not repent of their deeds."* Be prepared to witness this again as the darkness grows more intense.

DEEP DARKNESS

> *The path of the righteous is like the first gleam of dawn, shining ever brighter till the full light of day. But the way of the wicked is like deep darkness; they do not know what makes them stumble.* (Proverbs 4:18-19, NIV)

When there is great deception among a people, it is often referred to in the Bible as *"deep darkness."* Natural darkness resulting from the absence of physical light makes it virtually impossible for us to see our surroundings so that we can move in safety and security. In the same way the pervasive darkness (deception) released by the enemy makes it extremely difficult for people to clearly perceive who they are, what is happening around them, and what they are expected to do. I believe that people today are living in an era of exceedingly deep darkness. Politicians, media experts, news programs and newspapers have repeatedly been caught publishing fake news and giving distorted and false reports. They vigorously defend their behavior because they believe it will produce a greater good. How can people see and know the truth as they embrace a lie? Will this present deception change and improve as time progresses? If you believe the Word of God and have His light shining in the darkness you will have to answer this question with a "No!" It will get worse.

It is a lucrative business today to promote people, ideas and movements with words intended to distort reality in an effort to gain control over people and situations. An entire industry of deception has been created to meet the needs of power hungry individuals, political groups and activist organizations. A highly sought after skill today is the ability by worldly experts to twist the perceived results from so called research and make them say whatever the purchaser wants to hear. Research questions are often carefully and expertly crafted with the specific intent of gathering distorted data. As a result, once trusted organizations have lost their credibility because of their known practices of deception. The situation has grown so intense that no one person or group of people has been able to stop or control these practices. Perhaps it is because most people in positions of power do not desire this to change as long as it serves their purposes and keeps them in power.

I want to emphasis again that we are living in times when many people are being deceived by those they once trusted. Notice again one tragic truth. Those who are deceived do not understand they are being used by unscrupulous people. Think about it! Those who are deceived cannot discern the deception. The real problem they face is having a deception which works to prevent them from seeing their need or finding a solution. Here is an uncomfortable truth: The wisdom of the world simply cannot perceive the depth of this deception. Yeshua warned us that these times would come upon us.

> *And Jesus answered and said to them: "Take heed that no one deceives you. For many will come in My name, saying, 'I am the Christ,' and will deceive many. And you will hear of wars and rumors of wars. See that you are not troubled; for all these things must come to pass, but the end is not yet. For nation will rise against*

nation, and kingdom against kingdom. And there will be famines, pestilences, and earthquakes in various places. All these are the beginning of sorrows." (Matthew 24:4-8)

Paul gives us a diagnosis of our condition in 1 Corinthians 1:20, "*Where is the wise man? Where is the scholar? Where is the philosopher of this age? Has not God made foolish the wisdom of the world?*" In the absence of wisdom, people with no light of understanding are hopelessly searching the darkness for a solution. Know this: there are no solutions in the darkness. This brings up another question. How will we ever have victory over this problem? Well, I have some good news. The Lord has provided a way for us, and He is shining His light into the darkness. The Lord helped me to understand this through an early morning vision. I am sharing it with you in the paragraphs below.

One morning, in a vision, the Lord showed me a series of open doors. The first door opened into a room filled with amber colored light. On the opposite wall I saw another door leading into another room. The second room was filled with something like a powder blue light. As I entered each new place, I noticed there was another door on the opposite side of each room. As I reflected on these experiences, I noticed that I was standing in the middle of a large crowd of people. I was led by the Holy Spirit to understand that the open door was an invitation for all of us to enter, but no one entered the room. They remained standing outside in the darkness. I prayed to understand why this was happening. The Spirit led me to John 1:5, "*The light shines in the darkness, but the darkness has not understood it.*"

I moved toward the first door. Standing in the glow of the amber light, I received a revelation. This first room is a healing room. I began to get words of knowledge for healing. The release of healing is not limited by time or distance. The word "today" in this vision refers to the day you read it and to future days as the Lord chooses. Someone is being healed of chronic headaches today. Another person is being healed of pain and stiffness in the neck. Legs, knees and ankles are being healed right now. If you need any of these or any other type of healing, receive it now in the mighty name of Yeshua ha Messiach. Amen?

Then another revelation was given by the Holy Spirit. More than physical healings are being released in this room. In the light of His glory, people are being healed in spirit, soul and body. If you have been betrayed, cheated on or lied to by a person of significance in your life, there is healing for your hurts today. Let the oil of joy pour out from Heaven and cover over every hurt. As you are being healed, release the other person through forgiveness. This is necessary for you to retain your healing. If you have a deep spiritual hurt today, the Lord is releasing a powerful healing to bring restoration to your spirit as you read this account.

The next room, which is open right now, is a preparation room where you can receive help in moving to a higher level of glory. I thought about 2 Corinthians 3:18, "*But we all, with unveiled face, beholding as in a mirror the glory of the Lord, are being transformed into the same image from glory to glory, just as by the Spirit of the Lord.*" Looking into the mirror of His glory, light begins to shine on our needs revealing our shortcomings. It may feel like bad news when your short-comings are revealed, but not in this case. The good news of healing and forgiveness is being released for you right now. Those things which appeared to be shortcomings in His light are being healed today so that you can move to a higher level of glory. The Lord is inviting you to a deeper level of intimacy today. Are your ready for it?

As these visions continued, I began to wonder why people were choosing to stay in the darkness. Then the Spirit led me to John 3:19-21, "*And this is the condemnation, that the light has come into the world, and men loved darkness rather than light, because their deeds were evil. For everyone practicing evil hates the light and does not come to the light, lest his deeds should be exposed. But he who does the truth comes to the light, that his deeds may be clearly seen, that they have been done in God.*" I began to pray: "Lord please bring everyone into the light. Help people to be set free from the desire for darkness and from their fear of the light. Let healing in spirit, soul and body prepare them to enter the light of your glory. Help them not to miss the hour of their visitation! I pray these things in the mighty name of Yeshua ha Messiach! Amen and Amen! Then I stepped into the room filled with His awesome glory. Will you join me in this room?

DECEPTION IS RISING

One of the major threats for everyone in the spiritual seasons leading up to these "last days" is deception. We have been assured in the Word of God that the darkness of deception will increase more and more as we come closer to the end. A greater darkness than that which existed in any previous generation is manifesting in the world today as these perilous times approach. Here is a painful fact: many people you know and love will be deceived during this time. This includes people you know now as believers. I am convinced that we are already living in these prophesied times of deep darkness and deception.

> *Then if anyone says to you, "Look, here is the Christ!" or, "Look, He is there!" do not believe it. For false christs and false prophets will rise and show signs and wonders to deceive, if possible, even the elect. But take heed; see, I have told you all things beforehand.* (Mark 13:21-23)

Consider this question: How many "false christs" and "false prophets" have you been exposed to in your lifetime? Like you, I have difficulty counting because so many deceivers have come and gone during my lifetime. The apostle sums it up for us in 1 John 2:18, "*Little children, it is the last hour; and as you have heard that the Antichrist is coming, even now many antichrists have come, by which we know that it is the last hour.*" Where do all these false teachers and antichrists come from? This is the disturbing news. They are people who were once part of our fellowship of believers. "*They went out from us, but they were not of us; for if they had been of us, they would have continued with us; but they went out that they might be made manifest, that none of them were of us.*" (1 John 2:19) These people are not really like us. They are wolves dressed in sheep's clothing plotting now as you read this about the damage they can do to you when they depart from your group of believers. We must sadly acknowledge that the enemy has gotten into our camp.

In the midst of the lies and deceptions of this age, we still have a duty to discern what is true from what is false. It is up to you and to me to recognize and avoid the influence of false messiahs. To succeed with this mission, we must stay alert and watch carefully what is happening in the spiritual realm. Deceivers do not wear name tags announcing who they are or what they plan to do. Part of their plan is to keep you in darkness so that you will not be able to discern who they are or what they plan to do. This should not surprise you. Jesus warned us. Read the Lord's instructions again found in Matthew 24:4-8.

Remember, you have not been left alone to handle these challenges. You have resources provided by the Lord. You have the Holy Spirit to teach and guide you. You have an anointing from the Lord, which provides all you need to remain free from deception. Study the passage below from John and consider all the wonderful things the Lord provides for you in this anointing. Then receive it, give thanks for it and operate in the strength and wisdom you have received from the Lord. Always remember the "anointing" is a gift from the Lord and everything included with it is freely given to guide you to victory over all the deceptions of the enemy.

> *These things I have written to you concerning those who try to deceive you. But the anointing which you have received from Him abides in you, and you do not need that anyone teach you; but as the same anointing teaches you concerning all things, and is true, and is not a lie, and just as it has taught you, you will abide in Him.* (1 John 2:26-27)

GOOD GIFTS VS. BAD GIFTS

In an age of deep darkness and deception, it is challenging to discern the difference between the good gifts of the Lord and those counterfeit gifts the enemy is trying to give you. Advertisers are gifted and skilled at making their products look appealing to your eye, and to give you a desire to buy something, which very likely will not work for you. These ads are so pervasive that it is impossible to totally avoid them. This is how the enemy operates in the darkness of this age. He dangles things in front of you which appeal to your fleshly desires. Even if you are unable to avoid them, you must discern their intent and avoid being deceived. The appealing gifts of the enemy are designed to bring you to ruin. The gifts of the Lord are specifically given to bless, encourage and strengthen you. James gives a summary in the passage below. Notice how he begins by challenging you not to be deceived.

> *Do not be deceived, my beloved brethren. Every good gift and every perfect gift is from above,*

and comes down from the Father of lights, with
whom there is no variation or shadow of turning.
(James 1:16-17)

So how do we navigate ourselves through these perilous waters? The good news is that the Lord has given us powerful answers in His Word. In addition, He has given the Holy Spirit as our teacher and guide. He has taken care of our past mistakes, failures and sins through the completed work of Yeshua ha Messiach. He has made the way clear and provided all the help and resources we need. Now it is up to us to follow the old paths He has established for us. As an example of one way to do this consider the method the Apostle Paul revealed to his spiritual son, Titus. This is just one among many paths the Lord has provided for us. Perhaps you will think of others and take advantage of what the Lord has already provided.

Step one in the Lord's plan calls on us to avoid every temptation to operate under the influence of a rebellious spirit. The Lord hates rebellion. It never works as intended. It always leads to chaos, suffering and death. People in our generation have fallen victim to the rebellious spirit in unprecedented ways. In the USA and most other nations of the world the violence and chaos of anarchists plague the people and prevent us from living in the Shalom of the Lord. When Paul wrote this advice to Titus the situation was very bad throughout the so called civilized world. When despotic rulers were doing great harm to those who followed Yeshua, Paul advised:

> *Remind them to be subject to rulers and author-*
> *ities, to obey, to be ready for every good work,*
> *to speak evil of no one, to be peaceable, gentle,*
> *showing all humility to all men.* (Titus 3:1-2)

It is highly unlikely that this advice was well received in Paul's generation. In the USA, people have made a profession of attacking the President and seeking diligently to have him removed from office. Other nations are going through some of the same things. Those who identify themselves as globalists believe this is a good thing. They believe that opportunities to gain control are most readily available in the chaos of civil disobedience and protest. The enemy has always used these tactics to deceive the world. The political system known as "socialism" is an exact copy of the playbook the enemy has used since the beginning of time.

Those living in darkness and deception are as vulnerable to these tactics today as any previous generation. Wisdom and understanding do not emerge from darkness and deception. The enemy has no good plans for your life. Remember what Yeshua said in John 10:10a, "*The thief does not come except to steal, and to kill, and to destroy.*" When you are encouraged to rebel against your elected officials, remember this does not come from the Lord. Think about what Samuel said to King Saul in 1 Samuel 15:23, "*For rebellion is as the sin of witchcraft, and stubbornness is as iniquity and idolatry. Because you have rejected the word of the LORD, He also has rejected you from being king.*" Now as then, those caught up in rebellion are under the influence of witchcraft and idolatry. Those who have chosen to live by the wisdom of the world deny that either of these two influences truly exists. Don't be surprised by their behavior. You know they do this because they cannot see in the spiritual realm and they are ignorant of all the demonic influences presence in this age.

Paul continues with his advice for Titus by writing in Titus 3:3, "*For we ourselves were also once foolish, disobedient, deceived, serving various lusts and pleasures, living in malice and envy, hateful and hating one another.*" Don't return to the things you have been set free from by the Lord. This is foolishness, but it is a very real temptation. The human condition has not changed much over time. Like the apostles who swore to stand by Yeshua all abandoned him when He was arrested, people today abandon the wisdom of the Lord during perilous times. As foolish as it sounds, it still happens. The Apostle Peter gives a stark warning for people who are tempted to abandon the wisdom and counsel of the Lord.

> *For it would have been better for them not to have known the way of righteousness, than having known it, to turn from the holy commandment delivered to them. But it has happened to them according to the true proverb: "A dog returns to his own vomit," and, "a sow, having washed, to her wallowing in the mire."* (2 Peter 2:21-22)

In his letter to Titus, Paul gives a powerful summary of our spiritual condition when we are truly connected to the Lord. As you read the passage below from the book of Titus, I encourage you to celebrate what He has provided for you. We must hold to what the Lord has given us out of his kindness and love. We must always discern and receive the "good gifts and perfect gifts" of the Lord while we reject every other offer given by the enemy. Regardless of how good the offers may sound coming from leaders operating under the wisdom of the world, reject them immediately and totally. In fact, flee from the deceptive gifts of the world. They are meant to steal, kill and destroy. One way to do this is by reflecting on what the Lord has done for you. Think about what He is doing for you right now and what He has promised for you in the future.

> *But when the kindness and the love of God our Savior toward man appeared, not by works of righteousness which we have done, but according to His mercy He saved us, through the washing of regeneration and renewing of the Holy Spirit, whom He poured out on us*

abundantly through Jesus Christ our Savior,
that having been justified by His grace we
should become heirs according to the hope of
eternal life. (Titus 3:4-7)

DECEIVED DECEIVERS

How should we respond to those who are actively attempting to deceive us? Should we judge, criticize, or condemn them? I believe the answer is that we should intercede for them in prayer. First, acknowledge that you cannot help them break through their deception by means of logic and reason. The wisdom of the world helps to keep them in deception and never aids their escape from it. To have any hope of success, you must learn to look for a spiritual solution to a spiritual problem.

The temptation to react toward deceivers with a fleshly response of anger arises from the darkness rather than from the light. This is not our calling and does not come from the anointing we have from the Lord. We know from our study of the Word of God that evil will grow worse and worse during these perilous times. People will work harder to deceive and more will be vulnerable to deception. It must not be like this with true disciples of Yeshua. We must not give in to it and begin to operate under the directions coming from the side of darkness. Paul warned Timothy about these times and urged him to continue in the good things he learned from the Lord and to increase in the assurance he had received. Consider these things as you read Paul's advice in the passage below.

Yes, and all who desire to live godly in Christ
Jesus will suffer persecution. But evil men and
impostors will grow worse and worse, deceiving
and being deceived. But you must continue in
the things which you have learned and been

assured of, knowing from whom you have learned them, (2 Timothy 3:12-14)

In the last days these perilous times will be characterized by the pandemonium created by those being influenced by the powers of darkness. There will be no consistent truths and no fixed direction for those living in deception. Confusion will overwhelm many and bring danger and disaster to their souls. The majority of people will not be mentally tough or spiritually strong enough to handle what has been cast upon them by the enemy. Our struggles will seem very much like Luke described in Acts 19:32, *"Some therefore cried one thing and some another, for the assembly was confused, and most of them did not know why they had come together."* It does not have to be like that for you and for me, because the Lord has provide a way for us and has sent a counselor to teach and guide us – the Holy Spirit.

As always, Yeshua is our true example. I have always been fascinated by the response of the authorities sent to arrest Him. Remember how they responded in the garden when He declared the name "I AM." They fell back in awe. We must always remember the power and effect of the name of our Lord. Don't hesitate to speak the name of Yeshua or cry out in the name of Adonai. It is through the power of this name that you are enabled to break through the deepest darkness. Think about these things as you study the passage below. The awesome power of the Lord broke through the hardness of their hearts and minds.

Then the officers came to the chief priests and Pharisees, who said to them, "Why have you not brought Him?" The officers answered, "No man ever spoke like this Man!" Then the Pharisees answered them, "Are you also deceived? Have any of the rulers or the Pharisees believed in

Him? But this crowd that does not know the law is accursed." Nicodemus (he who came to Jesus by night, being one of them) said to them, "Does our law judge a man before it hears him and knows what he is doing?" They answered and said to him, "Are you also from Galilee? Search and look, for no prophet has arisen out of Galilee." And everyone went to his own house. (John 7:45-53)

CONDEMN OR INTERCEDE?

As I continued to ponder the appropriate response to those who are diligently trying to lead us into darkness and deception, I began to ask a question: Should we condemn them or intercede on their behalf? It is part of the darkness of deception, which leads us to believe that people are our enemies. Remember what Paul taught in Ephesians 6:12-13, *"For we do not wrestle against flesh and blood, but against principalities, against powers, against the rulers of the darkness of this age, against spiritual hosts of wickedness in the heavenly places. Therefore take up the whole armor of God, that you may be able to withstand in the evil day, and having done all, to stand."*

The real spiritual warfare is not against people. It is against the darkness of this age and those evil spirits which try to rule from within it. Filled with the love of Yeshua, we must continue to warn people as our brothers and sisters rather than attack them as enemies. They are all the children of Father God and it is His plan and purpose to help them to become free from the darkness and walk in the light. It is His plan to bring them home like prodigal sons and daughters. We must treat them in accordance with His love and grace.

*If anyone does not obey our instruction in this
letter, take special note of him. Do not associate
with him, in order that he may feel ashamed. Yet
do not regard him as an enemy, but warn him as
a brother.* (2 Thessalonians 3:14-15)

Isaiah gives us a clear description of the plight of those
caught up in darkness and deception: *"He feeds on ashes; a
deceived heart has turned him aside; and he cannot deliver
his soul, nor say, 'Is there not a lie in my right hand?'"* (Isaiah
44:20) It is clear that people in darkness are incapable of deliv-
ering themselves from deception. Deliverance is our assigned
task. With the help of the Holy Spirit we are called to work in
the Lord's deliverance business. Begin by keeping yourself
free from all deception. Our calling is to sow to the Spirit of
the Lord so we can reap a harvest of everlasting life.

*Do not be deceived, God is not mocked; for what-
ever a man sows, that he will also reap. For he
who sows to his flesh will of the flesh reap corruption, but he who sows to the Spirit will of the
Spirit reap everlasting life.* (Galatians 6:7-8)

To avoid deception store up the Word of God in your heart.
To protect yourself from deception avoid aligning yourself
with those who are in the deception business. You are vulnerable to being adversely affected by their darkness. There is no
spiritual inheritance for those who choose to remain in darkness so they can live for the fleshly desires of their hearts. Be
filled with compassion for the lost. Feel their pain and strive
to help them be set free. I am listing four key passages to help
you in this endeavor. I urge you to study them and put them
into practice.

But I fear, lest somehow, as the serpent deceived Eve by his craftiness, so your minds may be corrupted from the simplicity that is in Christ. For if he who comes preaches another Jesus whom we have not preached, or if you receive a different spirit which you have not received, or a different gospel which you have not accepted—you may well put up with it! (2 Corinthians 11:3-4)

Do not be deceived: "Evil company corrupts good habits." Awake to righteousness, and do not sin; for some do not have the knowledge of God. I speak this to your shame. (1 Corinthians 15:33-34)

Do you not know that the unrighteous will not inherit the kingdom of God? Do not be deceived. Neither fornicators, nor idolaters, nor adulterers, nor homosexuals, nor sodomites, nor thieves, nor covetous, nor drunkards, nor revilers, nor extortioners will inherit the kingdom of God. And such were some of you. But you were washed, but you were sanctified, but you were justified in the name of the Lord Jesus and by the Spirit of our God. (1 Corinthians 6:9-11)

And He said: "Take heed that you not be deceived. For many will come in My name, saying, 'I am He,' and, 'The time has drawn near.' Therefore do not go after them. But when you hear of wars and commotions, do not be terrified; for these things must come to pass first, but the end will not come immediately." (Luke 21:8-9)

PRIDE: THE ROOT OF DECEPTION

The primary goal of the spiritual prepper is to be fully prepared to meet and overcome the challenges of these perilous times coming on the earth. This means that we must become mentally tough and spiritually strong to fulfil our purpose and complete our mission for the Lord. A danger arises as people begin to experience these positive results. The danger is human pride. People are easily tempted to look down on those who have not achieved these goals. It is easy to begin to feel superior to them and be critical of their behavior and spiritual status. You must avoid pride if you are going to remain alert and be watchful for what the Lord is doing in these last days.

> *The pride of your heart has deceived you, you who dwell in the clefts of the rock, whose habitation is high; you who say in your heart, 'Who will bring me down to the ground?' Though you ascend as high as the eagle, and though you set your nest among the stars, from there I will bring you down," says the Lord.* (Obadiah 1:3-4)

Pride is definitely one of the main ways the enemy works to deceive you. Be aware that he also has other tools in his arsenal. In this spiritual season, many people feel justified in attacking others who hold different beliefs from their own. Some seem to feel they are like crusaders who are authorized to forcefully push their world view on those around them. The Lord warns us that the fierceness of our actions is also a source of deception. Ask yourself if there is any fierceness in your reactions to people who are different from you. Think about this as you study the passage below from the book of Jeremiah.

Your fierceness has deceived you, the pride of your heart, O you who dwell in the clefts of the rock, who hold the height of the hill! Though you make your nest as high as the eagle, I will bring you down from there," says the LORD. (Jeremiah 49:16)

Another source of deception which can take us by surprise is the belief that we are wise in this age. It is a short trip to a great fall when you begin to take credit for what the Lord has done. It is not our wisdom but His which will succeed in perilous times. We must always remain humble and give credit to the Lord where it is due. This challenge often goes hand in hand with a spirit of pride. Both are dangerous and deceptive. When you feel pride about your wisdom, it is most likely the wisdom of the world rather than the wisdom of God. This kind of wisdom is a snare for those who desire to overcome the challenges of these last days.

Let no one deceive himself. If anyone among you seems to be wise in this age, let him become a fool that he may become wise. For the wisdom of this world is foolishness with God. For it is written, "He catches the wise in their own craftiness"; and again, "The LORD knows the thoughts of the wise, that they are futile." (1 Corinthians 3:18-20)

You are able to diagnosis these things in others by looking at the results of their work. If the fruit of someone's labor is division, strife and/or offenses, this is not the work of the Lord. We are not called to satisfy our own desires or to deceive those who may be simple in their understanding. We need to exhibit the "fruit of the Spirit" rather than the fruit of the flesh. In the passage below, Paul tries to explain this to the body of believers in Rome. His warning and advice is also given for you and me.

> *Now I urge you, brethren, note those who cause divisions and offenses, contrary to the doctrine which you learned, and avoid them. For those who are such do not serve our Lord Jesus Christ, but their own belly, and by smooth words and flattering speech deceive the hearts of the simple.* (Romans 16:17-18)

Another way we see the forces of darkness working in people is their tendency to leave a group of believers when they get offended. Our strength of mind and spirit is increased as we stand in agreement with other believers. When we break away from our source of support, we are more vulnerable to being deceived. This often manifest when people begin to make up their own rules of holiness and try to control the behaviors of others. Remember that the spirit of Jezebel is primarily a spirit of control. We need to stay free from this very destructive and deceiving spirit.

> *Now the Spirit expressly says that in latter times some will depart from the faith, giving heed to deceiving spirits and doctrines of demons, speaking lies in hypocrisy, having their own conscience seared with a hot iron, forbidding to marry, and commanding to abstain from foods which God created to be received with thanksgiving by those who believe and know the truth. For every creature of God is good, and nothing is to be refused if it is received with thanksgiving; for it is sanctified by the word of God and prayer.* (1 Timothy 4:1-5)

CAN BELIEVERS BE DECEIVED?

I have been asked many times about the possibility of believers being deceived or oppressed by demonic spirits. Is this possible? Some say yes and others say no. What do you think? Jesus warns us of the possibility, but also assures us that having been warned we can stay free: "*For false Christs and false prophets will appear and perform great signs and miracles to deceive even the elect—if that were possible. See, I have told you ahead of time.*" (Matthew 24:24-25)

My purpose is not to start a debate, but to encourage everyone to remain watchful lest they too fall into temptation. The passage in the last paragraph is also found in the gospel according to Mark. It is a little different because Mark adds something important to this account. He reports that Yeshua called for his followers to remain on guard. This seems to suggest that it is possible for believers to be deceived if they do not stay watchful and pray at all times. Mark 13:22-23, (NIV), "*For false Christs and false prophets will appear and perform signs and miracles to deceive the elect—if that were possible. So be on your guard; I have told you everything ahead of time.*"

Paul gave the Ephesian Church a stern warning in Ephesians 4:27; "*...and do not give the devil a foothold.*" It is a good time for some introspection. Ask yourself if there are any ways in which you have given the devil a foothold? Look into your own life and the fruit of your work. Are you producing the fruit of righteousness or the fruit of the enemy? The great challenge is: "*...let no one deceive you.*" The work of the Lord was to "*...destroy the works of the devil.*" As His disciples, we have the same mission and purpose.

Little children, let no one deceive you. He who practices righteousness is righteous, just as He is righteous. He who sins is of the devil, for the devil has sinned from the beginning. For this purpose the Son of God was manifested, that He might destroy the works of the devil. Whoever has been born of God does not sin, for His seed remains in him; and he cannot sin, because he has been born of God. (1 John 3:7-9)

PROTECTED BY THE ANOINTING

Have you noticed that the Lord always gives us good news? One example is found in John 10:10 when Jesus warned us of the nature of the enemy's work. He didn't end with the warning. He went on to say, *"I have come that they may have life, and that they may have it more abundantly."* The enemy never has the last word. He may be working to deceive you, but the Lord has given you protection. This anointing will always be available to you and give you all you need to overcome the works of the devil. Reflect on the passage below once more and try to see a deeper level of revelation in it this time.

These things I have written to you concerning those who try to deceive you. But the anointing which you have received from Him abides in you, and you do not need that anyone teach you; but as the same anointing teaches you concerning all things, and is true, and is not a lie, and just as it has taught you, you will abide in Him. (1 John 2:26-27)

You have this assurance, but you also have the warning that perilous times are coming. This does not have to take you by surprise. You have been warned. You have been given signs to know when this is manifesting. One of the powerful signs is the *"falling away"* which must come first. I believe we are seeing this today as many churches and denominations are separating along the lines of who will follow the commands of the Lord and who will follow the ways of the world. Large groups have decided to make the church politically correct and to bring it in line with the declining moral base of their society. This is happening now. So take heed of the warning Paul gave to the church in Thessalonica.

> *Let no one deceive you by any means; for that Day will not come unless the falling away comes first, and the man of sin is revealed, the son of perdition, who opposes and exalts himself above all that is called God or that is worshiped, so that he sits as God in the temple of God, showing himself that he is God.* (2 Thessalonians 2:3-4)

In the two sections below, I want to give you two additional warnings from the Word of God. I encourage you to study them and evaluate yourself. The enemy does not give up easily. He is determined to continue to deceive people until the end of time. He will not stop. He will not give up. The threat is real. Consider it carefully as you study the two passages below, which give these warnings.

TEMPTATION TO THE FLESH

> *For this you know, that no fornicator, unclean person, nor covetous man, who is an idolater, has any inheritance in the kingdom of Christ and God. Let no one deceive you with empty words, for because of these things the wrath of God comes upon the sons of disobedience. Therefore do not be partakers with them.* (Ephesians 5:5-7)

DANGER OF SELF-DECEPTION

If we say that we have no sin, we deceive our-
selves, and the truth is not in us. If we con-
fess our sins, He is faithful and just to forgive
us our sins and to cleanse us from all unrigh-
teousness. If we say that we have not sinned, we
make Him a liar, and His word is not in us. (1
John 1:8-10)

GOOD NEWS

As I stated above, the Lord always gives good news. In the
midst of the worst of circumstances look for it. It is there even
though it is hidden from the world. It cannot be discerned by
the wisdom of the world, but it is not hidden from believers.
We have received the wisdom of the Lord. We have the Spirit
of Truth to guide us into all truth. I like the old adage: It is
always darkest just before the dawn. Always remember this
when you see deep darkness manifesting in the world.

For behold, the darkness shall cover the earth,
and deep darkness the people; but the LORD
will arise over you, and His glory will be seen
upon you. The Gentiles shall come to your
light, and kings to the brightness of your rising.
(Isaiah 60:2-3)

Darkness is here. It is real. It is pervasive. The whole
world is covered in it and many have lost the battle against
deception. It is not to be that way for you. As usual the Lord
has provided a way out. He has provided a solution for you.
He is still releasing the Good News of the Kingdom of God.
What was true in the time of the prophet Isaiah is true today.

You can count on the light of God, which will instantly overcome all darkness. Just look. It is already here and it is for you.

> *Lift up your eyes all around, and see: they all gather together, they come to you; your sons shall come from afar, and your daughters shall be nursed at your side. Then you shall see and become radiant, and your heart shall swell with joy; because the abundance of the sea shall be turned to you, the wealth of the Gentiles shall come to you.* (Isaiah 60:4-5)

This is the good news from the Lord. However, there is still one thing to do. You must put your faith and the gift of spiritual understanding into action. Don't be a mere spectator. Be in the action. Be the one who steps out of his/her dilemma and receives the good and perfect gifts from the Lord. It is time to take a stand. It is time to *"Arise, shine; for your light has come! And the glory of the LORD is risen upon you."* (Isaiah 60:1) Solomon understood this as he faced the darkness and deception of his day. Take the way of righteousness and avoid the way of the wicked.

> *The path of the righteous is like the first gleam of dawn, shining ever brighter till the full light of day. But the way of the wicked is like deep darkness; they do not know what makes them stumble.* (Proverbs 4:18-19, NIV)

Rather than getting caught up in the things which lead to deception, remain focused on your primary mission. Serve the Lord while you continue to serve others. Love the Lord as you continue to love one another. If your mind is fully occupied with your purpose and you continue to work out your Kingdom destiny, you will not fall into deception. Reflect on that as you study the guidance given by the Apostle Peter in the passage below. This is a powerful revelation of how you and I should respond in the deep darkness of our generation.

> *The end of all things is near. Therefore be clear minded and self-controlled so that you can pray. Above all, love each other deeply, because love covers over a multitude of sins. Offer hospitality to one another without grumbling. Each one should use whatever gift he has received to serve others, faithfully administering God's grace in its various forms. If anyone speaks, he should do it as one speaking the very words of God. If anyone serves, he should do it with the strength God provides, so that in all things God may be praised through Jesus Christ. To him be the glory and the power for ever and ever. Amen.*
> (1 Peter 4:7-11, NIV)

PRAYER

Father God, *"Who can understand his errors? Cleanse me from secret faults. Keep back your servant also from presumptuous sins; let them not have dominion over me. Then I shall be blameless, and I shall be innocent of great transgression. Let the words of my mouth and the meditation of my heart be acceptable in Your sight, O Lord, my strength and my Redeemer."* (Psalm 19:12-14)

MY BIBLICAL PRAYER FOR YOU

May the Lord answer you in the day of trouble; May the name of the God of Jacob defend you;

May He send you help from the sanctuary, and strengthen you out of Zion; May He remember all your offerings, and accept your burnt sacrifice. (Selah) May He grant you according to your heart's desire, and fulfill all your purpose. We will rejoice in your salvation, and in the name of our God we will set up our banners! May the Lord fulfill all your petitions! (Psalm 20:1-5) Amen and Amen!

CHAPTER FIVE
CONSPIRACIES ARISING

But mark this: There will be terrible times in the last days. People will be lovers of themselves, lovers of money, boastful, proud, abusive, disobedient to their parents, ungrateful, unholy, without love, unforgiving, slanderous, without self–control, brutal, not lovers of the good, treacherous, rash, conceited, lovers of pleasure rather than lovers of God—having a form of godliness but denying its power. Have nothing to do with them. (2 Timothy 3:1-5, NIV)

Are you mentally tough and spiritually strong enough to survive in the "*terrible times*" of these last days? As I studied this passage over and over, it occurred to me that this will be a time when both conspiracies and conspiracy theories will abound. As you read the list of traits which will manifest in many people around you, you may wonder who you can really trust. Even in our families we will experience treachery, deceit and rebellion. These deceptive traits will be the norm rather than the exception in the last days. If families behave this way, imagine what it will be like in groups of friends and casual acquaintances. Who will you be able to trust?

People do not have much time to prepare for these days, because they have already started to manifest. If an army plans to delay training until the war begins, it will most certainly fail in its mission. We understand this in regard to military units, but somehow we miss the importance of being trained and ready in the church for the arrival of the tribulations, which will manifest in the last days. When the enemy is attacking you, it is too late to begin to learn how to use your weapons of spiritual warfare. Consider this: our ancient enemy has been on the attack since he fouled up the Garden of Eden. We know this. Yet somehow we are still reluctant to get ready and watch for every move of the enemy.

One woman told me she didn't want to know what the enemy was doing because it made her uncomfortable. Perhaps more than any previous generation, we are living in an age of extreme deception when many people resist understanding the times because it makes them feel uncomfortable or challenges them to wake up and remain alert. This kind of attitude leaves us wide open to the wiles of the Devil. Remember Paul's warning to the church in Ephesians 6:11-12, "*Put on the whole armour of God, that ye may be able to stand against the wiles of the devil. For we wrestle not against flesh and blood, but against principalities, against powers, against the rulers of the darkness of this world, against spiritual wickedness in high places.*" The enemy is tricky, deceitful and determined. Don't make his job easier by choosing not to be ready. Always be found watching and remaining alert to all his wiles.

If you are an active participant in social media, you are aware that the enemy uses this communication resource as a tool of deception. Well-meaning people are unknowingly spreading all kinds of rumors, distortions and fake news over this open avenue of deception. Those who are mentally tough have the strength to resist these things. Think about what Paul wrote following the passage used at the beginning of this chapter. One warning: don't get caught up in the gender issues as you read his comment. The things Paul was warning Timothy to be cautious about, are common to both men and women.

> *For of this sort are those who creep into house-*
> *holds and make captives of gullible women*
> *loaded down with sins, led away by various*
> *lusts, always learning and never able to come*
> *to the knowledge of the truth.* (2 Timothy 3:6-7)

Be honest. Some of you got caught up with the reference to "*gullible women.*" Right? This is another trick of the enemy. He distracts us from the key principle being released in the Word of God by using our emotions to block our understanding. I will say it again: both gullible men and women are vulnerable to the wiles of the enemy. Paul had no idea of the easy access the enemy would have into the households of gullible people today through the use of social media. As people get caught up in social issues many are easily offended by any teaching which does not line up with their belief system or world view. The enemy will use your strength (strong belief systems) against you unless you remain on the alert always.

Many of the abuses of this age are being activated and transmitted via the promulgation of conspiracy theories. Many if not all of these theories have no actual basis in fact. On any given day you can read through your social media posts and encounter many of these theories. The deception is made stronger when bad things are carefully mixed with good things in these posts. At times I almost despair of finding any real truth in the postings of certain people. One thing I have decided and am firmly committed to is that I will not get caught up in any conspiracy theory. I will always take it to the Lord before I react. I will always claim Yeshua's promise of being guided by the Spirit of Truth. I refuse to be willingly deceived by the enemy. How about you? Will you join me by making these same decrees in your own life and ministry?

I will say it again: One of the worst things on social media is the spreading of false conspiracy theories. Many good people are being deceived by these postings. I urge you to try something I often do. I check out the date on the original post. These things tend to be repeated over time even after they have been thoroughly debunked. If you want to be mentally tough enough to handle the issues of these perilous times, refuse to get caught up in the fear and anxiety being release by another person. Stand strong on the Word of God. Be obedient to the Lord rather than being vulnerable enough to be led away from your mission and purpose in the Kingdom of God.

CONSPIRACY:
MIXING TRUTH AND LIES

The enemy has used conspiracies against the people of God from the beginning of time. The enemy is not very creative. He is not coming up with new things to use against us. He doesn't have to, because we keep being defeated by the same old methods. Old kingdoms fall and new ones arise when people carry out the plans of these destructive forces by allowing conspiracy theories to gain strength. As you study these events in the Bible, one thing becomes clear. The situation of the people almost never improves as a result of conspiracy and rebellion. The leaders of rebellions seldom have the needs of the people at heart when they carry out their destructive plans. Learn from this. The person posting a new conspiracy theory is not trying to help you. Many people are being deceived into rebellion against legal and authorized leaders by the twisting of words and the clever distortions of the enemy.

After this it happened that Absalom provided himself with chariots and horses, and fifty men to run before him. Now Absalom would rise early and stand beside the way to the gate. So it was, whenever anyone who had a lawsuit came to the king for a decision, that Absalom would call to him and say, "What city are you from?" And he would say, "Your servant is from such and such a tribe of Israel." Then Absalom would say to him, "Look, your case is good and right; but there is no deputy of the king to hear you." (2 Samuel 15:1-3)

Absalom's conspiracy against his father was a good example of someone mixing a little truth into a set of carefully crafted lies. Absalom knew that people had misgivings about the ability of the government to take care of their needs and concerns. He focused in on the anxiety and fear of the people to open a door for exploitation. He was careful to appear to be genuinely concerned for their welfare and to be viewed as being on their side. The political arena today is filled with those who have learned the same techniques used by Absalom. They will say whatever the people want to hear until they move into a position of power. Then the truth comes out. They are actually concerned for their own welfare, position and power rather than the needs of the people.

Moreover Absalom would say, "Oh, that I were made judge in the land, and everyone who has any suit or cause would come to me; then I would give him justice." And so it was, whenever anyone came near to bow down to him, that he would put out his hand and take him and kiss him. In this manner Absalom acted toward all Israel who came to the king for judgment. So

Absalom stole the hearts of the men of Israel. (2 Samuel 15:4-6)

After leading people into deeper feelings of fear and anxiety about their welfare, Absalom would present himself as the solution to all their problems. Does this sound familiar? Have you heard people running for office say some of the same things Absalom was saying? He reached out to take the hand of the people in order to reassure them that he would defend and protect them. I had a picture in my mind of politicians glad handing the people and kissing babies. Did you notice that Absalom would even give them a kiss like a father would give to a fearful child? This was how Absalom stole the hearts of the people and set up an environment for his rebellion with the sole purpose of gaining power and influence for himself.

Then Absalom sent for Ahithophel the Gilonite, David's counselor, from his city—from Giloh— while he offered sacrifices. And the conspiracy grew strong, for the people with Absalom continually increased in number. (2 Samuel 15:12)

Absalom began to win over more and more people with hollow promises of using his power and influence for their welfare. Does this sound familiar? Think of all the broken political promises you have heard in this generation. Absalom was so skilled in conspiracy that he persuaded some of David's closest associates to come over to his side. These things are still happening today, and people are still vulnerable enough to be led astray. Look again at what the Lord said about rebellion in 1 Samuel 15:23, "*For rebellion is as the sin of witchcraft, and stubbornness is as iniquity and idolatry.*" If we are going to successfully navigate the perilous times coming, we must avoid this kind of deception based in witchcraft and idolatry.

You need to search your soul and see if you are under the spell of someone practicing witchcraft. Is this really possible? Can believers actually come under the spell of others? Consider what Paul said to believers in the Galatian church: *"O foolish Galatians! Who has bewitched you that you should not obey the truth, before whose eyes Jesus Christ was clearly portrayed among you as crucified?"* (Galatians 3:1) Paul obviously thought that Galatian believers were bewitched. Examine yourself with the help of the Spirit of Truth and see where you stand right now.

I urge you to remain mentally tough enough and spiritually strong enough to resist every temptation to be caught up in the wiles of the Devil. The danger is real and ever present. Therefore you must remain vigilant and pray constantly for the strength to endure. After years of ministry, Paul was very aware of the dangers. However, many of his followers still needed encouragement to remain alert and to continue to stand in the power of the Holy Spirit. We are wise to carefully consider and take the sound advice of this old and experienced warrior. He had to issue the warning over and over to this community of believers. Perhaps we need to do the same.

> *Therefore take heed to yourselves and to all the flock, among which the Holy Spirit has made you overseers, to shepherd the church of God which He purchased with His own blood. For I know this, that after my departure savage wolves will come in among you, not sparing the flock. Also from among yourselves men will rise up, speaking perverse things, to draw away the disciples after themselves. Therefore watch, and remember that for three years I did not cease to warn everyone night and day with tears.* (Acts 20:28-31)

RESISTING CONSPIRACIES

People today continue to mistakenly believe they will gain power, influence and position by understanding and utilizing the wisdom of the world. They believe that it is good to dig into the depths of every new conspiracy theory. People today are still seeking to better understand their situation by listening to the voices of the real conspirators. The Lord has given numerous warnings of the dangers inherent in the lives of those who make decisions and operate under the fear of man rather than in the fear of God. The Lord spoke plainly about this through the prophet Isaiah.

> *For the Lord spoke thus to me with a strong hand, and instructed me that I should not walk in the way of this people, saying: "Do not say, 'A conspiracy,' concerning all that this people call a conspiracy, nor be afraid of their threats, nor be troubled. The Lord of hosts, Him you shall hallow; Let Him be your fear, and let Him be your dread. He will be as a sanctuary, but a stone of stumbling and a rock of offense to both the houses of Israel, as a trap and a snare to the inhabitants of Jerusalem."* (Isaiah 8:11-14)

There is a hidden key in this passage from Isaiah. Don't get caught up in the fear of man. Don't allow any man or woman to put a spirit of fear in you. Instead, fear the Lord and fear Him only. Those who fear the Lord will discover that He is a source of refuge and strength. He is like a tall tower of strength covering you with His protection and blessing. He is the one who will protect you and provide for you. Ironically, this wonderful news will be a stumbling block for those who do not recognize Him. Many will be offended by the Lord and in so doing reject the help and salvation He brings. This is tragic indeed. Isaiah gave an excellent summary of the real pitfalls in chapter eight of his book.

> *And many among them shall stumble; they shall fall and be broken, be snared and taken. Bind up the testimony, seal the law among my disciples. And I will wait on the Lord, Who hides His face from the house of Jacob; and I will hope in Him. Here am I and the children whom the Lord has given me! We are for signs and wonders in Israel from the Lord of hosts, Who dwells in Mount Zion.* (Isaiah 8:15-18)

It is always easier to see these problems in others than in ourselves. I believe we must avoid the temptation to place all the blame on those around us. We must seek first to see if any of these deceptions of the enemy are at work in or through us. As we explore these things, we must face and deal with these trials and temptations in our own lives. We must continue to grow in our mental toughness. This strength will serve us well during perilous times. We seldom learn things the easy way. Our best lessons often come through our own pain and struggles. Be willing to take the narrow and difficult path in order to build up your own strength and endurance.

WHISPERING AND MUTTERING

Asa was basically a good and faithful king in Judah for most of his time, but he didn't end well. After years of seeking to be faithful to the Lord and receiving the Lord's help and provision, he left the good path of trusting the Lord. When Israel came to war against him with the help of Syria, Asa made a tragic decision to use the wealth of Judah to bribe the King of Syria to switch sides. To a certain degree it worked. Syria turned on Israel, but the Lord was not pleased. He sent a prophet to let King Asa know that he made a huge mistake in seeking the help of man rather than the help of God. King Asa continued his downward spiral into spiritual darkness by rejecting the admonishment of the Lord, and in anger he made his situation worse by imprisoning the Lord's anointed prophet. Isaiah points out how those led into deception will be incapable of the mental toughness they need to survive in perilous times.

> *They will pass through it hard-pressed and hungry; and it shall happen, when they are hungry, that they will be enraged and curse their king and their God, and look upward. Then they will look to the earth, and see trouble and darkness, gloom of anguish; and they will be driven into darkness.* (Isaiah 8:21-22)

This rejection of the Lord's admonishment was the beginning of the end of Asa's reign in Judah. He became diseased in his feet, and in his pain and suffering he chose not to go to the Lord for healing. He sought help from the physicians. The result was a slow and painful death from a disease they were unable to heal. Who do you seek when you need help or healing? Do you go first to the lenders and doctors or do you seek the Lord first and always? Have you noticed that borrowing money to pay your debts does not solve your problems? Those who are mentally tough, trust the Lord more and more to provide for all their physical and spiritual needs.

> *And when they say to you, "Seek those who are mediums and wizards, who whisper and mutter," should not a people seek their God? Should they seek the dead on behalf of the living? To the law and to the testimony! If they do not speak according to this word, it is because there is no light in them.* (Isaiah 8:19-20)

YOU CANNOT DECEIVE THE LORD

The people of Judah are often used in scripture as examples of what happens when people make poor choices. When your situation gets really tough, where do you turn for help and guidance? After winning a big battle with the help of the Lord, people in Bible times would foolishly pick up the idols of their defeated enemy and worship them. How foolish can you be? These idols provided no help or protection for their original owners. What can they possibly do for you? As we see this happen with the Lord's people over and over in the Biblical accounts, we should be personally warned of a danger lurking around in what has been left behind by a previous generation. Think about it. Many people today need to be set free from generational curses handed down from parents to their children generation after generation.

One hundred years ago Adolf Hitler unleashed a great deception in order to lead the people into socialism. He used the youth of his country to rebel against authority as they protested and unleashed a radical form of anarchy. He focused their growing rage on others accusing them of the very things he was actually doing. He promoted various conspiracy theories, which placed the blame for all their problems on the legitimate democratic leaders of the nation. He called on the people to eliminate those he considered to be deplorable and unable to support and promote his socialist ideals. One of his cornerstone teachings was to declare one specific group of people as deplorable. Then he released what was called the "final solution." He led his people into a violent and radical form of antisemitism as a way of projecting the blame for his failures on a helpless group of people. This same antisemitism is growing in power and influence around the world today. To avoid the iniquities of our fathers and mothers in the last century, we need to harken once again to the word of the Lord coming through the prophet Jeremiah.

And the Lord said to me, "A conspiracy has been found among the men of Judah and among the inhabitants of Jerusalem. They have turned back to the iniquities of their forefathers who refused to hear My words, and they have gone after other gods to serve them; the house of Israel and the house of Judah have broken My covenant which I made with their fathers." Therefore thus says the Lord: "Behold, I will surely bring calamity on them which they will not be able to escape; and though they cry out to Me, I will not listen to them." (Jeremiah 11:9-11)

The work of Adolf Hitler was totally disastrous not only for his people, but for the entire world. Only one hundred years later, these same movements and ideologies are being taught, empowered and unleashed on the American people. You can also see it emerging again in Europe and other nations of the world. It appears that people have not learned any of the painful lessons of history. They continue to pick up the idols of defeated people and set them up for their own worship. The irony is that these modern socialists point to their opponents calling them NAZIs. The word NAZI was an acronym for the National Socialist movement in Germany. Then and now the true NAZIs are the socialist who bring division, discord and disaster everywhere their teachings are put into practice. In the midst of the great darkness and deception of these perilous times people are being led into disaster once again.

And the word of the Lord came to me, saying, "Son of man, say to her: 'You are a land that is not cleansed or rained on in the day of indignation.' The conspiracy of her prophets in her midst is like a roaring lion tearing the prey; they have devoured people; they have taken treasure and precious things; they have made many widows in her midst. Her priests have violated My law and profaned My holy things; they have not distinguished between the holy and unholy, nor have they made known the difference between the unclean and the clean; and they have hidden their eyes from My Sabbaths, so that I am profaned among them. Her princes in her midst are like wolves tearing the prey, to shed blood, to destroy people, and to get dishonest gain. Her prophets plastered them with untempered mortar, seeing false visions, and divining lies for them, saying, 'Thus says the Lord God,' when the Lord had not spoken. The people of the land have used oppressions, committed robbery, and mistreated the poor and needy; and they wrongfully oppress the stranger. So I sought for a man among them who would make a wall, and stand in the gap before Me on behalf of the land, that I should not destroy it; but I found no one. Therefore I have poured out My indignation on them; I have consumed them with the fire of My wrath; and I have recompensed their deeds on their own heads," says the Lord God. (Ezekiel 22:23-31)

Is there anyone today who will hear and respond to the calling of the Lord? Is there anyone willing to build a wall and stand in the gap before the Lord on behalf of a sinful people in this generation? Is there anyone who will be an intercessor in the deep darkness of this age? The Lord had a solution in the days of Ezekiel when no one would stand up for the kingdom. Does anyone really desire to experience the full power of His wrath and indignation? People are calling out for the fire of revival while ignoring the approaching fire of His wrath. Now is the time to repent and get right with the Lord. This is the kind of revival we need in this generation. How about you? Do you agree? Are you willing to take a stand on behalf of your people before the Lord?

CONSPIRACIES HAVE AN EVIL INTENT

Conspiracies are carefully crafted so they will appear to lead you to something good, but this is a deception. All conspiracies are based on the work of a rebellious spirit, which justifies its existence by making someone or something else appear to be devious, deceptive, or destructive. A good example of this is found in Acts chapter twenty three. A group of forty men presented themselves as potential heroes because they had bound themselves in a conspiracy to eliminate a man whom they claimed posed a threat to their security and endangered their way of life. Their conspiracy gained widespread support among the religious leaders of their day because it agreed with their spirits that were filled with jealousy and envy. At that time, they were completely unaware that they were fighting against the plan and purposes of the Lord. Does this sound familiar to you? It is happening again and people are as deceived now as they were then.

> *Now there were more than forty who had formed this conspiracy. They came to the chief priests and elders, and said, "We have bound ourselves under a great oath that we will eat nothing until we have killed Paul. Now you, therefore, together with the council, suggest to the commander that he be brought down to you tomorrow, as though you were going to make further inquiries concerning him; but we are ready to kill him before he comes near." (Acts 23:13-15)*

I always laugh a little when I read the passage above. I wonder how long they went without food since their plan completely failed. They believed they would succeed as they falsely thought they were doing the Lord's work. It is important to be aware that the Lord never supports a rebellious spirit. The prophet Samuel made this clear to King Saul in 1 Samuel 15:23, *"For rebellion is as the sin of witchcraft, and stubbornness is as iniquity and idolatry. Because you have rejected the word of the LORD, He also has rejected you from being king."* In addition to diagnosing the situation, Samuel gives the outcome of rebellion against the Lord. When you reject Him, He may reject and replace you.

David lived in an environment of continuous conspiracies against his kingship. He often prayed in the words of Psalm 64:2, *"Hide me from the secret plots of the wicked, from the rebellion of the workers of iniquity,"* As you read the words of his prayer you can feel some of the pain brought to him by those in rebellion. Perhaps you have gone through similar things in your own life. In his final words, he speaks of the outcome for those who rebelled against him vs. those who serve the Lord. He concludes that *"they shall be utterly burned with fire in their place."*

> *Although my house is not so with God, yet He has made with me an everlasting covenant, ordered in all things and secure. For this is all my salvation and all my desire; will He not make it increase? But the sons of rebellion shall all be as thorns thrust away, because they cannot be taken with hands. But the man who touches them must be armed with iron and the shaft of a spear, and they shall be utterly burned with fire in their place.* (2 Samuel 23:5-7)

When you are face to face with a rebellious spirit, and when you are suffering the effects of an unrighteous conspiracy against you, where do you turn? It is always right and appropriate to turn to the Lord for help. He is faithful to bless those who walk in righteousness. He is also faithful to bring judgment on the rebellious conspirators in every generation. Tragically, many people do not learn from history. We see it clearly in the history of Israel and Judah. A pattern emerges and then repeats itself through several generations. Dissatisfied people form a conspiracy to rid themselves of an unpopular leader. Each time they are hunted down and executed for their crimes. When will people ever learn about the end result of rebellion? As long as the enemy is allowed to oppress people with the rebellious spirit, these things will continue.

GOOD NEWS

The Lord is wonderful and faithful to release His good news in every troubling situation. The Lord has good news for those suffering at the hands of conspirators. He brings sudden judgment on them while he delivers, blesses and prospers those who stand with Him in faith. The dawn of His grace is about to shatter the darkness of the enemy in your life and ministry. Trust Him. He has a plan to deliver you from the thorny grasp of rebellious people. I like the way The Message Bible words the end results of rebellious people.

> *He aborts the schemes of conniving crooks, so that none of their plots come to term. He catches the know-it-alls in their conspiracies— all that intricate intrigue swept out with the trash! Suddenly they're disoriented, plunged into darkness; they can't see to put one foot in front of the other. But the downtrodden are*

saved by God, saved from the murderous plots, saved from the iron fist. (Job 5:12-15, TMSG)

PRAYER OF DEDICATION

Teach me, O Lord, to follow your decrees; then I will keep them to the end. Give me understanding, and I will keep your law and obey it with all my heart. Direct me in the path of your commands, for there I find delight. Turn my heart toward your statutes and not toward selfish gain. Turn my eyes away from worthless things; preserve my life according to your word. Fulfill your promise to your servant, so that you may be feared. Take away the disgrace I dread, for your laws are good. How I long for your precepts! Preserve my life in your righteousness. (Psalm 119:33-40, NIV)

PRAYER

Hear me, O God, as I voice my complaint; protect my life from the threat of the enemy. Hide me from the conspiracy of the wicked, from that noisy crowd of evildoers. They sharpen their tongues like swords and aim their words like deadly arrows. They shoot from ambush at the innocent man; they shoot at him suddenly, without fear. They encourage each other in evil plans, they talk about hiding their snares; they say, "Who will see them?" They plot injustice and say, "We have devised a perfect plan!" Surely the mind and heart of man are cunning. (Psalm 64:1-6, NIV)

PART TWO
ESTABLISHING SPIRITUAL STRENGTH

M ental toughness is the first of several strong foundation stones needed to prepare you to withstand the dangers and challenges of the coming perilous times. It is necessary to begin here, but you must not be tempted to stop here. To the natural mind this may appear to be enough, but the spiritual mind knows that much more is needed. To help in understanding this concept look again at Paul's teaching in 1 Corinthians 15:46, "*However, the spiritual is not first, but the natural, and afterward the spiritual.* This is the developmental sequence established in the Word of God. Following the way of the Lord is always the best decision you can make.

It is important to remember that as you move into this second part of the preparation process, you do not stop working on your mental toughness. You have made excellent progress, but you must never stop building the strength of character you need to resist the "wiles of the Devil." Now is the time to stand on the admonition Paul gave to believers in Romans 8:9a, "*But you are not in the flesh but in the Spirit, if indeed the Spirit of God dwells in you.*" It is clear that you must develop both mental toughness and spiritual strength as you prepare for the coming of the perilous times associated with the last days. Consider this as you study the passage below:

> *...we should no longer be children, tossed to and fro and carried about with every wind of doctrine, by the trickery of men, in the cunning craftiness of deceitful plotting, but, speaking the truth in love, may grow up in all things into Him who is the head—Christ—* (Ephesians 4:14-15)

Mental toughness will help you to make your stand for the Lord. Now is the time to "*grow up in all things*" as Paul directed in the passage above. Sometimes it helps to read these powerful passages aloud and put them into the first person. Say aloud now with confidence. I am no longer a child, tossed to and fro and carried about by every wind of doctrine. I am not led by the trickery of any man or woman. I will not be deceived by deceitful plotting because the Spirit of the Living God is in me. I am growing up in all the things as I become more and more like Yeshua Messiah. I urge you to make these decrees over and over as you develop the spiritual strength you need to survive, thrive and accomplish your Kingdom purpose for the Lord in this generation.

The really good news to get firmly establish in your mind at this time is the promise that the Lord will bless you, guide you and resource you to stand firm in times of trouble and tribulation. Say aloud: "He has given me everything I need to succeed!" Amen? I can hear someone saying, "I need a scripture for that." I'm glad you asked. Stand firm as you receive and believe the promise Paul released in Ephesians 1:3, "*Blessed be the God and Father of our Lord Jesus Christ, who has blessed us with every spiritual blessing in the heavenly places in Christ,*" How many blessings are promised? All of them have been given to you and will continue to flow as long as you love and serve the Lord. Amen? Continue to read this passage aloud as long as it takes to get it firmly anchored in your spirit. I take my stand and give the testimony that I have been blessed with every spiritual blessing in heavenly places in Christ. Amen?

> *For to be carnally minded is death, but to be spiritually minded is life and peace. Because the carnal mind is enmity against God; for it is not subject to the law of God, nor indeed can be. So then, those who are in the flesh cannot please God.* (Romans 8:6-8)

Building mental toughness is not the same as being carnally minded. In fact it is the exact opposite. To truly be mentally tough and spiritually strong, you must be "spiritually minded." This is the path to receive the promises of the Lord's provision for these perilous times. When you follow His path, you find that it leads you to the promise in the passage above. It leads you on the pathway of "*life and peace.*" In the next three chapters, we shift our focus to building spiritual strength. The Lord has not left us without resources. All we need to know, we can find in His Word.

THREE CRITICALLY IMPORTANT TASKS

As in part one, there are critically important tasks to be completed in order to develop the spiritual resilience needed for the last days. I received revelation about three of these tasks. Once again I pray that the Lord will reveal more to you as you work through these with me. We begin by cleaning the house and ridding ourselves of unnecessary baggage. You cannot move into your destiny if you are loaded down with spiritual hurts, failures and broken promises from your past history.

Next, we will look at the scriptural way of forgetting those things so you can move on unencumbered by what you are leaving behind. This is not a natural process. Only the supernatural power of God through the indwelling Holy Spirit can give you the forgetfulness you need. The ability to forget past hurts, betrayals and broken promises is not native to the human spirit. People are not able automatically to rid themselves of the negative effects of remembering past mistakes, failures and sins. You can only do this with the help, power and authority of the Lord.

In the third part of this section, we will look at what it means to walk by faith. Remember the promise in 2 Corinthians 5:6-7, "*So we are always confident, knowing that while we are at home in the body we are absent from the Lord. For we walk by faith, not by sight.*" It is important to understand that your natural eyes cannot see all you need to be aware of in these perilous times. You must trust the Lord and believe all He has promised in His Word. Always remember that faith is a power gift from the Lord and the good news is that He wants to give you all you need.

CHAPTER SIX
TRAVELING LIGHT

During almost 35 years of service as a military officer, I observed many interesting aspects of human behavior. One behavior which always caught my attention was the tendency of many people to unload their burdens during their farewell speech. These public displays of emotion are often filled with negative comments, which drastically diminished the joy of the party. Some departing unit members have embarrassed everyone present by unloading all their anger and bitterness toward the organization. Others have lashed out with harsh criticism for individuals they blamed for their hardships and troubles.

The tense moments arising during these emotional displays were difficult for many people to endure. This kind of behavior was not limited to young and inexperienced individuals. I remember a senior officer who spoke bitterly about a junior officer under his command. He said, "He couldn't have done more damage if he had been a communist agent." I decided very early in my military career to rise above the temptation to depart in this way. I established a cornerstone belief that it is always important to end well. At all costs, you should avoid burning any relationship bridges you might need to cross later. This personal philosophy served me well for the remainder of my career and I taught it to many subordinates through the years.

A rare exception to this pattern of unloading on the group occurred at the farewell of the unit physician during an overseas assignment. When it came time to give his farewell speech, he approached the podium in what looked like a very embarrassed and anxiety ridden manner. He let all of us know that during his tour of duty he had done some things that made him feel shame. He then said that he needed to make public confession before his departure to remove this burden from his soul. The eyes of everyone present were fixed on him and many people seemed concerned for his apparent stress and anxiety.

In a well-rehearsed and seemingly very sincere manner he explained that his burden was having secretly administered private and unreported treatment for various diseases contracted by the officers in the unit. He let us know the only way he could get free from the burden was to reveal the names of those he had treated. Panic swept through the room and a few people began to squirm in their chairs with obvious discomfort. He seemed to be shaking as he reached very slowly into his coat pocket to bring out a sheet of paper he claimed to contain all the names. At this point the tension was so heavy you could cut it with a knife.

He took an unusually long time to unfold that piece of paper as the stress and anxiety in the room continued to grow. In preparation for his talk, he had folded the paper over and over so that it took quite a bit of time to open it. He held the paper close to the microphone to allow it to make loud crackling sounds as he slowly opened it. His voiced seemed to quiver as he began to read from the list: "milk, eggs, bread and etc." Suddenly he said, "Oops, I brought the wrong list." The room broke out in laughter and the stress suddenly evaporated.

Why would I tell a story like this? It is a true story, but I had another point I wanted to make. I want you to understand from the beginning that confession has to do with revealing your own soul. People prefer to confess the sins, mistakes and failures of other people rather than their own. This is never right in the eyes of the Lord and will not lighten anyone's load. It is critically important for readiness that we reduce our burdens and only carry the spiritual loads which will enhance, bless and assist ourselves and others in our group. This often requires confession and repentance so that healing can begin.

Over the years, I have read several articles, magazines and books related to being prepared for the perilous times associated with the last days. In years past, I saw many attempts by Hollywood to release fear and panic through frightening movies based on their ideas of what the great apocalypse might look like. They often used distorted renderings of prophecies from the Bible to add credibility to the threat they attempted to make real. It didn't take a Bible scholar to recognize they had very little knowledge or understanding of what the Word of God actually says about the cataclysmic events, which are to manifest in the last days. I noticed that much of what was being presented was of very little potential help for the viewers who might face these challenges.

A few years ago, I began to seriously look into many sources of information for preppers. All of these teachings appeared to be based solely on the wisdom of the world. I noticed one other thing which was common in most of these presentations. Most "prepper" teachings focus a great deal of attention on how to lighten the load of your "bug-out bag." I also noticed there was little agreement as to what is actually needed in the bag. So I began to ask a question: When you need to travel with a light load, what will you take and what will you discard? I encourage you to think about that right now.

In addition to teaching about how to put together a bug-out bag, there were plenty of teachings available concerning what types of emergency food and provisions you need to stock up on as you prepare for the perilous times which are coming. As I went through a large number of these resources, it occurred to me there are already too many thoughts and ideas on this subject. I don't want to add to this burden. The focus I want to develop here is on learning how to lighten your spiritual load so you can better handle the challenges of the last days. My desire is for you to be set free from as many of these burdens as possible. I believe it is time for you to unload all the unnecessary baggage you are carrying around in your spiritual life.

> *Therefore, since we are surrounded by such a great cloud of witnesses, let us throw off everything that hinders and the sin that so easily entangles, and let us run with perseverance the race marked out for us. Let us fix our eyes on Jesus, the author and perfecter of our faith, who for the joy set before him endured the cross, scorning its shame, and sat down at the right hand of the throne of God. Consider him who endured such opposition from sinful men, so that you will not grow weary and lose heart.*
> (Hebrews 12:1-3, NIV)

Yeshua gives an excellent example of learning to travel light as He prepares His disciples for their first evangelistic outreach tour. As He sent out the first twelve missionaries, He gave them very specific instructions about what they should and should not carry with them. These things were specific to this particular journey, however they can also provide some insight for us in our preparation. Look at the Lord's instructions found in Mark 6:8-9, "*He commanded them to take nothing for the journey except a staff—no bag, no bread, no copper in their money belts—but to wear sandals, and not to put on two tunics.*" He gave similar instructions to the second group consisting of seventy missionaries.

Then He said to them, "The harvest truly is great, but the laborers are few; therefore pray the Lord of the harvest to send out laborers into His harvest. Go your way; behold, I send you out as lambs among wolves. Carry neither money bag, knapsack, nor sandals; and greet no one along the road. But whatever house you enter, first say, 'Peace to this house.'" (Luke 10:2-5)

The Lord then gave them some faith building advice in Luke 10:7, "*And remain in the same house, eating and drinking such things as they give, for the laborer is worthy of his wages. Do not go from house to house.*" There are several key concepts in Yeshua's statements. Expect and trust that the Lord will provide what you need when you need it if you are obediently going to places and doing those things He has specifically instructed you to do. Expect people to be a part of that provision. He is already preparing people to receive you and help you when it is time to move out into your area of assigned ministry. Always remember that as a worker in His harvest fields, you are worthy of your wages. Trust Him to provide what you need.

The main concept I want you to focus on in this study is that you need to lighten your spiritual load in order to accomplish your mission as you go where He sends you. This is not a new concept. The Lord revealed it in Isaiah 58:6, "*Is this not the fast that I have chosen: to loose the bonds of wickedness, to undo the heavy burdens, to let the oppressed go free, and that you break every yoke?*" You can be certain about two aspects of the Lord's will for you. It is the Lord's will for you to be set free from unnecessary and useless burdens. It is His will that you break free from every yoke which hinders you.

Here is the real question: Are you truly ready to let these spiritual burdens go? Many people hold on to their spiritual burdens as if there is something holy or pious about going around bent over with a heavy load. There are things you need to carry with you, but there are more things you need to release to effectively do His work and to survive in perilous times. I am providing a list of some of the things you need to let go for His purposes. You can probably add more to the list. In fact, I urge you to make your own list by adding the specific burdens you plan to release in your own life and work.

UNLOADING MAN-MADE DOCTRINE

The perilous times coming in the last days will be difficult for most people to navigate. Some people are already far along the way in their preparations for these perilous times. I hope you are one of them. Many others are totally unprepared. Some who read this may be in this category. Either way, work still needs to be done in this area. Whether you are focused on your own deliverance or working diligently to help others get free, you need a strategy to guide your efforts. We have been warned that many people will appear who are deceptively working to produce the opposite results in your life. These false leaders are intentionally deceiving people and actually adding to their load rather than helping them to be free and to succeed.

> *For the time will come when they will not endure sound doctrine, but according to their own desires, because they have itching ears, they will heap up for themselves teachers; and they will turn their ears away from the truth, and be turned aside to fables.* (2 Timothy 4:3-4)

I believe we are already living in the time prophesied by the Apostle Paul. You probably know several people who will not accept sound doctrine. I have heard many people claim that we should be free from all doctrine and just move with the

Spirit. This is unbiblical. Many spirits work to lead us. There are enemy spirits, which masquerade as the Holy Spirit. Our own spirits often appeal to the fleshly desires remaining in our souls. As people listen for the directions of the Holy Spirit, they have to navigate through a flood of conflicting words. This is why the Bible and sound doctrine are so important in these last days. Both of these resources will help you to discern that which is true from that which is false.

Some religious leaders are actually aligned on the wrong side. Yeshua was very aware of this situation and had to deal with it constantly. Listen to His warning in Matthew 16:6, *"Then Jesus said to them, 'Take heed and beware of the leaven of the Pharisees and the Sadducees.'"* The disciples with Yeshua that day totally misunderstood what He was saying. They were caught up in the concerns of the natural world. They thought He was accusing them of not bringing food for their trip. Yeshua had to wake up their spirits so they could understand what He was saying. Now spiritually awake, *"...they understood that He did not tell them to beware of the leaven of bread, but of the doctrine of the Pharisees and Sadducees."* (Matthew 16:12)

How many disciples are in the same boat today? How many are caught up in concerns about having enough food for the body, but unaware of what they need in order to be fed spiritually? How many are trying to feast on the bread of unrighteous religious leaders in our day? We do not need more man-made doctrine. We need to get back to the pure doctrine of God as revealed by Yeshua in His Word. Did you know that Jesus revealed and taught His doctrine, which had been given to Him by the Father?

> *Jesus answered them and said, "My doctrine is not Mine, but His who sent Me. If anyone wills to do His will, he shall know concerning the doctrine, whether it is from God or whether I*

speak on My own authority. He who speaks from himself seeks his own glory; but He who seeks the glory of the One who sent Him is true, and no unrighteousness is in Him." (John 7:16-18)

It is imperative that you be firmly anchored in the Lord as you make preparations for the increasingly difficult challenges you will face in the near future. It is not the time to be chasing around after some new and exciting theory based on the teachings of man. It is time to focus once more on the direction and purposes of the Lord. Paul states this very clearly in Ephesians 4:14, "...*that we should no longer be children, tossed to and fro and carried about with every wind of doctrine, by the trickery of men, in the cunning craftiness of deceitful plotting*," Manmade doctrine is a burden we need to drop now. It is time to lighten your load by ridding yourself of all false teaching no matter how much it appeals to your natural needs and desires. It is time to let go. Are you ready and willing?

UNLOADING UNRESOLVED SIN

From that time Jesus began to preach and to say, "Repent, for the kingdom of heaven is at hand." (Matthew 4:17)

Yeshua made a clear call for people to release the burden of sin in preparation for the coming of the "*kingdom of heaven.*" People responded to Yeshua's call in a variety of ways. Most missed the real point. Like today people then were seeking every new wind of doctrine. One of the main forms of entertainment in those days was to gather and listen to new ideas coming from charismatic speakers. People would hang on every word as long as their teachings appealed to their fleshly desires. Things haven't changed that much in the spiritual realm. People do the same thing today. Like those in the crowd that day, people travel for miles and lodge in faraway cities in order to hear some new and exciting preacher or prophet.

Peter spoke to a similar crowd gathered in Jerusalem for Shavuot. He spoke to them and made an appeal for them to get ready for the Kingdom of God. He said, "*Repent therefore and be converted, that your sins may be blotted out, so that times of refreshing may come from the presence of the Lord*," (Acts 3:19) His words are as powerful today as when they were first spoken. The truth he released is as real today as it was then. The spiritual realm has not changed. It has not been updated or modernized. Can you hear the truth of the Gospel right now? Are you ready to repent and drop your burdens of sin and darkness? Are you ready for a season of refreshing coming directly from the Lord? If so, I urge you to pause and do that right now. Get right with the Lord and let Him blot out every remnant of your past pain, brokenness and failure. The end is so near that it is clearly time for everyone to repent, to be converted and to receive the salvation of the Lord. Amen?

We would do well to heed Paul's warning in Romans 13:12, "*The night is far spent, the day is at hand. Therefore let us cast off the works of darkness, and let us put on the armor of light.*" Are you ready to lighten your load? Are you ready to "*cast off the works of darkness*?" One thing in short supply right now is time. The night is indeed far spent. The light of God is about to shine into our world and penetrate all the darkness around us. We will soon be covered with the glory of the Lord, which is about to appear. Hear the words of the prophet once more: "*For the earth will be filled with the knowledge of the glory of the Lord, as the waters cover the sea.*" (Habakkuk 2:14) Are you ready to receive it? Lighten your load right now by casting off all the works of darkness. Amen?

UNLOADING FALSE GUILT

The term false guilt describes a condition where people feel guilty about things outside their control or influence. We are living in an unprecedented time of the spread of false guilt. In the USA, the liberal left has been teaching for years that our nation is at fault for almost everything bad in the world. They ignore every good thing coming from our nation and wallow like pigs in the filth and mire of false guilt. They are not happy doing this alone. They want to spread the guilt to as many others as possible. These false teachers have mentored and brought up a generation of people overwhelmed by a burden of false guilt. It is time to let my people go. Amen?

We always supported our daughter by attending Parent's Night at her school as she went through Junior High and High School. I remember sitting in her history class room. The walls were plastered with posters made by students blaming our nation for every bad situation in the world. It was as if no other nation was responsible for the problems existing in their home countries. The atmosphere was extremely negative and the room was filled with the darkness of false guilt. As I sat in that room, I felt a great burden for our young people and for the future of our nation. If this is all they are taught, what kind of citizens will they become?

As I looked around that room, I thought about how different it was when I was in a high school history class. We were encouraged to have pride in the accomplishments of our nation and for the ways we have reached out to help others. Mistakes and flaws were presented in order to face the truth, but the entire focus was not on the negative. I felt happy that I had grown up in a different era and that I had learned to love and celebrate my own country. This is one of the reasons I served for almost 35 years as a US Army officer. We learned about the great heroes who stood up and fought for our freedom. In my experiences as a believer, I was also aware of the great heroes of our spiritual heritage and acknowledged always that we are standing on the shoulders of the giants of faith from the past. I am inspired by them. How about you? Who is inspiring this generation of young people to reach further than any past period and accomplish great things for the world and the Kingdom of God?

> *And what more shall I say? For the time would fail me to tell of Gideon and Barak and Samson and Jephthah, also of David and Samuel and the prophets: who through faith subdued kingdoms, worked righteousness, obtained promises, stopped the mouths of lions, quenched the violence of fire, escaped the edge of the sword, out of weakness were made strong, became valiant in battle, turned to flight the armies of the aliens. Women received their dead raised to life again.* (Hebrews 11:32-35)

I have always liked that old spiritual made famous by Mahalia Jackson, "Down by the Riverside." As I was writing this section, I began to quietly sing the opening words of this song. I felt a great desire to lay down my burdens beside the river of living water. How about you? Is it time to let go of the burdens which hinder your journey with the Lord? We are told by the Apostle Peter that we are being built up into a spiritual house. In the world today, we are the Temple of God where the Spirit of God resides. We don't need to store up any old spiritual trash in the Lord's house.

> *Coming to Him as to a living stone, rejected indeed by men, but chosen by God and precious, you also, as living stones, are being built up a spiritual house, a holy priesthood, to offer up spiritual sacrifices acceptable to God*

through Jesus Christ. Therefore it is also contained in the Scripture, "Behold, I lay in Zion a chief cornerstone, elect, precious, and he who believes on Him will by no means be put to shame." (1 Peter 2:4-6)

Can you come into agreement right now with what the Apostle Paul wrote in 2 Corinthians 4:2, *"But we have renounced the hidden things of shame, not walking in craftiness nor handling the word of God deceitfully, but by manifestation of the truth commending ourselves to every man's conscience in the sight of God."* We have laid our burdens of shame down. We have renounced the hidden things behind that old shame. We firmly stand in this powerful belief, *"For the Scripture says, "Whoever believes on Him will not be put to shame."* (Romans 10:11) Get rid of everything which hinders you right now. Let it go and let the Lord release you once and for all. In the passages below, I want you to receive the promises of God and to be set free from these burdens. Read them aloud, claim them for your own and spend the rest of your life thanking the Lord for what He has done.

> *Then you shall know that I am in the midst of Israel: I am the LORD your God and there is no other. My people shall never be put to shame.* (Joel 2:27)

> *Do not fear, for you will not be ashamed; neither be disgraced, for you will not be put to shame; for you will forget the shame of your youth, and will not remember the reproach of your widowhood anymore.* (Isaiah 54:4)

> *Instead of your shame you shall have double honor, and instead of confusion they*

*shall rejoice in their portion. Therefore in their
land they shall possess double; Everlasting joy
shall be theirs.* (Isaiah 61:7)

UNLOADING UNHEALTHY SOUL TIES

After the Lord had supernaturally delivered King
Jehoshaphat and the people of Judah, the king made a big mistake and allied himself with the enemy of the Lord. After the
Lord had caused all the nations surrounding him to be fearful,
which resulted in peace, he decided to go to war allied with
Ahab the worst king in Israel's history. Earlier, Jehoshaphat
made an unholy and unhealthy alliance by marrying someone
from Ahab's family. Now he voluntarily established an entire
grouping of unholy soul ties.

> *Jehoshaphat had riches and honor in abun-
> dance; and by marriage he allied himself with
> Ahab. After some years he went down to visit
> Ahab in Samaria; and Ahab killed sheep and
> oxen in abundance for him and the people who
> were with him, and persuaded him to go up with
> him to Ramoth Gilead. So Ahab king of Israel
> said to Jehoshaphat king of Judah, "Will you
> go with me against Ramoth Gilead?" And he
> answered him, "I am as you are, and my people
> as your people; we will be with you in the war."*
> (2 Chronicles 18:1-3)

Before going into battle with Ahab, Jehoshaphat asked the
king to seek wisdom from the prophets. Ahab brought in his
group of false prophets who encouraged him to fight an unholy
war. Jehoshaphat had enough spiritual discernment to know
that these were false prophets. He asked the king if he had
a prophet of the Lord. Ahab reluctantly brought in Micaiah

the son of Imla, but made it clear that he hated this man who never gave him a good word. Jehoshaphat admonished Ahab not to speak this way about one of the Lord's prophets. This sounds good and holy until you realize that Jehoshaphat continued to support Ahab contrary to the advice the Lord gave to him through the prophet. Micaiah said, *"I saw all Israel scattered on the mountains, as sheep that have no shepherd. And the Lord said, 'These have no master. Let each return to his house in peace.'"* (2 Chronicles 18:16)

Armed with this and some additional prophetic words from the Lord cautioning them not to go into battle, both Ahab and Jehoshaphat remained resolved to get into a hopeless and doomed fight. The outcome was exactly what the Lord had said through His prophet. Jehoshaphat asked for the word, heard what the Lord said, and then continued with his ill-advised decision. How many people have you seen do this same thing? Have you done something like this yourself? Think about it as you read the passage below describing their behavior.

> *So the king of Israel and Jehoshaphat the king of Judah went up to Ramoth Gilead. And the king of Israel said to Jehoshaphat, "I will disguise myself and go into battle; but you put on your robes." So the king of Israel disguised himself, and they went into battle.* (2 Chronicles 18:28-29)

You cannot effectively serve the Lord and hold on to unholy soul ties. It just doesn't work, and often produces tragic results. It is time to break all these soul ties so that you can freely follow the plans and purposes of the Lord. One man who effectively severed these types of soul ties was Nehemiah. This was not a quick and easy thing to do. He had to deal with the unholy soul ties of all the leaders who were supposed to be working with him on rebuilding the walls of Jerusalem. On his first mission in Jerusalem, Nehemiah thought he had dealt with these issues, but there was still work to be done on his second trip.

> *I arrived in Jerusalem and learned of the wrong that Eliashib had done in turning over to him a room in the courts of The Temple of God. I was angry, really angry, and threw everything in the room out into the street, all of Tobiah's stuff.* (Nehemiah 13:7-8, TMSG)

Eliashib had served as High Priest and had a great deal of influence on the other leaders in Jerusalem. Because of his unholy tie to Tobiah, he had desecrated the Temple by making a living room for the enemy in the courts of the Temple. This was a very clear violation of the Lord's commands and compromised the integrity of their worship and service for the Lord. Tobiah was determined to block the work of Nehemiah and had now been brought right inside the security area of their group. This was intolerable and Nehemiah took strong action to evict Tobiah and to break all ties to his influence. But it didn't end here. A few verses later in the Book of Nehemiah, we see another unholy soul tie effecting their work.

> *One of the sons of Joiada son of Eliashib the high priest was son-in-law to Sanballat the Horonite. And I drove him away from me.* (Nehemiah 13:28)

Once again Eliashib is at the center of the problem. He had allowed a member of his family to marry the daughter of another one of Israel's great enemies, Sanballat the Horonite. Every time Nehemiah turned over a stone, he found another tie between the people and their enemies. This is the nature of unholy soul ties. They have many tentacles like an octopus. When you are free from one, you find yourself attached to another. Getting free from soul ties is a process rather than an event. If you are involved in deliverance ministry, I am certain you have experienced this same problem. If you are going to be free, you have to persist until every tie is broken.

It is time to get free now. Don't wait any longer. There is much work to be done and you will be hindered until you are free. Listen to the advice from Isaiah 2:22, *"Sever yourselves from such a man, whose breath is in his nostrils; for of what account is he?"* In addition to continually seeking to sever the tentacles of these soul ties, be aware of another problem. Few people are alone in these unholy ties. Other members of the family or the group of believers are also likely to be tied along with you to that person. It is important to work the process as a group so that everyone is set free for the work of the Kingdom of God, and to prepare each member to deal with the challenges of these last days.

UNLOADING THE FEAR OF MAN

The fear of man brings a snare, but whoever trusts in the LORD shall be safe. (Proverbs 29:25)

The warning about the consequences of being ruled by the fear of man came too late for King Saul. This was probably his greatest weakness. It certainly led to his downfall as king. This character defect is visible from the very beginning of his kingship. As the announcement was being made concerning the Lord's choice for Israel's first king, he was nowhere to be found. *"So they inquired further of the Lord, 'Has the man come here yet?' And the Lord said, 'Yes, he has hidden himself among the baggage.'"* (1 Samuel 10:22) I believe it is significant that he was hidden *"among the baggage."* Are you hiding in any of the baggage you are carrying? Saul was hiding because of a basic fear of people. The Lord promised to be with him and help him overcome this defect in his character, however he chose not to take his difficulties to the Lord. Saul allowed his fear of man to rule over him instead of him ruling over it with the help of the Lord.

> *Then Saul said to Samuel, "I have sinned. I violated the Lord's command and your instructions. I was afraid of the people and so I gave in to them. Now I beg you, forgive my sin and come back with me, so that I may worship the Lord." But Samuel said to him, "I will not go back with you. You have rejected the word of the Lord, and the Lord has rejected you as king over Israel!"*
> (1 Samuel 15:24-26, NIV)

How are you doing with the human tendency to act or not act because of the fear of man? Almost everyone has this basic fear with the possible exception of sociopaths. It is not actually a question of whether you have it or not. The question is: What are you doing about it? Is it ruling over you or have you learned to rule over it? It is important to remember always the powerful truth released in 1 Corinthians 14:32, *"And the spirits of the prophets are subject to the prophets."* Your spirit is subject to you with the help of the Holy Spirit. You are expected to rule over it and never let it determine your actions. You must learn to fear God rather than failing because of your fear of man. Jesus spoke directly to this issue in the passage below:

> *And I say to you, My friends, do not be afraid of those who kill the body, and after that have no more that they can do. But I will show you whom you should fear: Fear Him who, after He*

has killed, has power to cast into hell; yes, I say
to you, fear Him! (Luke 12:4-5)

This fear of man is as old as the human race. Over and over people have let the Lord down because of their fear of other people. Moses struggled with this fear when the Lord called him to be the liberator of the Children of Israel. He is a hero of the faith because he trusted God and overcame his fears with the help of the Lord. This is the point: live by faith and not by fear! Tragically this character defect was not eliminated in ancient times. It continued even into the time of the prophet Ezekiel. The good news here is that he, like Moses, overcame his fear with the help of the Lord. The Lord is available to help you as well. Accept His advice and the promise that goes with it.

> *And you, son of man, do not be afraid of them*
> *nor be afraid of their words, though briers*
> *and thorns are with you and you dwell among*
> *scorpions; do not be afraid of their words or*
> *dismayed by their looks, though they are a*
> *rebellious house.* (Ezekiel 2:6)

Reflect on your own past. Have you ever been immobilized by the fear of man? It is very important for our preparations to honestly consider our own spiritual strengths and weaknesses so we can repent and return to the Lord who always helps us overcome. In the coming perilous times, the fear of man will be a greater challenge than it is today. Overcome it now and be ready for the days of deep darkness as we like David are called to walk through the valley of the shadow of death. The Lord gave us a powerful and overcoming word in the book of Proverbs.

Do not be afraid of sudden terror, nor of trouble from the wicked when it comes; For the Lord will be your confidence, and will keep your foot from being caught. (Proverbs 3:25-26)

THE BURDEN EXCHANGE

This is the good news of the Gospel. The Lord is offering us the greatest exchange in human history. I like the thought of that. How about you? He wants to exchange your heavy burdens for His light ones. He wants to exchange His rest for all your wearisome struggles. He wants to take your heaviest burdens and replace them with easy and light ones. Are you ready to make a deal? Are you ready to let go?

> *Come to me, all you who are weary and burdened, and I will give you rest. Take my yoke upon you and learn from me, for I am gentle and humble in heart, and you will find rest for your souls. For my yoke is easy and my burden is light.* (Matthew 11:28-30, NIV)

There is no hidden trap here. There is no deceit in His promise to set you free from one burden so that you can be caught up in another. The Lord wants you to experience total freedom from you burdens of sin and shame. The Lord wants you to be free from every tie, which holds you back from your purpose and destiny in the Kingdom. All you have to do is accept the wonderful gift and live in freedom for eternity. Will you accept His offer today?

> *It is for freedom that Christ has set us free. Stand firm, then, and do not let yourselves be burdened again by a yoke of slavery.* (Galatians 5:1, NIV)

When the thief comes to steal, kill and destroy (John 10:10a), are you ready to answer the challenge by asking him: Is that all you've got? Then turn to the Lord and believe His word, "*I have come that they may have life, and that they may have it more abundantly.*" (John 10:10b) Are you ready to declare with the Apostle Paul, "*Yet in all these things we are more than conquerors through Him who loved us.*" (Romans 8:37) Be the conqueror you were called, anointed, blessed and equipped to be in the service of Yeshua ha Messiach! Amen and Amen!

CHAPTER SEVEN
FORGETTING THE PAST

I t is not enough to merely leave things behind, you must also remove them from your memory. To be totally free from the burdens, which hinder your readiness for the challenges of the last days you must learn to forget what you have left behind. I do not intend to deceive you by saying this is something easy for you to do. In fact, forgetting is not normal. Forgetting is not characteristic of human behavior. Being able to forget is in fact something divine. It is something supernatural. As we continue to grow into the image of God, we need to assimilate more and more of His divine characteristics. One of those godly characteristics is the ability to choose to forget.

> *No more shall every man teach his neighbor, and every man his brother, saying, 'Know the Lord,' for they all shall know Me, from the least of them to the greatest of them, says the Lord. For I will forgive their iniquity, and their sin I will remember no more."* (Jeremiah 31:34)

This passage of scripture reveals one of the greatest mysteries of the nature of God. How can an omniscient (all knowing) God forget things? At first glance, it appears to be completely impossible, but know this: God does not lie. This is the point given to us in Hebrews 6:18, *"God did this so that, by two unchangeable things in which it is impossible for God to lie, we who have fled to take hold of the hope offered to us may be greatly encouraged."* By His design and decree, it is impossible for God to lie. If He says He will remember no more, then you can take that to the bank. In fact, He testifies to this truth over and over in both the Old Testament and the New Testament.

> *This is the covenant that I will make with them after those days, says the LORD: I will put My laws into their hearts, and in their minds I will write them,"* then He adds, *"Their sins and their lawless deeds I will remember no more."* (Hebrews 10:16-17)

This is the nature of God. Someone may ask if we can actually aspire to take on part of the nature of God. I believe this is the point of being created in His image. We will never be equal to Him, but we are to be like Him. If He can forget the sins, iniquities and lawless deeds of others, so can you. Of course you will need His help to do this. The Lord made a decision to forget. It is time for you to make a similar decision. It is time to forget the things of the past (the burdens you have released). You can do it because the Lord created you that way. Like forgiving others, forgetting is a choice. Now is the time to declare and decree that you will remember them no more. I can hear someone saying, I need a scripture to back that up. Good! I thought you would never ask. Here it is.

> *Do not fear, for you will not be ashamed; neither be disgraced, for you will not be put to shame; for you will forget the shame of your*

*youth, and will not remember the reproach of
your widowhood anymore.* (Isaiah 54:4)

You can do it because the Lord decreed it for you. Now is
the time to receive this powerful spiritual gift from the Lord.
Embrace it and give Him thanks for it. The Lord wants to do
this for you because He knows that painful memories can be
a heavy burden to carry. Memories of your past failures, mistakes, lost opportunities and sins may be like a veil, which
prevents you from seeing your true destiny for the Kingdom
of God. Memories of the hurts you received from others will
keep you from forgiving people, and block you from deciding
to trust them once more. The kind of unity and agreement necessary to survive the perilous times of the last days can only
be achieved if we forgive, forget and move on.

Here is one example of how this works. As you read the
last chapter it spoke of letting go of unholy soul ties. Hopefully
you worked through this process and let go of one or more of
these soul ties. That is good, but you are only half finished
with the deliverance process. To complete this process you
need to forget about those you were once tied to in unhealthy
ways. If you continue to think about the other person or per-
sons, you are not yet free from your ties to them. If you repeatedly let your mind go over things in those past relationships
and think about the ill effects they had on you, you are not
free. In the same way, if you spend time remembering the
parts of those relationships which appealed to your flesh, you
are not free from those soul ties. You must finish the process
by choosing to forget.

The key to this is to develop a strategy to stop yourself
every time these memories arise. Have a strategy in place
to do something to stop the pattern of your thinking, which
maintains those ties. The best way to do this is to add something new to the pattern, which causes you to turn your attention to something else. One powerful way to do that is to stop

your train of thought by singing praise songs. Get your eyes back on the Lord and away from the unhealthy past. You can do it. God created you with the ability to choose to forget. It is in your DNA. So the issue is not about your ability. It is a matter of choice. Choose to forget and make that choice again every time the old patterns arise.

The enemy wants to remind you of every negative thing, which has happened to you and keep you tied to your burdensome past. Don't continue to fall for his tricks. Choose to forget as many times as it takes to set yourself free. This works well with your past unholy soul ties, but it doesn't stop there. You can also use this technique with every type of memory which blocks you from moving forward in the Kingdom of God. If you are burdened by past mistakes and failures, decree aloud that you have chosen to remember them no more. Each time they arise immediately break it off by making the same decrees. Then begin to give praise and worship to the Lord. Remember how important it is to refuse to give the enemy a foothold.

Some people are completely immobilized by the pain and trauma of past events. These debilitating influences can block them from their destiny in the Kingdom. If you are not gaining spiritual ground as you try to move forward, you are in fact losing ground. There is no neutral point in this present spiritual warfare. The refusal to forgive and forget amounts to allowing the enemy to have victory over your life and work. It is imperative for each of us to shake off these burdens. Paul had a plan for dealing with his painful memories which he shared with the Philippian Church.

> *Not that I have already attained, or am already perfected; but I press on, that I may lay hold of that for which Christ Jesus has also laid hold of me. Brethren, I do not count myself to have apprehended; but one thing I do, forgetting*

those things which are behind and reaching for-
ward to those things which are ahead, I press
toward the goal for the prize of the upward call
of God in Christ Jesus. (Philippians 3:12-14)

The Apostle had learned how to be more like the Lord and forget the things in his past. He was determined to prevent the things he left behind from blocking him spiritually, and from hindering his ability to accomplish his destiny in the Kingdom. It is time for you to do the same thing. It is time for you to make the same decision. Don't ever underestimate the enemy. He will do everything he can to block your ability to forget the past. He will bring it up over and over until he gives up. He will only give up if you steadfastly refuse to allow these things to hinder your walk with the Lord. When he tries to hold you back, double your efforts to reach out for the prize of the upward call as Paul did.

At one time, I became aware that the enemy was doing this in my life. I brought something new into the pattern. As soon as I recognized what he was doing, I would say to the enemy: "Wait a minute. Let's talk about your past. You were one of the morning stars giving praise in front of the Father. Then you made the dumbest mistake in history by thinking you could replace Him. Now let's talk about your present. You have no worthwhile purpose in all of eternity. Now let's look to your future in the lake of fire...." Before I could finish, he was gone. Learn to use his tricks against him and get yourself free.

I urge you to consider beginning another spiritual practice, which has worked well for me. Every time the enemy reminds you of the past and encourages you to hold a grudge toward others, stop and declare forgiveness over them once again. Each time you do this, you will have a victory over the enemy. Each time you do this, you are rubbing his nose in defeat once again. As you continue to decree forgiveness over and over, you will also increase your spiritual strength. Then add to this your choice to forget about it. Never give the enemy a foothold in your spirit, soul, or body. Amen? I remind you again of Paul's instructions in Ephesians 4:26-27 (NIV), "*In your anger do not sin: Do not let the sun go down while you are still angry, and do not give the devil a foothold.*"

One morning as I went upstairs to worship the Lord, I noticed a very sweet fragrance at the entrance to our worship room. It smelled like banana bread baking in the oven. I checked with Gloria and confirmed there was nothing baking in our oven. Then she began to smell this same sweet fragrance. Before, during and after this fragrance manifested, I was led to pray for specific people, but I didn't know what they needed. So, I just trusted that the Holy Spirit would pray the needed prayers through me. Romans 8:26, "*Likewise the Spirit also helps in our weaknesses. For we do not know what we should pray for as we ought, but the Spirit Himself makes intercession for us with groanings which cannot be uttered.*" I encourage you to spend more time praying for others in the Spirit. Let the power of the Lord flow through you as you obey and trust the Holy Spirit to effectively pray through you.

As I continued to worship and pray, the Lord began to bring to my mind some very specific times when I had not responded well to other people. I prayed for forgiveness and I asked Him to help me break off any word curses I may have unintentionally spoken over others during these times. I had never realized that these old things (over 20 years old and mostly forgotten) were still a blockage, but I was glad to be rid of them. It was a relief and joy for me when I set others free from anything negative I may have spoken over their lives or ministry. Then I understood that this is part of the cleansing the Lord began in me the day before. Once it has been cleaned up, there is still one more task. Now I could forget in the proper way because I had left the past in the past.

All the unresolved issues in your past which are contrary to the Word and will of God will hinder you in the time of your greatest need. They will hinder your prayer life, your evangelistic outreach and your daily service to the Lord. These are all things which we must learn to avoid, but there is also an even greater danger. If left unresolved, these spiritual defects will eventually grieve the Holy Spirit. If you grieve Him to the point of His departure, what will you be able to accomplish alone during perilous times. Consider the warning the Apostle Paul gave to the Ephesian Church.

> *And do not grieve the Holy Spirit of God, with whom you were sealed for the day of redemption. Get rid of all bitterness, rage and anger, brawling and slander, along with every form of malice. Be kind and compassionate to one another, forgiving each other, just as in Christ God forgave you.* (Ephesians 4:30-32)

I encourage you to consider your own spiritual condition as you continue to prepare yourself to be able to deal with the hardships and challenges of the last days. Start by asking yourself some important questions. Do you have any old baggage you need to let go of in this season? Now is the time to allow the Lord to set you and others free in the spiritual realm. Do you have any bitterness or unforgiveness in your soul? These things will hinder your walk with the Lord and block your much needed spiritual effectiveness. Once you have repented and released them, it is now time to forget them. Please understand that this is very different from forgetting unresolved issues in your past. You must deal with them and let the Lord release you before you can effectively forget and move on. Every root of bitterness and all the spiritual problems which accompany them, must be removed. The passage below has helped me with this task and I pray it will also help you.

Therefore strengthen the hands which hang down, and the feeble knees, and make straight paths for your feet, so that what is lame may not be dislocated, but rather be healed. Pursue peace with all people, and holiness, without which no one will see the Lord: looking carefully lest anyone fall short of the grace of God; lest any root of bitterness springing up cause trouble, and by this many become defiled; (Hebrews 12:12-15)

Forgiving is the Key to Forgetting

The Lord is longsuffering and abundant in mercy, forgiving iniquity and transgression; but He by no means clears the guilty, visiting the iniquity of the fathers on the children to the third and fourth generation. (Numbers 14:18)

For many people this is a very uncomfortable truth. I have seen it over and over in the past. People will walk out of your meetings when you focus on forgiveness. As a result of past hurts, they feel justified in holding on to anger and bitterness. They are not inclined in the least to speak forgiveness over those they believe caused them pain or emotional harm. One great tragedy in the spiritual realm is that people don't seem to realize that refusing to forgive others, keeps the hurt within their own hearts alive. Holding on to old hurts and refusing to forgive will continue to block you from your destiny. If not dealt with, unforgiveness will likely grow stronger with time.

When the command to forgive is mentioned, I have heard many people find ways to deny what the Lord taught in Matthew 6:14-15, *"For if you forgive men their trespasses, your heavenly Father will also forgive you. But if you do not forgive men their trespasses, neither will your Father forgive your trespasses.*" People have actually listed for me some things in Paul's writings to counter the clear focus given by Yeshua. It is as if anything Paul said is more powerful than the words of Yeshua. It is important to remember this principle: you cannot and must not try to change the Word of God to align with your thoughts, feelings and desires. We must allow ourselves to be transformed by the Word of God in order to align ourselves with Him. Remember once again the imperative given by the Apostle Paul to the believers in Rome.

> *And do not be conformed to this world, but be transformed by the renewing of your mind, that you may prove what is that good and acceptable and perfect will of God.* (Romans 12:2)

I pray that you will allow the Lord to renew your mind and transform your soul as you allow Him to prepare you for the tribulation of the last days. Remember that forgiveness is the nature of God. This is one of His thirteen attributes, which He revealed to Moses on the mountain. If we want to serve Him fully, we must change to meet His will rather than explaining away what He has decreed over us. If we want Him to forgive and forget our shortcomings, failures and sin, we must be willing to do the same for His other children.

> *For I will be merciful to their unrighteousness, and their sins and their lawless deeds I will remember no more.* (Hebrews 8:12)

Declare Bankruptcy over Lost Things

As I pondered the spiritual necessity of forgiving and forgetting, it occurred to me that in the natural world bankruptcy is a way of being released from old debts and getting a fresh start for the future. Many people who declare bankruptcy in the natural are in fact giving up on hopes and dreams for their future. They have come to realize that continuing in their failing endeavors will never result in success. It is never easy to give up on hopes and dreams even when we come to realize that they are not a part of the Lord's plan and purpose for our lives.

You have most likely found it necessary to let go of your own plans from the past in order to take hold of the things which are possible for you in the future. As I pondered this idea, I began to think about all the little girls I have known who wanted to grow up to be ballerinas, pop singers, models, or modern dancers. At some point, most of them had to realize they were not born with the natural gifts and talents to succeed in these career choices. It is not easy to accept something less than your first hopes and dreams for the future. I thought about all the little boys who wanted to grow up to be firemen or police officers, but had to let go because their opportunities and abilities led them in a different direction.

For many people, some aspects of these long lost dreams and desires are still present in the depth of their hearts and in distant but powerful memories. In moments of weakness, the deep feelings of loss from unrealized dreams can come back to haunt the strongest among us. These burdens of memory also need to be resolved for us to move forward in our spiritual preparations. Perhaps the Apostle was thinking of his own past dreams and ambitions of becoming a powerful influence in the religious and political organizations in his culture when he wrote the passage below. He realized he needed to put away "childish things" in order to take hold of his calling and anointing in the Kingdom of God. Perhaps you need to go through a similar process as you work to prepare for the perilous times of these last days.

> *When I was a child, I spoke as a child, I understood as a child, I thought as a child; but when*

I became a man, I put away childish things. For now we see in a mirror, dimly, but then face to face. Now I know in part, but then I shall know just as I also am known. (1 Corinthians 13:11-12)

Growing up is never easy. This is partially due to the fact that you have to let go of many things in your past and present in order to take hold of other things more appropriate for your current level of maturity and future life and ministry. Are you ready to let go of outdated hopes and dreams in order to take hold of the new things the Lord is placing before you now? This is the challenge of the hour and season we are in right now. Your choices are important for your life and your Kingdom destiny. I encourage you to take some time to intentionally let go of things from your past so you can be set free for the future. Then intentionally choose to forget and remember them no more. Accept your new hopes, dreams and possibilities for the true destiny given to you for the Kingdom of God.

No Pining Away

Not that I have already obtained all this, or have already been made perfect, but I press on to take hold of that for which Christ Jesus took hold of me. Brothers, I do not consider myself yet to have taken hold of it. But one thing I do: Forgetting what is behind and straining toward what is ahead, I press on toward the goal to win the prize for which God has called me heavenward in Christ Jesus. (Philippians 3:12-14, NIV)

Have you ever known someone who has been emotionally and spiritually frozen in their past? It is sad to see someone immobilized and debilitated by their past. Some are frozen

143

in time because the past was seemingly the best time of their lives, and try as they might they cannot get back to it. Others are immobilized because of the pain and trauma which persists from old emotionally overwhelming events. Still others are blocked because they cannot let go, forgive and forget. It is a tragic loss for both that individual and for the Kingdom of God. They were created for a purpose, which they are not able to accomplish because of these burdens. They were born with a wonderful and powerful destiny for the Kingdom of God, which is unlikely to be reached. In the past, people would say that they are "pining away."

The phrase "pining away" describes someone who is both thin and weak because of sadness and loss in their lives. They are often overwhelmed by both a sense of hopelessness and helplessness. People often become thin because they are too sad, lonely and depressed to feel the normal hunger, which drives others to eat what they need. They are both physically and spiritually weak because they are unable to embrace the strength of the Lord needed to lift them out of the deep darkness in their lives. Many have exhausted every natural resource and remedy without making any real progress. The problem is that their situation is more spiritual than natural, but their eyes have been blocked from seeing the nature of their problem. You will never resolve a spiritual problem with a natural solution. It is time for them to seek and find a spiritual solution to resolve their distress.

If you are struggling at any level with this issue, it is time to look to the Lord for help. Ask Him to help you break free from the grasp of the enemy. Only the Holy Spirit can truly liberate you from your deep darkness. The world will not support you in switching to a spiritual solution. Natural science will lead you to the use of many kinds of prescription medicines. Many of these medicines have worse side effects than the disorder they claim to fix. I am not recommending that you give up a particular medication. This can often lead to worse problems. I am recommending that you add to your current health care plan, a new and more powerful prescription — the Holy Spirit and the Word of God. When it is appropriate for your health, the Lord and your physician will agree that you no longer need the help of medication. Don't make rash and unwise decisions which might do more harm than good.

> *These things we also speak, not in words which man's wisdom teaches but which the Holy Spirit teaches, comparing spiritual things with spiritual. But the natural man does not receive the things of the Spirit of God, for they are foolishness to him; nor can he know them, because they are spiritually discerned.* (1 Corinthians 2:13-14)

The powerful presence and influence of the Holy Spirit is always the best solution for every problem. I always pre-scribe more of Him and more of the Word of God. I use the Word of God like medication. When I feel weak, I take several doses of Joel 3:10b, *"Let the weak say, 'I am strong.'"* When I feel the symptoms of an illness, I start taking repeated doses of Isaiah 53:5. I paraphrase this to make it mine. I say, "By His stripes I am healed!" I urge you to find other passages of scripture which can be medication for your needs and speak them aloud over and over until they manifest. Don't just read these things and move on. Put them into practice so that you will not "pine away" any longer. Take the recommendation of another James:

> *Do not merely listen to the word, and so deceive yourselves. Do what it says. Anyone who listens to the word but does not do what it says is like a man who looks at his face in a mirror and, after looking at himself, goes away and immediately*

forgets what he looks like. But the man who looks intently into the perfect law that gives freedom, and continues to do this, not forgetting what he has heard, but doing it—he will be blessed in what he does. (James 1:22-25, NIV)

GOOD NEWS

There is always good news in the Lord. He never leaves us without hope and a promise during our times of weakness, illness, or hardship. The Lord is good and His love and mercy endure forever. Amen? It is always a good thing to look back on the powerful revelations of the nature of God in His Word. As you find these powerful and empowering messages in the Word, begin to say them aloud and claim all the promises for your own life and ministry. Even before solutions manifest, begin to give Him thanks, praise and worship. This will unlock many spiritual gifts for you. Praise as in the Psalm below.

You are forgiving and good, O Lord, abounding in love to all who call to you. Hear my prayer, O Lord; listen to my cry for mercy. In the day of my trouble I will call to you, for you will answer me. (Psalm 86:5-6, NIV)

Instead of going over a long list of your problems and needs, focus on Who He is and What He does. He has not changed. He is the same yesterday, today and forever. You can trust His promises and you are encouraged to claim them for yourself, your family and your work. The more you speak aloud words of praise for His awesome character as your loving Father, amazing Savior and powerful Holy Spirit, the more you will tend to take on these same characteristics. Paul charged the Colossian Church to become more and more like the Lord. This charge is also for you. I pray that you will grow into this awesome image more and more each day. Receive the advice of a seasoned Apostle of the Lord in the passage below.

> *Therefore, as the elect of God, holy and beloved, put on tender mercies, kindness, humility, meekness, longsuffering; bearing with one another, and forgiving one another, if anyone has a complaint against another; even as Christ forgave you, so you also must do. But above all these things put on love, which is the bond of perfection.* (Colossians 3:12-14)

I want to close this chapter by sharing another speech given at a military farewell party. The person leaving was a senior member of the Commanding General's Staff. As a member of the staff, I was required to be present. In fact I was charged to help prepare for the party, but I had no idea about what would happen during this gathering. One side note: as I wrote this another memory flashed back into my mind. I took off the jacket of my Class A (green) uniform and hung it over a chair as I helped set up the tables, chairs and decorations. I had no idea until much later that someone had rearranged the items pinned to my blouse. I wore it incorrectly throughout the party to someone's great pleasure. Someone enjoyed seeing me out of uniform at the General's party. Now I need to forgive and forget about this memory hidden for such a long time. Expect these things to continue to manifest as you work through this process. However this is not the primary point I want to make.

When we got to the point in the ceremony where the farewell speech was to be given, the departing colonel appeared to be very emotional. As he began to talk, his voice quivered and then began to break up as he wiped tears from his eyes. He meekly said this had been his greatest fear leading up to this moment. He realized he was too emotional to continue. Then he let us know that he had prepared for this moment by recording his farewell comments the night before. He asked us to bear with him as he tearfully set up the recorder. It took some time, but it was finally ready. No one was prepared for what would happen when he pushed the "Play" button. In a very loud voice, we heard Johnny Paycheck blast out the words to his hit song: "Take this job and shove it. I ain't workin here no more."

The tension in the room burst like a balloon as outrageous laughter followed. I looked at the head table to see how the Commanding General was handling this. As my eyes moved in his direction, I couldn't believe what I was seeing. The General was laughing so hard that he was sliding out of his chair. He sat on the floor for a very long time before he was able to gather himself together to make some closing comments. The Colonel told us that his job had been difficult and he didn't want to take any of that stress into his retirement. He found a way to let it go so that he could truly forget about it. This was a very creative and fun way to accomplish his purpose.

Maybe it is time for you to find a creative way to let go and forget the things of your past. Remember you were created in the image of God and He is the most creative person in the Universe. Use you God given gifts to find ways to set yourself free so that you can be more like Him each day. Find ways to lay your burdens down and never return to pick them up again. Amen?

CHAPTER EIGHT
WALKING BY FAITH

But someone will say, "You have faith, and I have works." Show me your faith without your works, and I will show you my faith by my works. You believe that there is one God. You do well. Even the demons believe—and tremble! But do you want to know, O foolish man, that faith without works is dead? Was not Abraham our father justified by works when he offered Isaac his son on the altar? Do you see that faith was working together with his works, and by works faith was made perfect? (James 2:18-22)

There is an age old dilemma faced by every generation as they try to understand the relationship between faith and works. As you can see in the passage above, this struggle was present in the New Testament church. Now it is the struggle of our generation as we prepare for the coming of the Lord. Should we simply walk by faith and expect the Lord to provide all our needs or is there some action required on our part? Should we store up things now which we may need when perilous times come upon us? Are we showing a lack of faith when we trust in our storehouses to meet our needs? People have strong opinions on both sides.

For some people storing up money, food and supplies is logical and is the obvious choice. For others, trusting in what you can store demonstrates a profound lack of faith in the Lord's promised provision. It often appears that these two positions are too far apart to work out a compromise or to resolve the arguments. Of course there is a third alternative actually taken by the majority of people. They choose not to think about it. They simply refuse to believe perilous times will come during their lifetime. You can always spot these people in the news reports covering a major disaster. They are the ones doing panic shopping, which depletes all the supplies in local stores. They are the ones who suddenly change from mild mannered and generous people into a hostile mob of hoarders who are gathering everything they can get their hands on in the time of crisis.

Both panic shopping and hoarding can make any troubling situation much worse. During the hurricane season this year, all the storm watchers were predicting that the big one would make landfall near where we live. News programs were predicting that panic shopping would deplete the supplies in local stores and it might take several days to get the trucks back on the road with fresh supplies. As you have already guessed panic hit our region. Even the superstores were depleted of water and emergency food. To everyone's surprise, the storm changed directions and we only received a nice rain shower. The stores were empty and many people had enough bottled water to last for months. Proper prior planning by people in our area would have yielded much better results. What do you think about stocking your storehouse to be safe in case perilous times suddenly come upon you?

TO STORE OR NOT TO STORE?

Over the years, I have met several people who decided to live by faith alone. They quit their jobs and sat down to wait on the Lord's provision. This hasn't worked very well for those I have known. I have listened to various explanations given by these people for making their choice to stop working. These explanations are carefully designed and worded to make this behavior sound both righteous and honorable. I have many questions about the choices these individuals make. Is this a choice blessed by the Lord? Has He made a commitment to provide for them while they rest and wait? Did He really tell them to do this? I have one answer which seems right to me. If no provision comes, it is very unlikely that the Lord told them to do this. The Lord does not call individuals or families to live under conditions of deprivation or starvation.

As I stated in the beginning of this chapter, this struggle has been going on since the days of the early church. Paul also had to deal with this issue in the church at Thessalonica. Some people had stopped working and were depending on others to provide for them while they waited for the Lord's return. After a short period of time, people realized it was too great a burden for them to take care of their own families as well as those who refused to work. They appealed to Paul and he gave his solution to the problem in 2 Thessalonians 3:10 *"For even when we were with you, we commanded you this: If anyone will not work, neither shall he eat."* Paul was willing to apply a little tough love for those unwilling to work. It is unrealistic, unwise and unholy to expect others to work hard to provide for you during a long season of resting. Those people I know who chose the path of refusing to work were so entrenched in their beliefs that they continued until they ran out of people willing to support them.

With the current rise of the age old blight on humanity known as socialism, we hear people once again teaching and plotting to give away the wealth and wages of others to support those who do not work. The false teachers promoting this system of government are able to convince many people that they can transfer the wealth of the rich and provide for the needs of everyone. This system of government has failed miserably throughout history. No matter how wealthy a country may be, it will soon run out of wealth to transfer. The people who are constantly paying the bills for others will soon stop producing. The result has always been great deprivation, suffering and chaos followed by violent outbursts and radical anarchy. Socialism is in effect a constant effort by the enemy to push us too quickly into perilous times. This is clearly demonstrated in every socialist government in the world today. It is and always has been the economic system of the antichrist.

RESPONDING TO THE SITUATION

At first glance it may seem that Yeshua gave conflicting information to the disciples according to Luke's account of the Gospel. In the ninth chapter, He told the disciples to take nothing with them on their ministry trips. *"And He said to them, 'Take nothing for the journey, neither staffs nor bag nor bread nor money; and do not have two tunics apiece.'"* (Luke 9:3) Later in chapter twenty two Yeshua instructed them to take everything they would need on their missionary journey. What changed? In addition to food, money and clothes, He told them to take a sword. As you read Luke's account in chapter twenty two, ask yourself what is the difference between these two plans for the future?

> *Then He said to them, "But now, he who has a money bag, let him take it, and likewise a knapsack; and he who has no sword, let him sell his garment and buy one. For I say to you that this*

which is written must still be accomplished in Me: 'And He was numbered with the transgressors.' For the things concerning Me have an end." So they said, "Lord, look, here are two swords." And He said to them, "It is enough." (Luke 22:36-38)

Was Yeshua unable to provide for them on the second trip? Were they now unable to simply live by faith and expect things to be provided? Clearly this is not the case. Yeshua reminded them of the provisions which came to them by faith on the earlier trip. *"And He said to them, 'When I sent you without money bag, knapsack, and sandals, did you lack anything?' So they said, 'Nothing.'"* (Luke 22:35) It is clear that the point Yeshua is making is not about faith. So what is His point? As I prayed about this, I received an answer from the Holy Spirit which works for me. The Lord was urging His disciples to be attentive to the leadership of the Holy Spirit rather than standing on an old principle which may have worked in the past. The key here is to be ready to respond immediately to the guidance of the Holy Spirit.

I urge you now to be prepared to receive differing instructions as your situation changes. The point of the Lord's message to us is about obedience. It is also about being flexible and remaining prepared for rapid change. There is no doubt the Lord can provide for us. There is no doubt there is great power in faith. Certainly we should always have more faith in the Lord than in our storehouses. We need to keep our eyes on the prize. We need to stay focused on the Lord even when we stand in faith for His provision. Think about this as you study the passage below.

Life is more than food, and the body is more than clothing. Consider the ravens, for they neither sow nor reap, which have neither storehouse

*nor barn; and God feeds them. Of how much
more value are you than the birds? And which
of you by worrying can add one cubit to his
stature? If you then are not able to do the least,
why are you anxious for the rest? Consider the
lilies, how they grow: they neither toil nor spin;
and yet I say to you, even Solomon in all his
glory was not arrayed like one of these. If then
God so clothes the grass, which today is in the
field and tomorrow is thrown into the oven, how
much more will He clothe you, O you of little
faith?* (Luke 12:23-28)

PREPARING

Here is one powerful truth: the Lord is all about preparing.
He constantly prepared himself and His followers for things
happening in the near term as well as those things which will
happen in the distant future. He made this clear in many of
His teachings. Near the end of His ministry on Earth, He told
His disciples that He was starting a new program of preparation for them. He was planning to go to Heaven in order to
prepare a place for them in His Father's house. Here is some
good news for you. He is preparing a place for you too.

*Let not your heart be troubled; you believe in
God, believe also in Me. In My Father's house
are many mansions; if it were not so, I would
have told you. I go to prepare a place for you.
And if I go and prepare a place for you, I will
come again and receive you to Myself; that
where I am, there you may be also.* (John 14:1-3)

This passage is often read in funeral services. Many people
choose not to think much about it because it brings up painful

memories of the loss of loved ones. This passage actually describes the process once followed in preparation for a Jewish wedding. After the bride and groom became engaged, they considered themselves to already be married in the spiritual realm. The actual wedding and moving in together would come at a later date. Until that time came, the groom was tasked to go back to his family home and make provisions for his bride to move in after the wedding process was complete. This is what Yeshua was promising to the believers. He was letting them know that the church is His bride and He is preparing a place for her in His Father's house. He is fulfilling His part of the marital arrangement.

Preparations have been completed and your home in Heaven is ready for you now. Now is the time to accept this good news and stand on it by faith. All true believers are invited to the wedding feast of the Lamb. This promise is for you and me. Look again at the promise given in Revelation 19:9, *"Then he said to me, 'Write: Blessed are those who are called to the marriage supper of the Lamb!' And he said to me, 'These are the true sayings of God.'"* When you complete your purpose for the Kingdom on earth, you have an eternal place of residence in the Father's house. Trust His word. It is the truth.

The messages in the Bible about storing things to meet future needs all have a double meaning. As I told you at the outset, the purpose of this book is to prepare you spiritually and mentally for the perilous times ahead. There is a pattern to the Lord's teaching and we can see it clearly in this instance. Remember what Paul wrote to the believers in 1 Corinthians 15:46, *"However, the spiritual is not first, but the natural, and afterward the spiritual."* When we teach, study and prepare for our storehouse in the natural, it is all working to help us visualize and establish provisions for our future spiritual needs.

A good example of this is revealed in the Biblical story of Noah and the flood. The Lord gave Noah very detailed information about building a floating storehouse in preparation for a great flood. On the surface this all seems to focus only on the natural provisions needed to feed people and animals for several months while the earth remained under water. Later, you can see and understand that the Lord was preparing Noah's heart and mind for establishing a brave new world. With Noah and his family the Lord was establishing a new spiritual order. He released the same spiritual instructions to Noah first given to Adam and Eve in the garden.

> *By faith Noah, being divinely warned of things not yet seen, moved with godly fear, prepared an ark for the saving of his household, by which he condemned the world and became heir of the righteousness which is according to faith.* (Hebrews 11:7)

After the perilous times released in the generation of Noah, human beings were once again given great spiritual authority over the earth and everything which lives on it. The Lord made this very clear in the instructions given in Genesis 9:1-2, "*So God blessed Noah and his sons, and said to them: 'Be fruitful and multiply, and fill the earth. And the fear of you and the dread of you shall be on every beast of the earth, on every bird of the air, on all that move on the earth, and on all the fish of the sea. They are given into your hand.'*" In his natural situation on the Ark, Noah was daily demonstrating his spiritual role as the dominate one who would take care of the needs of all animals.

Think through the process of this restoration of spiritual authority once more. Noah was given authority and was told to have dominion over every living thing on earth. This authority was first established in the natural when he prepared for them by storing food to meet their needs during that extended period of time. When they stepped off of the ark, Noah and his descendants were told to maintain the kind of dominion over the earth, which was given to Adam in the beginning. This new spiritual reality followed what he had to do in the natural. The spiritual authority which had been lost has now been restored. This command to have dominion has been passed down through the ages and now rests on you. This is how we continue to move from understanding in the natural first and then in the spiritual realm.

People often have difficulty understanding these things. With the natural mind these spiritual truths are beyond our reasoning abilities. Remember what Paul wrote in 1 Corinthians 2:14, "*But the natural man does not receive the things of the Spirit of God, for they are foolishness to him; nor can he know them, because they are spiritually discerned.*" As you study the passage below, think about it from the perspective of the spiritual as well as the natural. How is the Lord preparing you for these perilous times and what will He release to you through them? The clue is found in the last verse in this passage. Every promise the Lord has made will be fulfilled. Be prepared. Watch and wait for the fulfillment of the prophetic words and promises of Yeshua concerning the last days.

> *But when you see Jerusalem surrounded by armies, then know that its desolation is near. Then let those who are in Judea flee to the mountains, let those who are in the midst of her depart, and let not those who are in the country enter her. For these are the days of vengeance, that all things which are written may be fulfilled.* (Luke 21:20-22)

STORING WITH WRONG MOTIVES

It is possible to limit or block the benefits and blessings of every good thing if you respond to the situation with wrong motives. You would do well to heed the advice of Solomon released in Proverbs 16:2, *"All a man's ways seem innocent to him, but motives are weighed by the Lord."* We must learn not to choose solely based on what our natural mind or flesh feels is right. The worst despots in history believed they were doing the right things for the right reasons when in fact their actions were more like those of a monster. It is much better for everyone if you follow the advice given in Proverbs 16:3, *"Commit to the Lord whatever you do, and your plans will succeed."*

The point is that motives matter. They matter a great deal, because they are important to the Lord. Always go to the Lord for guidance when you decide to establish your natural and spiritual storehouses. Yeshua gave a powerful parable to the people to help them understand this truth. Once again the natural mind cannot fully understand this teaching of the Lord. Ask the Holy Spirit for wisdom to fully grasp what the Lord is saying to you. In the natural, you may wonder what is wrong with the plans of the man in this parable. It all seems to make sense to the natural mind. Once again, Yeshua is using things in the natural to reveal spiritual truths. The man's time was short and he didn't know it. He should have been storing spiritual treasures and working to get right with the Lord. Your time is short. What should you be doing right now?

> *And he thought within himself, saying, 'What shall I do, since I have no room to store my crops?' So he said, 'I will do this: I will pull down my barns and build greater, and there I will store all my crops and my goods. And I will say to my soul, "Soul, you have many*

goods laid up for many years; take your ease; eat, drink, and be merry "' But God said to him, "Fool! This night your soul will be required of you; then whose will those things be which you have provided?" (Luke 12:17-20)

STORING WISELY

With the wisdom given by the Lord, Solomon provided a treasure trove of powerful spiritual keys to help people understand how to be wise rather than foolish. He speaks of wise things for us to store up for the future. You can find one of these wise choices in Proverbs 10:14, *"Wise people store up knowledge, but the mouth of the foolish is near destruction."* How are you doing at filling your storehouse with the knowledge of the Lord? Are you making wise choices about the things you choose to store? Are you growing in your understanding of His plans and purposes for your future? It is my goal to add to my storehouse every day as I begin each morning by immersing myself in the Word of God. I want to store up His word, understand His ways and prepare myself to obediently follow Him. How about you? What are you doing to store up the knowledge of the Lord? Are you daily growing in the grace and knowledge of the Lord? I recommend a thorough study of Peter's second letter to help you learn to store what you will truly need in the perilous times ahead. Below is one example.

> *You therefore, beloved, since you know this beforehand, beware lest you also fall from your own steadfastness, being led away with the error of the wicked; but grow in the grace and knowledge of our Lord and Savior Jesus Christ.* (2 Peter 3:17-18)

The Lord was also working to help people understand these spiritual truths during the time of Isaiah the prophet. The people often missed the point of the Lord's messages because they were only able to see with their natural eyes, believe with their natural heart and hear with their natural ears. It must not be that way with you and me. Consider Isaiah's advice in Isaiah 33:6, (NIV), "*He will be the sure foundation for your times, a rich store of salvation and wisdom and knowledge; the fear of the Lord is the key to this treasure.*" Consider this profound truth. The Lord is a rich store of everything you need in the spiritual realm. To prepare for the perilous times ahead consider what you are doing to build up this storehouse.

In Biblical times there were only brief periods of safety and security before the next outbreak of danger, war and peril. Some wisely prepared for those times. One example is Jehoshaphat. His preparations are reported in 2 Chronicles 17:12-13, (NIV), "*Jehoshaphat became more and more powerful; he built forts and store cities in Judah and had large supplies in the towns of Judah. He also kept experienced fighting men in Jerusalem.*" King Jehoshaphat was adept at preparing for the natural needs of the future. He was not always so effective in his spiritual readiness. The Lord continuously sent prophetic words to help him. Unlike many of the kings of both Israel and Judah, He was almost always wise enough to heed the word of the Lord spoken by His prophets. Who are you listening to today?

Many people today struggle over the issue of tithing. I learned early on that people react in very visible ways to every mention I made about giving from the pulpit. I love to watch people respond when I teach on giving. Often people will grasp their wallet or purse and hold on with a firm grasp as if I am planning to walk up and take what I want. I never teach about giving in order to get something for myself. I always teach because it is in the Word of God and He will bless those who obey. I want people to receive the blessing and favor the

Lord has promised to those who are generous in their sowing. This is why I teach about these spiritual truths. What are your thoughts on tithing? Consider the Lord's purposes for tithing in the passage below.

> *At the end of every three years, bring all the tithes of that year's produce and store it in your towns, so that the Levites (who have no allotment or inheritance of their own) and the aliens, the fatherless and the widows who live in your towns may come and eat and be satisfied, and so that the Lord your God may bless you in all the work of your hands.* (Deuteronomy 14:28-29, NIV)

People who are obsessed with storing up money in the bank or food in the closet often reject these teachings. Some claim these teachings and commands were only valid for those people at that time. I recommend further study. If you want access to the Lord's storehouse, you need to be investing in the Kingdom. This is how you access the promises of God like the one below. Store wisely my friend. Your future depends on it.

> *Now he who supplies seed to the sower and bread for food will also supply and increase your store of seed and will enlarge the harvest of your righteousness. You will be made rich in every way so that you can be generous on every occasion, and through us your generosity will result in thanksgiving to God.* (2 Corinthians 9:10-11, NIV)

FAITH

Do any of these things diminish the role of faith in your life? Of course not! Study once again the powerful lessons of faith and outcomes in the eleventh chapter of the book of Hebrews. One powerful truth revealed in this chapter is that true heroes of the faith understand both the natural and spiritual implications of faith. As an example consider the teaching about the faith of Abraham. He was not only focused on the natural, but understood that the real meaning of the Lord's promises were eternal. He was not looking for a pleasant place to visit or live on the earth. His eyes were fixed on a city built by God. We might call this the New Jerusalem; our eternal home with the Lord.

> *By faith Abraham obeyed when he was called to go out to the place which he would receive as an inheritance. And he went out, not knowing where he was going. By faith he dwelt in the land of promise as in a foreign country, dwelling in tents with Isaac and Jacob, the heirs with him of the same promise; for he waited for the city which has foundations, whose builder and maker is God.* (Hebrews 11:8-10)

Faith is listed among the spiritual gifts in 1 Corinthians 12:9 *"...to another faith by the same Spirit..."* Some people act as if they believe faith is one of the works of the natural man. They make accusations to and about people they see as having too little faith. There is a powerful spiritual truth released in this brief reference to faith as a spiritual gift. This is not about a simple belief or acknowledging that the Lord exists. This is about something much more powerful. This kind of faith is a power gift of the Spirit by which supernatural things are brought into manifestation. This is believing beyond any doubt that the Lord will heal someone. This kind of faith opens the windows of Heaven so that miracles, healings, signs and wonders pour out on you and me. This is the kind of faith which can affirm with certainty: "*For we walk by faith, not by sight.*" (2 Corinthians 5:7)

People often ask me why their prayers have not been answered. There are many possible answers to this question; most of which are not very helpful at that moment to the one asking. It takes spiritual maturity to understand the Lord's answers. The natural mind simply cannot understand the deep spiritual truths, which will provide answers to these questions. As you grow in the Lord, look for some of these answered questions in His Word.

For now, here is one key to understanding why some prayers are not answered. James 4:3, "*When you ask, you do not receive, because you ask with wrong motives, that you may spend what you get on your pleasures.*" Again the answer has to do with motives. Get your heart right with the Lord and always evaluate and correct your motives to line up with His Word and His will. It is always good to live and walk by faith as long as it is lined up with the Lord's plans and purposes for your life. Store as He tells you to store. Wait for provision when He tells you to wait.

FAITH PLUS PREPARATION

The real answer to our questions about faith vs. storing, is that both things are necessary. It is not about either/or, but about maintaining a wise balance between the two. We always trust the Lord and commit our lives to Him firmly maintaining that He will provide for His own now and forever. At the same time, we understand that we must also do our part. The Lord promised provision for Egypt during a great and protracted famine. Through the wise advice of Joseph His plan was understood. They needed to store up supplies to last for seven years.

This solution sounds one way to the natural mind but an entirely different way for those who understand the ways of the spiritual realm. Something very supernatural happened in Egypt. Joseph stored up 20 percent of the crops each year while the people lived on 80 percent. When the famine came, Joseph's 20 percent was more than enough for the people. They had as much as when they were living on 80 percent. In addition, Egypt had enough to feed numerous people from other nations. In the spiritual realm, the Lord's 20 percent is greater than the natural world's 80 percent.

We too have the opportunity to store up now the provisions we need in the perilous times ahead. This all seems very natural until we factor in the supernatural power of the Lord. The little which we store becomes much when the Lord blesses it. Remember what the Lord did for the Children of Israel in their collection of manna. *"Then the children of Israel did so and gathered, some more, some less. So when they measured it by omers, he who gathered much had nothing left over, and he who gathered little had no lack."* (Exodus 16:17-18a) The Lord's plan is for you to have no lack as you store what is needed while you continue to stand on faith.

As we close out this chapter, I want to share one more pearl of spiritual wisdom with you from the book of James. Throughout the text of this powerful book, James considers the connection between faith and works. In his day, people who were living during perilous times were also wrestling with these issues. They struggled to understand how they should live for the Lord. Some said one thing while others said something else. We haven't really moved past this struggle and we can still profit from the wisdom and understanding of the brother of Yeshua, head of the church in Jerusalem. Look again at his powerful lesson on faith and works.

But someone will say, "You have faith, and I have works." Show me your faith without your works, and I will show you my faith by my works. You believe that there is one God. You do well. Even the demons believe—and tremble! But do you want to know, O foolish man, that faith without works is dead? (James 2:18-20)

PART THREE
MAXIMIZING RESOURCES, MINIMIZING SHORTFALLS

I n the next three chapters we will again use the Biblical principle of looking first at the natural then at the spiritual. Remember once again how Paul summarized this way of getting at spiritual truths in 1 Corinthians 15:46, "*However, the spiritual is not first, but the natural, and afterward the spiritual.*" The created order is based on what already exists in the spiritual realm. Since the natural order is a limited copy of the spiritual, many of the same principles are at work in both. When you are enabled to more fully understand the natural order, hidden truths are revealed. These revelations do not come from the wisdom of the world, but through the wisdom of the Lord. In this manner, He reveals the hidden mysteries of the Kingdom to those who are willingly led by His Holy Spirit.

> *But the natural man does not receive the things of the Spirit of God, for they are foolishness to him; nor can he know them, because they are spiritually discerned.* (1 Corinthians 2:14)

Spiritual discernment is one of the nine powerful gifts of the Spirit revealed in 1 Corinthians 12:4-10. In verse eleven, Paul writes: *"But one and the same Spirit works all these things, distributing to each one individually as He wills."* It is important to understand and accept the fact that all these gifts are worked by the Holy Spirit and given to those He chooses. This does not mean that we sit back and wait for Him to decide what He will give to us. The Holy Spirit inspires us to seek more and when we are spiritually ready He gives more. Now is the time to press in for the gift of spiritual discernment. I will share with you one of these hidden mysteries in the section below.

PRINCIPLE OF MULTIPLICATION

One important kingdom mystery is revealed when we are enabled to learn and work with the Lord's math. In the natural realm, math skills are viewed as one of the most important things to be taught in the world's education systems. Every modern culture follows this same principle. If we align with the assumptions in the opening of this section, we understand that the skills taught in the natural also need to be taught in the spiritual realm. You quickly learn that Kingdom math is not like what we must learn in the natural. Take for example the doctrine of the Trinity. In this doctrine we learn first that the Lord is one (Deuteronomy 6:4). Then we learn that there are three in this one (Father, Son and Holy Ghost). Do you have an understanding of the Lord's spiritual math to help you grasp the fullness of this message?

The doctrine of the Trinity was a great challenge to me in the beginning because one of my best skills in the natural realm was math. I kept asking: How can three be one? The key to understanding this is revealed in the Hebrew language. They have two totally different words to indicate oneness. The word used in Deuteronomy (*Echad*) indicates one set or one group. The word used to describe Yeshua as the only begotten Son of God (*Yachid*) is different and indicates one and only one. Knowing the language helps you to understand the math. It is time for you to move from the natural to the spiritual.

Another principle to understand about Kingdom Math is that the Lord prefers multiplication to addition. He prefers addition to subtraction. This is how the Lord operates in His relationship with those who follow Him. Notice this principle at work in the passages below. First look at the Lord's promise to Abraham in Genesis 22:17, "*...blessing I will bless you, and multiplying I will multiply your descendants as the stars of the heaven and as the sand which is on the seashore; and your descendants shall possess the gate of their enemies.*" This principle is reaffirmed in the New Testament: "*For when God made a promise to Abraham, because He could swear by no one greater, He swore by Himself, saying, 'Surely blessing I will bless you, and multiplying I will multiply you.'*" (Hebrews 6:13-14) I don't know about you, but I like the Lord's math. I like multiplication.

Combining the principle for the natural realm with that of the Spiritual realm the Apostle Paul released a very powerful promise for you and me as we go through perilous time. First we take the principle from the natural realm given in Isaiah 55:10, (NIV), "*As the rain and the snow come down from heaven, and do not return to it without watering the earth and making it bud and flourish, so that it yields seed for the sower and bread for the eater,*" In this passage, the Lord promised to be a source of things His followers needed in the natural realm. I believe this promise of provision in the natural is for me. So, I receive it and give thanks for it. Then the Lord expands this to include a promise of provision in the spiritual realm.

Now may He who supplies seed to the sower, and bread for food, supply and multiply the seed you

have sown and increase the fruits of your righ-
teousness, while you are enriched in everything
for all liberality, which causes thanksgiving
through us to God. For the administration of
this service not only supplies the needs of the
saints, but also is abounding through many
thanksgivings to God, (2 Corinthians 9:10-12)

This blessing specifically speaks of *"the fruits of your righ-*
teousness," You and I can expect the Lord to multiply our
resources in the natural and then receive this as a promise
to multiply to us every spiritual blessing in heavenly places
(Ephesians 1:3, *"Blessed be the God and Father of our Lord*
Jesus Christ, who has blessed us with every spiritual blessing
in the heavenly places in Christ,"). Yeshua often taught His
followers in this same manner. He taught spiritual lessons
through parables which described natural situations. In private, He gave the spiritual meaning to His disciples. If you are
His disciple, these same things are available to you.

For example Mark 4:8, (NIV), *"Still other seed fell on*
good soil. It came up, grew and produced a crop, multiplying
thirty, sixty, or even a hundred times." The crowds as well
as His chosen disciples often had difficulty understanding
His parables, because their minds were only open to the natural realm. When the disciples asked why He taught this way,
Yeshua gave an answer in Matthew 13:11, *"He answered and*
said to them, 'Because it has been given to you to know the
mysteries of the kingdom of heaven, but to them it has not
been given.'"

Where do you fit in? Are you one of those who only sees in
the natural or are you a Spirit filled believer enabled to understand the mysteries of the Kingdom? This is a good time for
self-reflection. If you have difficulty understanding kingdom
mysteries, perhaps you need another outpouring of the Spirit
of truth to guide your heart and mind. The good news is that

all you have to do is ask. Speak to the Holy Spirit and claim the promise of Yeshua once more as you read aloud Luke 11:13, "*If you then, being evil, know how to give good gifts to your children, how much more will your heavenly Father give the Holy Spirit to those who ask Him!*"

DIVINE PROTECTION

I want to add one more dimension to the promise of the Lord's provision for your needs and His desire to multiply all these blessings to you. The Lord not only gives, He also protects what He has given to you. Consider the promise in Malachi 3:11, "*And I will rebuke the devourer for your sakes, so that he will not destroy the fruit of your ground, nor shall the vine fail to bear fruit for you in the field, says the Lord of hosts;*" I have met many people who seem to be in the grips of a spirit of poverty. This is not a gift from the Lord. This spirit works for the thief, which Yeshua described in John 10:10a. The promise of what the Lord has done for us is found in the second part of the same verse (John 10:10b). Yeshua came that you might live in abundance. Amen?

There is one action you need to take in order to unlock this mystery in your own storehouse. The Lord did not mince words. He stated this kingdom principle as bluntly and directly as possible. Yet to this day people still attempt to misunderstand it. As I mentioned above, when I read this promise aloud in meetings, I have noticed women grasping their purses with a more firm grip. I have seen men move their hands to protect their wallets from a spiritual invasion. By their responses, they choose to block the blessing flow of provision in their own lives.

Bring the whole tithe into the storehouse, that there may be food in my house. Test me in this, says the Lord Almighty, and see if I will not

171

throw open the floodgates of heaven and pour
out so much blessing that you will not have
room enough for it. (Malachi 3:10, NIV)

Will you open yourself to the blessing flow of the Lord or try to hold on to the meager supplies in your bank account? This is the teaching in the natural. Now it is time to unpack the spiritual part of this teaching. It is not all about money. It is not about how to get rich and stay rich. It is about the great end time harvest. It is about opening the flow of spiritual and natural resources to meet every ministry need and opening the door of blessing to the lost so they will be inspired to return to the Lord before it is too late. This has been clearly revealed to those who operate in the spiritual realm. Check it out once more in the passage below.

And with great power the apostles gave witness
to the resurrection of the Lord Jesus. And great
grace was upon them all. Nor was there anyone
among them who lacked; (Acts 4:33-34a)

Would you like to receive these spiritual gifts of great power, great grace and no lack? All these promises are for you. Consider this as you study the next three chapters. Chapter nine gives more detail on the spiritual mission of preparing your storehouse. In chapter ten we will unpack the Kingdom mystery of the extra oil. In chapter eleven, we will look closely at our mission to equip the saints for the ministry of the Kingdom. May the Lord release the Spirit of truth to guide you in this study! Amen and Amen!

CHAPTER NINE
PREPARING THE STOREHOUSE

But know this, that in the last days perilous times will come: For men will be lovers of themselves, lovers of money, boasters, proud, blasphemers, disobedient to parents, unthankful, unholy, unloving, unforgiving, slanderers, without self-control, brutal, despisers of good, traitors, headstrong, haughty, lovers of pleasure rather than lovers of God, having a form of godliness but denying its power. And from such people turn away! (2 Timothy 3:1-5)

A t first glance the title of this chapter looks contrary to the principle I stated at the beginning to focus on the spiritual aspects of prepping rather than the natural. I remind you that there is a spiritual law at work in this situation. For me this means that powerful hidden mysteries are found in both natural law and the normal ways people do things. These mysteries are totally hidden from those who only understand with their natural minds. This spiritual law is revealed in 1 Corinthians 2:14, "*But the natural man does not receive the things of the Spirit of God, for they are foolishness to him; nor can he know them, because they are spiritually discerned.*" In order to get at these hidden mysteries, we will look briefly at some of the standard means of prepping in the natural.

During my military career, I learned the importance of proper preparation. As in spiritual warfare, situations shift rapidly in military operations. One principle we were taught is that every plan is perfect until the first shot is fired. People who are limited in their ability to adapt to rapid change do not do well in a military setting. During my first assignment, I experienced extreme frustration with the daily change in plans and operations which characterize military operations. I was so frustrated that I seriously considered getting out of the army after my initial obligation was complete. Have you ever struggled with frustration because people and situations constantly change in your environment? If so, you probably understand what I am talking about. How are we to deal with all this frustration?

One day something changed all this for me. It was something people often call an epiphany. Suddenly the spiritual lights came on and I knew what I needed to change in me. I was reading through an operations order so that I could properly prepared to do my job during the upcoming mission. When I got to "Appendix J," my eyes stopped moving forward. I was almost frozen in time and place. I knew instantly that this was the answer for me to be able to handle my frustration over constant change. The entire appendix simply read: "Keep plans flexible." I knew at that moment this was to be the principle which would help me to survive. I decided to have an "Appendix J" in every plan I made from that day forward. For me it worked. Think about it. What will work for you? Ask the Lord to reveal something to help you deal with your frustration. I believe He will do for you what he did for me.

Another powerful principle I learned in my military career was how unwise it is to allow your commander to be caught off guard and surprised in front of others. No one likes to get caught off guard. No one likes being hit with a surprise attack. A good soldier learns personal protection and is also committed to protecting his/her leaders. Paul expressed this idea in His letter to Timothy: *"No one serving as a soldier gets involved in civilian affairs—he wants to please his commanding officer."* (2 Timothy 2:4, NIV) To me this means that a good soldier stays focused on the mission while remaining aware of a commitment to please the commander. Never surprise your commander by running out of needed supplies or equipment. Never surprise your commander by having a hidden agenda which gets revealed in front of others.

You may be wondering about the spiritual principle behind the things I wrote in the paragraph above. Consider your relationship with the highest commander in your spiritual chain of command. After reading the description of Yeshua in Revelation 1:16 (*"He had in His right hand seven stars, out of His mouth went a sharp two-edged sword, and His countenance was like the sun shining in its strength"*) I started to call Him my Seven Star General. I always want to please Him above everyone else. Therefore, I will always put His spiritual mission above everything in the natural realm. I will not make plans contrary to His mission and purpose for my life. I will not suddenly blurt out things or behave in a way, which brings shame upon His Name. My deepest desire is to please Him and get closer every day. How about you?

A VISION REPORT

One morning I found myself especially thirsty for more intimacy with the Lord. The strength of my spirit rose up in me and I began to stand on the promise of Isaiah 55:1-3, *"Ho! Everyone who thirsts, come to the waters; and you who have no money, come, buy and eat. Yes, come, buy wine and milk without money and without price. Why do you spend money for what is not bread, and your wages for what does not satisfy? Listen carefully to Me, and eat what is good, and let your soul delight itself in abundance. Incline your ear, and come to Me. Hear, and your soul shall live; and I will make an everlasting covenant with you— the sure mercies of David."* I am thirsty and my soul cries out for the living water that Yeshua gives to those who ask.

It seemed clear at that moment that what I was thirsty for and what I needed most cannot be purchased with money. I was longing to hear the Lord inviting me to come to Him and buy what I needed without money because it is priceless. I made a personal claim on the promise given through Isaiah. I want what the Lord is offering. I am hungry and thirsty for these gifts and I am ready to press in more and more to receive them. Listen carefully to what the Lord is offering to you right now, *"…eat what is good, and let your soul delight itself in abundance."* Whatever you are doing right now: Stop, turn to Him and let your spiritual ears hear Him inviting you to come to the table. Receive what He is offering to you in that passage from Isaiah, *"Hear, and your soul shall live; and I will make an everlasting covenant with you."* Claim it for yourself and begin to give Him thanks and praise.

The Holy Spirit assured me this invitation is not being offered to just one person. We cannot truly receive it apart from our fellowship with other hungry and thirsty believers. I am constantly seeking to be with a group of people as hungry and thirsty as I am so we can press in together for what the Lord is ready to pour out to us. Will you join with me as we sincerely cry out to the Lord? Will you join me in pressing in to get into His presence and receive what David was praying for in Psalm 132:7-8 (NIV), *"Let us go to his dwelling place; let us worship at his footstool—arise, O Lord, and come to your resting place, you and the ark of your might."*

At this point it became crystal clear that all I needed and all I wanted in that hour was Him! This is still my most passionate spiritual desire. I want to be in His presence. I want to be in the Holy place where the ark of His might is located.

May He be drawn near to us as we draw near to Him with hearts ready to receive whatever He is willing to release to us! Do you feel the hunger? Do you feel that thirst? Are you ready to press in for more of Him? Stop and do it right now! Amen and Amen!!!!

HIDDEN MEANING FOR YOU

On that morning which I described above, the Lord was teaching me something profound that is also being released to you right now. We need things in our storehouse, which we may not recognize or understand in this moment. It is important to understand that you can't get a full list of the things you need from some magazine, book or documentary. These natural sources are all based on the wisdom of the world. You can never become fully prepared armed only with the wisdom of the world. Only the wisdom of God can make clear to you what you need, and how the Lord will provide it. Only the Lord can help you keep your plans flexible enough to change and move instantly at His command. Consider what Paul is saying to you in the passage below?

> *However, we speak wisdom among those who are mature, yet not the wisdom of this age, nor of the rulers of this age, who are coming to nothing. But we speak the wisdom of God in a mystery, the hidden wisdom which God ordained before the ages for our glory, which none of the rulers of this age knew; for had they known, they would not have crucified the Lord of glory.* (1 Corinthians 2:6-8)

In the two verses following this passage of scripture, Paul challenges us to open our spiritual eyes to see and our spiritual ears to hear what the Lord has for us. It is obvious in these passages that this is not a new idea or new command. Paul was quoting from Isaiah 64:4. This is an age old powerful principle which you and I need to embrace in our generation. You need to apply these powerful spiritual principles in your preparations for the perilous times, which are coming. Consider this as you study these two verses.

> *But as it is written: "Eye has not seen, nor ear heard, nor have entered into the heart of man the things which God has prepared for those who love Him." But God has revealed them to us through His Spirit. For the Spirit searches all things, yes, the deep things of God.*
> (1 Corinthians 2:9-10)

There is no other source for what we need to know and understand in order to prepare for the last days. There is no other source but the Holy Spirit to reveal these things to us. No other source can give you the truth and help you to understand what you need to store up for the times of stress and tribulation, which will soon manifest. You must get close to the Lord and be totally committed to staying close to Him until the end. This means getting ready now and remaining on alert for His return.

The rules and principles are still the same. No one knows the day or hour. As I am writing this, someone is prophesying that the world will end in nine days. I cannot count the number of times people have made these kinds of predictions during my lifetime. When they do not come true in the time predicted, we cannot give up and stop. Our task is to remain vigilant and never give up on the idea that it could happen any moment. Listen again to Yeshua's teaching on this in the passage below.

> *Likewise as it was also in the days of Lot: They ate, they drank, they bought, they sold, they*

planted, they built; but on the day that Lot went out of Sodom it rained fire and brimstone from heaven and destroyed them all. Even so will it be in the day when the Son of Man is revealed.
(Luke 17:28-30)

The end will come suddenly. There will be no time to prepare when it manifests. In one day, all the store shelves will be empty and the delivery trucks will remain motionless. Things will seem still, but it will not be quiet. The sudden stopping of the flow of supplies and services will be accompanied by a loud and panic ridden mob of people who did not listen to the warnings and are now caught without food, water and medicine. The only alternative for many will be to steal, to kill and to destroy those who possess what they want and need. These mobs are more likely to become violent because they have also failed to prepare spiritually. They will be focused on their personal needs and the desires of their flesh. They will have no heart or compassion for others. These will indeed be perilous times. Are you ready for it?

Then He said to the disciples, "The days will come when you will desire to see one of the days of the Son of Man, and you will not see it. And they will say to you, 'Look here!' or 'Look there!' Do not go after them or follow them. For as the lightning that flashes out of one part under heaven shines to the other part under heaven, so also the Son of Man will be in His day. But first He must suffer many things and be rejected by this generation. And as it was in the days of Noah, so it will be also in the days of the Son of Man: They ate, they drank, they married wives, they were given in marriage, until the day that

Noah entered the ark, and the flood came and destroyed them all." (Luke 17:22-27)

Our Seven-Star General, Yeshua, does not want His troops to be caught off guard by the things, which are coming. He spent a great deal of time teaching about the things, which will happen before and after His return. He was often asked to speak about these issues by both His followers and those who wanted to destroy Him and His work. A great mystery is revealed in one of His answers to the Pharisees. We can only understand spiritual things with the help of the Holy Spirit. Pray for wisdom and revelation as you read the passage below.

Now when He was asked by the Pharisees when the kingdom of God would come, He answered them and said, "The kingdom of God does not come with observation; nor will they say, 'See here!' or 'See there!' For indeed, the kingdom of God is within you." (Luke 17:20-21)

How can we prepare for something which is already in us? The hidden key to unlock this mystery is available to you. Ask the Holy Spirit to reveal what you need to know as you prepare. It is important to understand that you need to stop and examine yourself. Is the kingdom of God really inside you now? Do you need to take steps to make this happen for yourself right now? There is only one way to get it. There is only one source for it. The Pharisees needed to get the kingdom of God into the empty shells of their souls and spirits. They didn't understand it because they were using the wisdom of the world. Things are different for you. You have the Holy Spirit residing in you. He can reveal these things to you.

This is very important. So I want to emphasis it again. If you are uncertain about whether the kingdom of God is inside you or not, now is the time to get this resolved in your life. You do this with the help of the Holy Spirit. Take care of this issue before you move on. Remember another powerful kingdom principle. In Luke 11:13, Yeshua said, *"If you then, being evil, know how to give good gifts to your children, how much more will your heavenly Father give the Holy Spirit to those who ask Him!"* Why not ask right now. If you have the Spirit residing in you, ask for a greater awareness of His presence and an increased ability to see and understand those things which are real in the spiritual realm. Ask for an increase in your seer anointing. Trust Him. He wants to help you.

Yeshua should be your primary instructor for the things of the spirit. Go to Him first and stay with Him until the end. The other New Testament writers provided added details and helped to clarify some of the teachings, but Yeshua is always the primary instructor for all things spiritual. Listen carefully to what He is telling you in the passage below. Ask for the Spirit of wisdom and revelation to reveal what you need to understand about the Lord's teaching. Above all, remain teachable. I have met many people who believe they know everything about the last days and are unwilling to learn. They try to sound wise and righteous, but they are actually more like the Pharisees than the followers.

> *In that day, he who is on the housetop, and his goods are in the house, let him not come down to take them away. And likewise the one who is in the field, let him not turn back. Remember Lot's wife. Whoever seeks to save his life will lose it, and whoever loses his life will preserve it. I tell you, in that night there will be two men in one bed: the one will be taken and the other will be left. Two women will be grinding together: the one will be taken and the other left. Two men will be in the field: the one will be taken and the other left.* (Luke 17:31-36)

All these things will manifest suddenly. Remember it is too late to train and prepare after they manifest. When these perilous times appear, you will only be able to access those things which you have already prepared. Prep wisely now. Continue to ask the Holy Spirit to reveal more to you. Remember and claim the promise of Yeshua in John 16:13, *"However, when He, the Spirit of truth, has come, He will guide you into all truth; for He will not speak on His own authority, but whatever He hears He will speak; and He will tell you things to come."* Understand this: the Holy Spirit will *"tell you things to come."* This is your sole source for the truth about what is to come in the last days. Ask now and prepare for all He reveals to you. Amen?

IS IT RIGHT TO STORE THINGS

This is an age old question we looked at in chapter eight. In traumatic times we see the worst in the character of many people. Remember that during natural disasters or any other threat of shortages in the supply chain, many people panic and begin to horde things. In their vain attempt to take care of all their physical needs they begin a pattern of panic buying and the shelves in stores are quickly emptied. It is immediately clear they have done little or no prepping in the natural and have done even less in the spiritual realm.

True followers of Yeshua love their neighbors as they love themselves. True spiritual preppers have a storehouse of things to meet their own needs and enough to help others. Remember this principles was revealed as the Lord worked through Joseph to prepare for Egypt and their neighboring countries. People are only able to have this kind of love with the help of the Lord. We look at His teachings and prepare much more than food, medicine and personal defense supplies. We have learned many of the lessons in the spiritual realm and will know things unavailable to those who only have the wisdom of the world.

One powerful example is revealed by Yeshua in the passage below. We looked at this passage in the previous chapter. I am using it again because you need to read it aloud over and over until it is fixed in your spirit. Each time you read it, expect the Holy Spirit to reveal to you a deeper level of understanding about how to understand and apply the spiritual principles Yeshua is revealing to you. Trust me you don't want to hear him say to you on that day, *"O you of little faith."*

> *Life is more than food, and the body is more than clothing. Consider the ravens, for they neither sow nor reap, which have neither storehouse nor barn; and God feeds them. Of how much more value are you than the birds? And which of you by worrying can add one cubit to his stature? If you then are not able to do the least, why are you anxious for the rest? Consider the lilies, how they grow: they neither toil nor spin; and yet I say to you, even Solomon in all his glory was not arrayed like one of these. If then God so clothes the grass, which today is in the field and tomorrow is thrown into the oven, how much more will He clothe you, O you of little faith?* (Luke 12:23-28)

FOOD, WATER, MEDICINE

> *Bring all the tithes into the storehouse, that there may be food in My house, and try Me now in this,"* says the LORD *of hosts, "If I will not open for you the windows of heaven and pour out for you such blessing that there will not be room enough to receive it.* (Malachi 3:10)

I know several believers who are caught up in wrestling with this passage today. The people I know who are straining at these teachings are only focused on protecting the money in their storehouses. Their eyes are fixed on the natural and they miss the hidden mystery in this passage. Read it again and ask the Holy Spirit to reveal what you need to know in the spiritual realm as revealed by the Lord through the prophet Malachi. Be prepared to let go of useless religious baggage so that you will be able grasp the spiritual promises of the Lord.

When I hear people struggling with this passage, a question comes into my mind. Where is the house of the Lord today? Some people say it is the local church where you are being fed. I have heard other people twist it to say their ministry is the storehouse and people need to give to them. I think they are all missing the spiritual point the Lord is trying to make. Two powerful passages have helped me to formulate a spiritual answer in my life and ministry. The first is from the Apostle Peter and the second one is from the Apostle Paul. Can you apply these two teachings to the question about the location of the storehouse of the Lord?

>*...you also, as living stones, are being built up a spiritual house, a holy priesthood, to offer up spiritual sacrifices acceptable to God through Jesus Christ.* (1 Peter 2:5)

>*Do you not know that you are the temple of God and that the Spirit of God dwells in you?* (1 Corinthians 3:16)

Of course we give to the local church where we are fed. Of course we partner with and give to ministries reaching out to the lost sheep. These are things in the natural, which actually open the windows of heaven to provide for our spiritual needs as we obey the Lord's commands. Using the resources the Lord has entrusted to us to bless others will open the windows of Heaven. The Lord gives seed to the sower along with bread (resources) to eat. Like Abraham, we have inherited promises from the Lord. He blesses us so we can be a blessing for others.

The Lord has a plan to supply the needs of someone special through what He has stored up in your life. He plans to use the gifts you give to feed someone else both physically and spiritually. He is allowing you to participate in the blessing flow. Only you can block the blessing flow by closing the doors to your storehouse out of self-centered motives. Only you can open them again by supplying what is needed in the Lord's House. Perhaps you need to help the Lord open the windows of heaven again in your life and work. This is a good time to begin. Amen?

PERSONAL PROTECTION

Is it right to have weapons for personal protection? This is a controversial issue. I am choosing to be confessional at this point. I have thought about this for a long time and I have prayed about it over and over. The conclusion is that I believe it is right to have a means to protect yourself, your family and others who will be with you in the troubled days, which are certainly coming. I base that on one of Jesus' teachings. He told the disciples to buy the most powerful weapon of personal defense available in their day – a sword.

> *Then He said to them, "But now, he who has a money bag, let him take it, and likewise a knapsack; and he who has no sword, let him sell his garment and buy one. For I say to you that this which is written must still be accomplished in Me: 'And He was numbered with the transgressors.' For the things concerning Me have an*

*end." So they said, "Lord, look, here are two
swords." And He said to them, "It is enough."*
(Luke 22:36-38)

Did you notice that Yeshua said to sell your garment if necessary to buy a sword. The way my mind works when I read
a passage like this is to ask a question. What kind of garment
is Yeshua talking about? I researched to find an answer and at
the same time asked for wisdom and revelation from the Lord
to help me understand. Here it is. Yeshua is telling them to sell
their Prayer Shawl to buy a sword. This would be unthinkable
to most Hebrew men.

This revelation tells me that something very important is
being revealed here. The Lord had previously pointed out how
important this garment is by telling His followers to return this
garment before the end of the day. The outer garment was their
daily covering and their blanket in the cold air of the night.
In the morning, the tallit was their prayer tent as they began
each day in the presence of the Lord. How could Yeshua ask
them to sell this garment in order to buy a sword?

*He said to them, "Therefore every teacher of
the law who has been instructed about the
kingdom of heaven is like the owner of a house
who brings out of his storeroom new treasures
as well as old." (Matthew 13:52, NIV)*

One of the great challenges for those under the influence of a religious spirit is to open up to learn new things. I
believe Yeshua said something shocking in order to awaken
their sleeping spirits. Peter only heard with his natural mind
and found two swords among the group to show the Lord.
He missed the spiritual revelation in this word from the Lord.
Will we miss it as well? Keep these teachings in mind as we

go deeper into this mystery of the two swords revealed in the following section.

MYSTERY OF THE TWO SWORDS

What is the best form of personal protection? If you asked ten people, you might get ten different answers. Almost everyone has an opinion and many are unwilling to change with time or more information. Remember the old saying: "My mind is made up. Don't confuse me with facts." Arguments about gun control are raging at this time in the USA. Most people are entrenched in their personal beliefs and are unlikely to be changed in their opinions. Many have made a conscious choice to refuse to listen to factual information and honest data. This is our dilemma as we seek to understand the teaching of the Lord.

Jesus told the Disciples to own a sword. On the one hand, we know that a sword was the most powerful personal weapon in that generation. Have you ever wondered what the Lord might tell us to buy in our generation? Think about it. It may seem repetitious, but I am asking you to read the passage from Luke again. Think of this from the spiritual and not merely the natural point of view. Study again the Lord's teachings in the passage above from Luke 22:36-38.

I am intentionally repeating some passages and principles because this is such a fascinating account to me. I want you to unpack everything the Lord wants you to understand as we go through this together. Please understand that I was trained as an instructor by the US Army and served on the faculty of the US Army Chaplain Center and School for a number of years. Repetition is one of the primary principles in military instruction. Military doctrine maintains that people learn more effectively as key concepts are taught over and over.

Why two swords? Perhaps a more significant question is: How could two swords be enough during the tribulation they were about to face? If we apply our principle that there is hidden spiritual truth in the natural things we see, consider how this principle works in the passage above. This is what I have been building up to slowly so we are ready to hear it with our spiritual ears. Perhaps the reason for two swords is that one is a natural weapon and one is a spiritual sword. It is clear that the focus of Yeshua is not totally on physical swords because He blocked Peter's use of one in the garden.

> *Then Simon Peter, having a sword, drew it and struck the high priest's servant, and cut off his right ear. The servant's name was Malchus. So Jesus said to Peter, "Put your sword into the sheath. Shall I not drink the cup which My Father has given Me?"* (John 18:10-11)

When I read this, I wonder how this sounded to Peter. I reflected on this by putting myself in Peter's shoes. Perhaps you can do the same and think of it from the first person view. Here is how I believe Peter's inner dialogue sounded. "First, Yeshua told me to buy a sword even if I had to sell my tallit to do so. He seemed to confirm this was correct when He told me two were enough. Now I am confused. When we really seem to need that sword the most, He tells me not to use it. How can I understand these seemingly conflicting pieces of information?" Are you getting a feel for Peter's dilemma? Perhaps this confusion is one of the reasons he fled the scene after hearing this from Yeshua.

Now let's try to understand it from our point of view. We have more information available to us than was available to Peter in the garden. He had not yet received the Spirit of truth. We have received this powerful gift from the Lord and we need to use what was given to understand this. Perhaps Yeshua was talking about what Paul would later refer to as "the sword of the Spirit." Remember what he wrote in Ephesians 6:17,

"Take the helmet of salvation and the sword of the Spirit, which is the word of God." This knowledge then points us to an even more powerful weapon than the sword. It is the "word of God." This is abundantly clear when you read Hebrews 4:12, *"For the word of God is living and active. Sharper than any double-edged sword, it penetrates even to dividing soul and spirit, joints and marrow; it judges the thoughts and attitudes of the heart."*

STORE SWORDS IN YOUR HEART

Many years ago church youth groups would have training sessions called "sword drills." They were taught to memorize Bible verses so these passages would be stored in their hearts as weapons of spiritual warfare. In these groups you would be tested on your ability to quickly and accurately reference a verse of scripture directly associated with a particular spiritual challenge. This kind of training is strongly supported by the method Yeshua used to deal with the Satan during His period of testing. Each time the devil attacked, Yeshua drew out a Biblical passage and used it like a spiritual sword. Each time, He won the battle.

Back when I was a member of those groups, young people were actually taught to study and use the Bible. The teachers viewed these passage of scripture as being like swords for spiritual protection. They hoped these verses would help protect the spiritual wellbeing of their students during times of youthful temptation and trouble. Think about this as you read what John was saying in 1 John 2:14b, *"Because you are strong, and the word of God abides in you, and you have overcome the wicked one."* This sword, the Word of God, is available to you and me in times of need. It will be there to protect us as we go through perilous times. We need to learn and practice in order to be able to draw out the right sword at any given time to strike the enemy and win the spiritual battle.

Pause a moment and reflect on Hebrews 4:12 once again to be certain that it is stored and ready in your heart.

Great blessings are promised to those who hold and use the "sword of the spirit." Think about what Yeshua meant in Luke 11:28, *"But He said, "More than that, blessed are those who hear the word of God and keep it!"* More blessed are those who learn to use the sword of the Lord and constantly train themselves and others as they prepare for the times when they will need it most. Imagine how the situation in the garden might have been different if Peter had used the correct sword. The word of God works. It worked for Yeshua and it will work for you. As a teacher, I am filled with joy when I see my students properly using the sword of the spirit, which is "the word of God."

> *And we also thank God continually because, when you received the word of God, which you heard from us, you accepted it not as the word of men, but as it actually is, the word of God, which is at work in you who believe.* (1 Thessalonians 2:13, NIV)

SPIRITUAL SUPPLIES

Remember the Biblical principle which instructs us to learn natural things first and then move on to receive an understanding of spiritual things. When you apply Biblical principles to your study, you can rightly expect to understand the mysteries of the Kingdom of God. As these mysteries are revealed, you will be enabled to understand more about what you need in your spiritual prepping. We learned in this lesson that the sword represents a greater spiritual truth than the natural need to have a weapon.

Now we apply that to other parts of our preparations. Ask yourself a few questions. What great spiritual truths will be revealed as you consider placing physical supplies in your storehouse? What did you learn earlier from your study of Proverbs 10:14, *"Wise people store up knowledge, but the mouth of the foolish is near destruction?"* Solomon was making a connection between the use of the mouth (something in the natural) and the storing of the knowledge and wisdom of the Lord (something spiritual).

If you look at the natural realm with the eyes of faith enlightened by the Holy Spirit, mysteries will be revealed. The natural order was established through the wisdom of the Lord and that wisdom is stored up in animals and even insects. The natural man calls these things instincts but is ignorant about their source. Who created them with the instinctual knowledge to survive and thrive? Consider Proverbs 30:24-25 (NIV), *"Four things on earth are small, yet they are extremely wise: Ants are creatures of little strength, yet they store up their food in the summer;"* If an ant was created with instructions to store food for the winter, what is the Lord saying to you about the perilous times to come? Is He telling you to store up for your natural needs as well as your spiritual needs?

Look again at the account of Joseph who spent time as both a slave and then a prisoner in Egypt. He went from serving the needs of others in the prison to ruling the palace and all of the land. I doubt that he was able to see himself ruling Egypt as he began to interpret Pharaoh's dream. Through God given revelation knowledge he actually provided the means for his promotion, which was later released by Pharaoh. Think about this as you study Joseph's words in the passage below.

> *Now therefore, let Pharaoh select a discerning and wise man, and set him over the land of Egypt. Let Pharaoh do this, and let him appoint officers over the land, to collect one-fifth of the produce of the land of Egypt in the seven plentiful years. And let them gather all the food of*

those good years that are coming, and store up grain under the authority of Pharaoh, and let them keep food in the cities. Then that food shall be as a reserve for the land for the seven years of famine which shall be in the land of Egypt, that the land may not perish during the famine." (Genesis 41:33-38)

Looking at it another way, Joseph began a process in the natural, which brought His entire family out of famine and positioned them in the exact place where the Lord planned to release a great spiritual destiny for them. In Egypt, Israel was built up by the Lord to become a powerful nation, which would operate under a new kingdom economy birthed during perilous times. Consider the words of David in Psalm 17:14b (NIV), *"You still the hunger of those you cherish; their sons have plenty, and they store up wealth for their children."* The Children of Israel learned these powerful spiritual lessons during times of tribulation and hardship. Then they applied these special life lessons when they entered the Promised Land. Will we access the wisdom of God and be enabled to do the same in our generation?

Yeshua made it plain that these spiritual teachings go far beyond mere information for the natural realm. He often quoted an often used Biblical teaching. *"He who has ears to hear, let him hear!"* This admonition used by Yeshua is recorded in Matthew, Mark and Luke. Moses cried out in frustration to the people who had witnessed the mighty power of God in miracles, signs and wonders: *"Yet the LORD has not given you a heart to perceive and eyes to see and ears to hear, to this very day."* (Deuteronomy 29:4) Has the Lord given you a heart to perceive, eyes to see and ears to hear what is happening in the spiritual realm? Wise men and women continue to seek more spiritual wisdom so the Lord can elevate them to a higher level of glory.

Rebellion is the primary reason our eyes and ears do not work well in the spiritual realm. The spirit of rebellion was working powerfully in the days of both Moses and Ezekiel. This is a tenacious spirit. Once it takes hold of a person or group of people, it is incredibly difficult to root it out. The persistence of the rebellious spirit is as frustrating for us as it was for the prophets of old. It was also frustrating for the Lord as He dealt with the Children of Israel. You can feel that frustration as the Lord speaks in Ezekiel 12:1-2, *"Now the word of the LORD came to me, saying: 'Son of man, you dwell in the midst of a rebellious house, which has eyes to see but does not see, and ears to hear but does not hear; for they are a rebellious house.'"*

This same rebellious spirit is working in our generation. It always comes against us to block our ability to clearly hear and see in the spiritual realm. It is time to break free from this spirit and then work to stay free. I gave detailed information on how to accomplish these tasks in the book, "A Warrior's Guide to the Seven Spirits of God, Part 1." It is time to stop focusing so much attention on our physical needs and focus more on the spiritual issues in our day. To make this spiritual need clear, Yeshua gives a powerful command to those who would follow Him. Ask for wisdom and revelation to fully understand the spiritual dimension in Yeshua's teaching in the passage below.

> *Do not store up for yourselves treasures on earth, where moth and rust destroy, and where thieves break in and steal. But store up for yourselves treasures in heaven, where moth and rust do not destroy, and where thieves do not break in and steal. For where your treasure is, there your heart will be also.* (Matthew 6:19-21, NIV)

A WORD TO THE WISE

My son, keep my words and store up my commands within you. Keep my commands and you will live; guard my teachings as the apple of your eye. Bind them on your fingers; write them on the tablet of your heart. Say to wisdom, "You are my sister," and call understanding your kinsman; (Proverbs 7:1-4, NIV)

CHAPTER TEN
CARRYING EXTRA OIL

In this chapter we continue the process of seeing spiritual truth in the instructions for dealing with the natural world. I remind you that Yeshua often taught parables, which the people were unable to fully understand because they only used the wisdom of the world. Most if not all the parables are filled with many layers of meaning. These various levels of meaning are accessible to those who have allowed the Holy Spirit to have more influence on their thoughts and actions.

The words of Proverbs 20:27 came to me as I studied the parable in the passage below this paragraph, "*The spirit of a man is the lamp of the LORD, searching all the inner depths of his heart.*" Let the Lord search your inner depths as you study this chapter. Ask the Holy Spirit for wisdom and revelation to understand the fullness of what Yeshua was teaching in this parable. I have a custom of asking the Lord to give you more revelation and understanding as you study than He gave me while writing. I am praying this for you right now.

> *Then the kingdom of heaven shall be likened to ten virgins who took their lamps and went out to meet the bridegroom. Now five of them were wise, and five were foolish. Those who were*

195

foolish took their lamps and took no oil with them, but the wise took oil in their vessels with their lamps. (Matthew 25:1-4)

With natural wisdom, it is difficult to make a comparison between the "kingdom of heaven" and ten virgins. The natural mind likes to compare things which are very similar to one another. If there is a similarity here, it is difficult to see. It is unlikely that any of his listeners fully understood what Yeshua was teaching that day. His parables were often clouded even in the minds of His closest disciples because they had not yet received the indwelling Holy Spirit. After the resurrection, Yeshua breathed on them and released the Spirit of wisdom and revelation to them so they could understand more of His teachings on the Kingdom of God. I believe they actually received it because we see that He was able to give them more Kingdom instruction before His ascension. I also believe it because there was a major change in their behavior after this moment. I pray right now for the Lord to breathe on you and speak those powerful words over you.

And when He had said this, He breathed on them, and said to them, "Receive the Holy Spirit. If you forgive the sins of any, they are forgiven them; if you retain the sins of any, they are retained." (John 20:22-23)

Did you notice in this passage that Yeshua did it again? He wrapped two seemingly different topics together in one teaching. What does forgiving have to do with being enabled to understand the mysteries of the Kingdom of God through the indwelling Holy Spirit? You probably got it because you already have the Holy Spirit in you. You cannot make these spiritual things work in your life if your spirit and soul are still filled with unforgiveness. You need to deal with this problem before you attempt to understand the mysteries of the Kingdom. This would be a good time for you to examine yourself to see in there is any unforgiveness in your spirit or soul. If there is, take care of it right now. Make a choice to forgive. Forget about your feelings. We walk by faith and not by our feelings. Forgiveness is a choice. It is a choice we must make if we want our eyes and ears to be open to understand the hidden mysteries in the spiritual realm. It is a choice you will have to make over and over every time the enemy tries to use your feelings against you.

Look back at the primary teaching in this parable and understand that Yeshua is focusing on the fact that five of the virgins were wise and five unwise. Somehow the presence of a mixture of the wise and unwise is being compared to the "kingdom of heaven." People who are preparing for the manifestation of the kingdom are not all wise in their beliefs or actions. We must understand this spiritually. This teaching directly challenges each of us to examine ourselves to determine the level of our spiritual wisdom. The difficult part is recognizing that we can only accomplish this when we are listening to the guidance of the Holy Spirit and totally committed to obediently following Him. How can you know about your own spirit? Remember again what we heard in Proverbs 20:27, *"The spirit of a man is the lamp of the LORD, searching all the inner depths of his heart."* Ask the Lord to use His lamp (your spirit) to examine you and reveal these things to you.

Yeshua highlights another spiritual problem in this parable. Look again at Matthew 25:5, *"But while the bridegroom was delayed, they all slumbered and slept."* Did you get it? All were asleep. Even the wise ones striving to enter the Kingdom of God have fallen asleep. Over and over in the scriptures we hear a cry similar to what we read in Joel 3:9, *"Proclaim this among the nations: 'Prepare for war! Wake up the mighty men, let all the men of war draw near, let them come up.'"* Are you a mighty man or woman of God? Is this cry from the Lord coming to you today? Can you hear the Lord calling to you right now: "Mighty warrior it is time for you to wake up."?

Consider how many times this wakeup call was given by the Lord in the Bible and yet followers are still being found asleep on the job. Believers have been deceived into allowing their flesh to rule over their spirit. Paul wrote to the believers in Rome, *"And do this, understanding the present time. The hour has come for you to wake up from your slumber, because our salvation is nearer now than when we first believed."* (Romans 13:11, NIV) In the garden of Gethsemane, Yeshua challenged His disciples, *"Are you still sleeping and resting? Behold, the hour is at hand, and the Son of Man is being betrayed into the hands of sinners."* (Matthew 26:45b) In spiritual time, it is later than most Christians believe. In his first epistle, John says it is the last hour. Are you living like a "last hour disciple"? So many believers think there is still plenty of time left so there is no urgency. They falsely believe there is nothing to worry about and nothing to hurry about.

In the parable of the ten virgins, these women are awakened by a cry. It was midnight and the bridegroom was almost there. What were they going to do now? They all began to trim their lamps. When midnight comes and the cry is heard, it is a little too late to begin making your preparations. The time was far spent and none of them were ready. Even the wise ones were caught off guard. I urge you to ask yourself some questions before you move on. Is there a challenge coming to you from the Holy Spirit today? Is He asking about your readiness in this late hour? Can you see yourself in the parable when they hear the cry?

> *And at midnight a cry was heard: "Behold, the bridegroom is coming; go out to meet him!" Then all those virgins arose and trimmed their lamps.* (Matthew 25:6-7)

As I looked at this parable again several questions began to emerge. Where do you go for help when you have waited too long? Are there any stores selling the spiritual oil you need after the midnight hour? Will any of the other sleeping disciples give you their supplies at this late hour? Most likely you are on your own when these things happen. So I leave off here with one more question. If Yeshua returns at midnight tonight will you be ready?

> *And the foolish said to the wise, "Give us some of your oil, for our lamps are going out." But the wise answered, saying, "No, lest there should not be enough for us and you; but go rather to those who sell, and buy for yourselves."* (Matthew 25:8-9)

When perilous times fully manifest, it is too late for a shopping trip. It is too late to expect the Lord to open doors for you when you did not listen to his teachings or heed his warnings. At some point, you have to be held accountable for your failure to obey. At some point you have to face the lack of oil in your lamp and be held responsible for the outcome. Is the time of accountability close at hand? Are you waking up now so you will be ready for it?

> *And while they went to buy, the bridegroom came, and those who were ready went in with him to the wedding; and the door was shut. Afterward the other virgins came also, saying, "Lord, Lord, open to us!" But he answered and said, "Assuredly, I say to you, I do not know you."* (Matthew 25:10-12)

What is the conclusion of this parable? Jesus summed it up for them and for us in one short sentence. "*Watch therefore, for you know neither the day nor the hour in which the Son of Man is coming.*" (Matthew 25:13) In the garden of Gethsemane, the Lord woke them up three times and they were still not prepared. He gave a very sobering conclusion: "*Watch and pray, lest you enter into temptation. The spirit indeed is willing, but the flesh is weak.*" (Mark 14:38) Can you see the spiritual danger here? Temptations are likely to overtake and overwhelm all those who are not prepared for the Lord's return. Which part of you is winning the battle for readiness? Is it the flesh which is weak or the spirit which is willing?

EXTRA OIL FOR SPIRITUAL LAMPS

As with all of Yeshua's parables, there are multiple levels of meaning found in this story of the plight of ten virgins on their way to a wedding ceremony. On the surface this is merely a cute story about the ten women who have been invited to this wedding reception. In the natural, this story focuses on wisdom among some of the ten women and the lack of it among others. People listening on this level usually identify with the five wise women and feel good about their own nature. They are happy not to be counted among those who lack wisdom. Overall, this is a very comfortable level of meaning. But there is more to the story.

Another level of meaning in this story is focused on one of the primary subjects in this book: spiritual readiness. Those listening on this level begin to understand that a disciple must plan ahead and be prepared for whatever may come in the future. As some would say: If you don't want to be left behind when the Lord returns, get ready and stay ready. Making a commitment to being ready for the Lord's return is a good decision for believers and many are content to leave it at that point. Even though many are content to leave it at this level, there is more to the story.

I believe the most important level of meaning in this parable is something other than the plight of the 10 women. The key to unlocking this third level of meaning is found in the multiple references to oil in the story. Oil had many very important purposes in the culture of that period and meant many things to the various listeners. Oil was at the center of their agricultural economy. It was a commodity needed by every citizen, and it provided a healthy income for many living in that economic system. Oil was used in cooking and was an important key to meeting the nutritional needs of every citizen in Israel. As directly referenced in this story, oil was a fuel which brought light into their homes and workshops allowing them to work during the hours of darkness. It provided light to move around without tripping, falling and being injured. Light from the oil helped them maintain the security of their homes.

Oil was also a key ingredient in the sacrificial system at the center of their religious beliefs. It was intermingled with various sacrifices to produce a sweet fragrance in the offerings lifted up to the Lord. In addition, oil was used ceremonially for anointing, ordination and blessing. Oil was also a key ingredient in their ministry of healing and restoration. It would be difficult to overstate the value of oil in the lives of the people listening to the teachings of Yeshua.

Do you have the oil you need in your natural and spiritual life? Do you have enough? Yeshua took His listeners to another level of spiritual understanding as He taught with this story. He connected the oil in this story with spiritual readiness. Those listening at this level are left with a few questions about their own readiness. These questions are still pertinent today. It would be wise to ask the questions of yourself. Have you stored up enough for your future needs? Are you ready in both the natural and spiritual realms for the return of the Lord?

Interestingly the idea of carrying extra oil speaks of being ready to wait and watch as long as it takes for the Lord to appear. Many people have a limited ability to patiently wait for things to happen. We like fast food, fast cars and electronics which are immediately ready when we hit the switch. Patience is difficult to learn and more difficult to practice. I found it more difficult to be patient when I was young, because there were so many things I wanted to see and do. I didn't like waiting for those things to manifest. Now, I am usually very content waiting and watching for things in both the natural and spiritual realms. Patience seems to grow with time as we receive more and more of the fresh oil of heaven.

As we unpack the meaning of this parable, I want to focus on what oil still represents for us today. To be very clear, I am not talking about the fossil fuels which drive the economies of all of the countries in the world. I am focused on the uses of oil to help us become spiritually ready, resilient and focused. At this point, I prayed over a long period of time for wisdom and revelation to be able to effectively share these ideas with you. I searched the Word of God for references to oil and found an abundance of spiritual treasures. I will share several of these passages with you as we look together for their meaning in our lives and ministries.

OIL OF GLADNESS

You love righteousness and hate wickedness; therefore God, Your God, has anointed You with the oil of gladness more than Your companions.
(Psalm 45:7 and Hebrews 1:9)

The passage above fascinated me for various reasons. First, it felt good and focused on a special blessing the Lord has for those who strive to build on their character so it will be more and more like His. I would like to receive some of the "oil of gladness" today. How about you? The good news is that the Lord is ready and willing to provide what you need

202

as well as what you desire in this area. The path to receiving it seems clear. The door to the supply of this oil is open to those who love righteousness and hate wickedness. Does this describe you?

If you are reading this book, I believe you are one of those who want to please the Lord and develop the character which will bring blessing to you. Most likely this is already at work in you. The question arising here is not about what you desire but about your willingness to take the steps necessary to demonstrate in your life what you love and want to see manifested. Pause for a moment and examine your own spirit and soul. Do you truly love righteousness or do you merely believe you should? Does your daily walk demonstrate your hatred for evil or reflect some remaining love for the things of the flesh? It is important to get right with the Lord and stay right with Him if you plan to be spiritually ready for His return. Think about it. Building character is one of the most important tasks in preparing for the Lord's return and for the perilous times, which will accompany it.

LIGHT OF REVELATION

For it is the God who commanded light to shine out of darkness, who has shone in our hearts to give the light of the knowledge of the glory of God in the face of Jesus Christ. (2 Corinthians 4:6)

I found this passage of scripture very fascinating. It also has multiple levels of meaning for us. Paul begins by focusing the attention of the readers to one of the cornerstone aspects of the Torah. In his day, those reading or hearing this reference to the first chapter of Genesis would immediately connect with what Paul was sharing. Then he pulls a switch and focuses on a much deeper meaning. He is no longer talking about Sun light. He is talking about Son light. Always walking in the light is one of the powerful keys for succeeding in your preparations for Yeshua's return.

Is the light of revelation shining in your heart? Is the Word of God bringing light in your darkness and allowing you to see the Glory of God in the face of Yeshua ha Messiach? When the light of God is truly shining in your heart, you should be receiving new knowledge of His glory. When His light shines in your mind you will receive a deeper understanding of how Yeshua is leading you into a closer relationship with Father God. Is the fresh oil from heaven burning in the lamp of your heart to reveal the deeper things of God? We should live in expectancy of an ever growing awareness of the spiritual dimension in our lives and our future.

OIL OF ANOINTING

Then Moses took some of the anointing oil and some of the blood which was on the altar, and sprinkled it on Aaron, on his garments, on his sons, and on the garments of his sons with him; and he consecrated Aaron, his garments, his sons, and the garments of his sons with him. (Leviticus 8:30)

One of the first uses for the oil of anointing was to ordain and consecrate the priests who would serve in the newly constructed tabernacle. This is the first level of meaning for the use of this oil, but it is not the last word. Shortly after this was introduced to the Children of Israel, the Lord gave it a deeper meaning when He declared, "*And you shall be to Me a kingdom of priests and a holy nation.*" (Exodus 19:6) The Lord extended this powerful anointing to the whole nation, but it doesn't stop there. In the last chapter of the Bible, this anointing is extended to every true believer. "*You have made them to be a kingdom and priests to serve our God, and they will reign on the earth.*" (Revelation 5:10, NIV) As a kingdom priest you need the oil of anointing. This speaks of the Lord helping to prepare you for the challenges of the times to come. Are you anointed and prepared for His return?

The Lord also gave another amazing prophecy about the anointing oil through the prophet Isaiah. The focus is on what will happen in the last days. The Lord is pointing to the time and season of this generation. This prophetic word is given for you if you are willing to receive it. The Lord says the time will come when he frees His people totally from the yoke of the enemy. This yoke will be destroyed forever. If you are in Christ Jesus, you have been set free from the yoke of sin and death forever. Hallelujah! As you study the passage below receive this promise in your own life. If you haven't already done so, accept the Lord's willingness to transport you right now into the kingdom of the Son of His love. Amen? Notice what destroys the enemy's yoke of oppression. It is the anointing oil.

> *It shall come to pass in that day that his burden will be taken away from your shoulder, and his yoke from your neck, and the yoke will be destroyed because of the anointing oil.* (Isaiah 10:27)

HEALING: SPIRIT, SOUL AND BODY

> *Is anyone among you suffering? Let him pray. Is anyone cheerful? Let him sing psalms. Is anyone among you sick? Let him call for the elders of the church, and let them pray over him, anointing him with oil in the name of the Lord. And the prayer of faith will save the sick, and the Lord*

will raise him up. And if he has committed sins,
he will be forgiven. (James 5:13-15)

The oil of healing is also one of the ways the Lord helps you to become prepared for His return. When the oil of healing is applied a number of powerful spiritual blessings are released. The physical act of obedience to the Word of God aligns the spirit and soul with the plans and purposes of the Lord. As a result of this alignment, powerful spiritual gifts are released and begin to flow. There is a release of the power gift of faith. This is not mere belief but a gift of the Spirit, which releases a powerful spiritual force. When it is released, this spiritual force is so powerful that things change in the natural realm.

Miracles, healings, signs and wonders manifest when disciples faithfully obey the command to anoint those who are sick. This spiritual force is still available and can be released once again for you. In the atmosphere of this spiritual power, the "prayer of faith" (released in obedience to the Lord) breaks the power of the enemy, which has been holding people in the grip of infirmity, sickness and pain. It is clear in this brief passage from the book of James that healing occurs on multiple levels. The first and obvious level is the healing of the physical body. But releasing the oil and the prayer of faith also brings forgiveness to the soul and spirit of the one in need.

OIL OF JOY

To proclaim the acceptable year of the LORD,
and the day of vengeance of our God; to com-
fort all who mourn, to console those who mourn
in Zion, to give them beauty for ashes, the oil
of joy for mourning, the garment of praise for
the spirit of heaviness; that they may be called
trees of righteousness, the planting of the Lord,
that He may be glorified. (Isaiah 61:2-3)

The Lord made it clear through the prophet Isaiah that the release of the oil of joy is associated with the ministry of Messiah and will emerge during *"the acceptable year of the Lord."* This is the Lord's way of preparing you to handle all the challenges and troubles coming in the last days. This oil is extremely powerful and is only available through Yeshua. This oil blesses people in so many ways, but it also has another purpose. It is released so that the Lord may be glorified. You are invited to receive these blessings and also to have the honor of helping to bring glory to the Lord.

At this point, I want to make one thing clear: having joy is much better than feeling happiness. Your circumstances may diminish your feelings of happiness. You can often see the ebb and flow of expressions of happiness in the lives of other people. Perhaps you have gone through some of these ups and downs in your own life. The Lord wants to anoint you with something far better. He wants to cover you and fill you with the oil of joy. I like the way the Apostle describes it in 1 Peter 1:8b-9, *"Though now you do not see Him, yet believing, you rejoice with joy inexpressible and full of glory, receiving the end of your faith—the salvation of your souls."* Are you ready for some of that inexpressible joy which is full of the Lord's glory and brings grace to meet every need? I am ready. How about you?

The oil of joy is something very powerful. It has the ability to break the power of mourning off of the Lord's people. Some grief and loss are inescapable as we live in the natural realm. This is normal. However, there is something deeper and darker, which manifests in the lives of many people. I often see people who are overcome by a spirit of grief and appear to be immobilized by their inability to break free. Here is the good news. The Lord has provided the means of escape for you. He will anoint you with the oil of joy, which releases you from the power of grief. I want to give you some really good news. Nothing can take the joy of the Lord from you.

OIL OF READINESS

Oil ultimately speaks of readiness for the wedding supper of the Lamb. This truth is made clear by Yeshua in the parable of the ten virgins. This teaching focuses on our readiness for the great feast of the bridegroom at the end of this age. Are you ready for it? I want to apply more and more of the oil of readiness over myself and then release it to as many people as possible. The Lord released so much good news in this parable that it inspires me to press in for more and more. It is time to put into practice all the things made available by the Lord. Think about this as you embrace the powerful promises in the passage below. You have been invited to the most joy filled celebration in human history.

> *Let us rejoice and be glad and give him glory! For the wedding of the Lamb has come, and his bride has made herself ready. Fine linen, bright and clean, was given her to wear. (Fine linen stands for the righteous acts of the saints.) Then the angel said to me, "Write: 'Blessed are those who are invited to the wedding supper of the Lamb!'" And he added, "These are the true words of God."* (Revelation 19:7-9, NIV)

LIGHT FOR YOUR DARKNESS

Are you ready to carry the light of God even in the deep darkness of these perilous times? Are the wicks of your lamp trimmed and made ready for the arrival of the bridegroom? Have you been wise and brought extra oil as you journey toward that great celebration? The purpose of this parable is to encourage you to be ready on all the levels revealed by the Lord. The purpose is to awaken you before the midnight hour. Time is short and His return is closer now that when we first believed. Take the advice of Yeshua released in the passage below and always be found faithfully waiting and watching.

> *Watch therefore, for you do not know when the master of the house is coming—in the evening, at midnight, at the crowing of the rooster, or in the morning—lest, coming suddenly, he find you sleeping. And what I say to you, I say to all: Watch!"* (Mark 13:35-37)

CHAPTER ELEVEN

EQUIPPING THE SAINTS

Every soldier is taught the importance of maintaining all assigned equipment. This process usually begins with learning the proper maintenance of their weapon. There is an old adage that goes something like this: the first rule in a gunfight is to have a gun. You are unlikely to win a fight without a properly maintained and working weapon. This applies to the weapons of our spiritual warfare as well as those carried by soldiers, police and security guards.

In order to pay for my seminary education, I took on many different jobs. In one of these jobs, I served as a night security guard at construction sites located in a part of town some police officers told me were very dangerous. I was warned that people would probably try to steal my weapon to sell and pay for their drugs. Therefore I needed to be most vigilant to guard and protect my own property from theft. The second warning I received was to never draw the weapon regardless of the circumstances. Stories were told of previous guards who had gotten into serious trouble from the improper use of their weapons. This was the extent of my weapons training from this employer. I was glad that I already had several years of military training to go along with this extremely inadequate company training. As you read the passage below, think about how you can apply your understanding of things in the natural to these powerful spiritual truths.

> *For though we walk in the flesh, we do not war according to the flesh. For the weapons of our warfare are not carnal but mighty in God for pulling down strongholds, casting down arguments and every high thing that exalts itself against the knowledge of God, bringing every thought into captivity to the obedience of Christ, and being ready to punish all disobedience when your obedience is fulfilled.* (2 Corinthians 10:3-6)

I wonder how many believers have received essentially the same level of training I described above on the proper use, protection and maintenance of their weapons of spiritual warfare. Think about it. How much training have you received in this area? I am guessing that for most readers the answer will be very little or perhaps no training at all. Am I right? I have met many believers who have never received any advice or training on the use of these extremely powerful spiritual weapons. When I talk with some of these people, they are unable to name, describe or identify what these weapons are. They are as unprepared as I was when assigned as a security guard in a dangerous neighborhood overnight with no real training.

The Lord's plan as identified in the Bible is for every spiritual soldier to be well trained and equipped for their spiritual tasks. I will give you an example. I have noticed something which has emerged in the body of Christ in recent times. There is a new doctrine being propagated by many believers that the only valid office of ministry is the evangelist. Those holding this view tend to judge every believer and especially pastors and teachers by the standards of the evangelist. This may sound good on the surface to some people. After all, the last days are at hand and we are tasked to bring as many lost souls as possible back to the Lord in this great end-time harvest. The shortfall in this doctrine begins to emerge as we send more and more untrained and inexperienced people into the harvest fields. These novice evangelists don't understand how to do their tasks appropriately and are left vulnerable to the attacks of the enemy. They are in danger and are not aware of it. They are somewhat like the seven untrained sons of Sceva who recklessly jumped into deliverance ministry on their own authority.

> *Also there were seven sons of Sceva, a Jewish chief priest, who did so. And the evil spirit answered and said, "Jesus I know, and Paul I know; but who are you?" Then the man in whom the evil spirit was leaped on them, over-powered them, and prevailed against them, so that they fled out of that house naked and wounded.* (Acts 19:14-16)

The imagery in this account is somewhat funny and many people laugh at the seven foolish sons of Sceva, but miss the real point of this story. These seven men paid a huge price for their error and probably dropped out of the ministry. We have all seen this happen to young ministers who are improperly or inadequately trained. Luke adds a note to this story: *"This became known both to all Jews and Greeks dwelling in Ephesus; and fear fell on them all, and the name of the Lord Jesus was magnified."* (Acts 19:17) The good news was that the name of Yeshua was magnified. The bad news was the humiliation of potential disciples and the release of a spirit of fear. The fear of the Lord is a good thing, but the spirit of fear falling on people will likely produce the wrong kind of fruit. Remember what Paul told his spiritual son in 2 Timothy 1:7,

"For God has not given us a spirit of fear, but of power and of love and of a sound mind."

The Lord has another plan, which has been revealed to us. He has called people into a variety of ministerial offices. He has done this for a purpose. This plan insures the training and equipping of the saints for ministry. When Paul lists the offices of ministry in his first letter to the church in Corinth, he doesn't even mention the office of the evangelist (See 1 Corinthians 12:27-31). The point he clearly makes is that a variety of offices are needed to make the church complete and that no one is called to all of these offices of ministry. We each have a unique calling and purpose in the Kingdom of God. The church works best when it embraces all of them. In the passage below the office of evangelist is mentioned, but Paul's focus in this passage is on the purpose of the offices: *"equipping of the saints."*

> *And He Himself gave some to be apostles, some prophets, some evangelists, and some pastors and teachers, for the equipping of the saints for the work of ministry, for the edifying of the body of Christ, till we all come to the unity of the faith and of the knowledge of the Son of God, to a perfect man, to the measure of the stature of the fullness of Christ; that we should no longer be children, tossed to and fro and carried about with every wind of doctrine, by the trickery of men, in the cunning craftiness of deceitful plotting, but, speaking the truth in love, may grow up in all things into Him who is the head—Christ—from whom the whole body, joined and knit together by what every joint supplies, according to the effective working by which every part does its share, causes growth*

of the body for the edifying of itself in love.
(Ephesians 4:11-16)

Are you well equipped to accomplish the ministry of your calling? Are you well trained in the maintenance and use of your spiritual equipment? This is the time to train. Don't wait for the outbreak of spiritual warfare to learn what you need to know. The truth is we are at war whether we are prepared or not. We are at war whether we are ready or not. We are at war whether we want to fight or not. We have a fully committed enemy who has openly declared war on all believers. It is time to grasp the facts of our situation and learn to do everything possible to complete our purpose and reach our destiny in the Kingdom.

In the following paragraphs we will look at some of the training you need to properly operate in this present warfare. Some training focuses on the care and maintenance of the equipment you have been issued by the Lord. Some will focus on the use of your weapons of spiritual warfare. Proper training helps people to understand that some old patterns need to be dropped and some new patterns of behavior need to emerge. Once again, I pray that the Lord will give you more revelation as you read and study these principles than He gave to me as I fulfilled His command to write them down for you.

Controlling Your Body

It is God's will that you should be sanctified: that you should avoid sexual immorality; that each of you should learn to control his own body in a way that is holy and honorable, not in passionate lust like the heathen, who do not know God; (1 Thessalonians 4:3-5, NIV)

Here is an interesting thought: your body is part of your equipment. You are primarily a spiritual being who has been placed in a body in order to accomplish your spiritual mission. You are not merely your body. You are much more than that. The part which is the essential you will live far beyond the lifetime of the body in which you are currently residing. The proper thing to do is to sanctify your body to the Lord. In other words set it apart for the primary mission of pleasing the Lord rather than merely satisfying the desires of the flesh.

Paul tells the believers in Thessalonica they need to learn to control their bodies. They are expected to use their bodies in holy and honorable ways so they can faithfully serve the Lord. If they give in to the *"passionate lusts of the heathen,"* they will fail to accomplish what the Lord has called them to do. People who do not learn to control their bodies are in effect telling the world they do not actually know the Lord. What is your body telling the world? Is it demonstrating that you know and honor the Lord or that you are just like all the heathens.

Paul takes this further as he urges the Philippian believers to remember who they are and whose they are. If you truly belong to the Lord, He will help you to take and maintain control over your physical body. Think about it. When we give the Lord control over our bodies, he will transform them to be like His glorious body. I really like this imagery. How about you? Are you allowing the Lord to have control over your body or are you still giving up your control to the desires of your flesh?

> *But our citizenship is in heaven. And we eagerly await a Savior from there, the Lord Jesus Christ, who, by the power that enables him to bring everything under his control, will transform our lowly bodies so that they will be like his glorious body.* (Philippians 3:20-21, NIV)

Controlling Your Tongue

It is essential that we learn how to control our bodies if we are going to serve the Lord well. He has provided a manual for us to use in this part of our training mission. Everything we need to know about training, equipping and controlling the body is in this special manual. The owner's manual for the human body is the Bible. The problem is that too few people actually read it. To better understand this concept, we once again look first at the natural and then move on to learn its spiritual meaning. Few people who own automobiles actually read the owner's manual. Many problems could be resolved by the use of the manual and others could be avoided if the prescribed maintenance is done on a regular basis. It is important to take certain preventative measures to keep your automobile running problem free.

I believe the same principles for the use and care of automobiles applies to the use of the human body. Failure to read the manual can also result in many problems and challenges, which could have been avoided for most owners of the human body. I don't want to take this comparison too far, but there is one more thing I would like for you to consider. Like an automobile you come equipped with various options and special features not readily visible to the untrained eye. One part of the body with something like super powers is the tongue. It is small but powerful. It can be used for good or for evil.

One part of the body which seems to defy every attempt to establish control over it is the tongue. In many ways, this is the most dangerous part of our bodies. Please understand that it is not only dangerous for other people, but it can actually endanger our own spiritual wellbeing. Think about Solomon's warning in Proverbs 18:21, *"Death and life are in the power of the tongue, and those who love it will eat its fruit."* What kind of fruit are you eating? Add to this the lesson in Proverbs 18:20, *"A man's stomach shall be satisfied from the fruit of*

his mouth; from the produce of his lips he shall be filled."
What kind of fruit is your tongue releasing to fill your spiritual stomach? In the paragraphs below, you will see five of the controls you need to apply for the proper use of the tongue. All five are fully discussed in your owner's manual.

1. Stop confessing the power of the enemy

As I travel for ministry, I continually meet people who are confessing more about the power and works of the enemy than they are about the power and works of the Lord. As you listen to them, it begins to sound like they have more faith in the enemy to harm them than faith in the Lord to protect and save them. This should not be the case in the Body of Christ. This is not the witness we want to give to the world. I want to tell all the lost souls that Yeshua has all the authority and power in the universe. This is what he taught. Consider the teaching in Matthew 28:18, *"And Jesus came and spoke to them, saying, 'All authority has been given to Me in heaven and on earth.'"* If Yeshua has it all, how much is left for the enemy? If you believe what Yeshua said, stop confessing what the enemy is doing. Stop confessing your weakness and vulnerability and confess what Yeshua has already given to you.

> *Behold, I give you the authority to trample on serpents and scorpions, and over all the power of the enemy, and nothing shall by any means hurt you.* (Luke 10:19)

When Yeshua received all this power and authority after the resurrection, He immediately released it to us. At that time, He added this amazing authority to what He had already spoken over us in the past. Think about it. The enemy only has as much authority as we release to him through our confessions and professions. He knows you have the authority given by Yeshua and he wants you to pass it along to him. He uses illegitimate authority to do his work. Don't let him have any more of your authority. Confess the power and authority of Yeshua and claim what He has released to you. What do you do with the devil? Follow the process released in James 4:7, *"Therefore submit to God. Resist the devil and he will flee from you."* Now that doesn't sound too difficult does it? Just use your tongue to release the power of the Lord with the authority He has already bestowed on you. Amen?

2. Stop accusing other believers

Another thing I hear over and over among people who claim to be believers is the vicious accusations heaped on others by the unruly tongues of immature disciples. Examine yourself. How often do you heap accusations on other believers? I see it all the time on social media. I call these people unlicensed heresy hunters. Are you hunting without a license? Think about what you are doing with this behavior. Think about whose work you are doing when you accuse other believers. I encourage you to store the passage below in your heart and let it be a constant reminder of who you are and what you are called to do.

> *Then I heard a loud voice saying in heaven, "Now salvation, and strength, and the kingdom of our God, and the power of His Christ have come, for the accuser of our brethren, who accused them before our God day and night, has been cast down. And they overcame him by the blood of the Lamb and by the word of their testimony, and they did not love their lives to the death."* (Revelation 12:10-11)

One of the names of the enemy used in the Bible is *"the accuser of our brethren."* Please don't help him do his destructive work. As you think about this, study want is being taught in Jude 1:9 (NIV), *"But even the archangel Michael, when he was disputing with the devil about the body of Moses, did not dare to bring a slanderous accusation against him, but said, 'The Lord rebuke you!'"* If the Archangel Michael refuses to accuse the devil, who am I to accuse a fellow believer. I choose to let the Lord rebuke others through the work of the Holy Spirit. I trust Him to take care of it without my help. I try to always practice this unless I receive a very specific order from the Lord. Even then I am careful to be certain this came from the Lord and not from my own spirit. I am also careful to only say what the Lord said and not embellish it with my own words of condemnation or judgment.

3. Speak the wisdom of God

The truth is that we have a choice about what we speak. I have heard some people claim they are innocent of the terrible things they do with their tongues because it is beyond their control. Controlling the tongue may be difficult but it is not impossible. Like any other skill, it takes training and practice to replace one habit with another. You may begin by correcting yourself after you speak. Each time you do this you tend to get closer to establishing control over the tongue before it speaks. Then that day comes when you are able to correct your speech before it leaves your mouth. Wise disciples will remember what Yeshua said in Matthew 12:36-37, *"But I tell you that men will have to give account on the day of judgment for every careless word they have spoken. For by your words you will be acquitted, and by your words you will be condemned."*

There are two kinds of wisdom at your disposal and it is up to you to decide which you want to speak. The most popular wisdom for the majority of speakers is what the Bible calls the wisdom of the world. In his first letter to the church at Corinth, Paul warns that the wisdom of the world and those who use it are both coming to an end. In fact He uses the phrase "coming to nothing." I do not want my works and words to come to nothing. How about you? Think about it as you study the passage below and then make a decision for your own life.

> *However, we speak wisdom among those who are mature, yet not the wisdom of this age, nor of the rulers of this age, who are coming to nothing. But we speak the wisdom of God in a mystery, the hidden wisdom which God ordained before the ages for our glory, which none of the rulers of this age knew; for had they known, they would not have crucified the Lord of glory.* (1 Corinthians 2:6-8)

You will not get blessed by the rulers of this age for speaking the wisdom of God. For one thing, they cannot understand it. Rather than confessing their shortcomings, they will most likely attack you and your use of the hidden wisdom of God. Always remember that God's wisdom is called hidden for a reason. It is hidden from the unbelieving rich, famous and powerful people of this age. Many who hear it will feel convicted by the wisdom of the Lord and they do not like that. They would rather silence the prophet than hear the truth. As with the kings of old, powerful people attack the prophets of God who release the much needed truth of God into this generation.

4. Continue to confess the power and presence of the Lord

As you confess the power, authority and presence of the Lord you are releasing these powerful spiritual forces against the enemy. A beautiful description of the work of those in the winner's circle in Heaven is given in Revelation 12:11, *"And they overcame him by the blood of the Lamb and by the word of their testimony, and they did not love their lives to the death.*" When you add your testimony about the power and authority of Yeshua to His shed blood, you have unleased the most powerful weapon of spiritual warfare. This is what overcomers do all day every day.

Continuously confessing the power, authority, wisdom and presence of the Lord takes training and practice. Remember that changing a habit requires constant attention and correction. Ask the Holy Spirit to help by correcting you as needed. Ask the Holy Spirit to teach you the things you need to know and speak. I pray that you will receive the powerful promise Yeshua released in John 14:16-17, "*And I will pray the Father, and He will give you another Helper, that He may abide with you forever—the Spirit of truth, whom the world cannot receive, because it neither sees Him nor knows Him; but you know Him, for He dwells with you and will be in you.*" You never have to take on these battles alone. The Lord will always be with you to help you. In fact, He has already sent help in the person of the Spirit of truth.

> *Now we have received, not the spirit of the world, but the Spirit who is from God, that we might know the things that have been freely given to us by God.* (1 Corinthians 2:12)

5. Store good treasures in your Heart (spirit)

In the previous chapters of this book I have referred to the practice of storing the swords of the Lord in your heart. This means to store powerful promises from the Word of God where you can easily access them when needed. The way to do this is to establish a practice of memorizing passages of scripture, which will help you in the future. The Lord created you with this capacity to store things in your heart. Take advantage of this gift. Too many people are storing harmful things in their hearts. They are storing up things the Lord calls "evil" in their hearts. Listen to His advice and make a practice of storing good things and purging every evil thing.

> *A good man out of the good treasure of his heart brings forth good; and an evil man out of the evil treasure of his heart brings forth evil. For out of the abundance of the heart his mouth speaks.* (Luke 6:45)

When someone says something harmful or painful to another believer, two things happen. First the words go forth like arrows bringing emotional pain and spiritual harm to their target. Here is a powerful truth we must understand: Words intended to harm others will also do harm to the one who speaks them. They may go forth, but they also return to the heart and become a part of what is stored there. In the future, you are more likely to release these things again because they are in your storehouse. As you do it again, you also store more of it in your heart. This character defect gets stronger and stronger as it is allowed to continue to manifest. The more you store these things the greater the challenge of purging them out will become. Begin quickly to replace the evil things with the good things of the Holy Spirit. I pray that very soon you can confess with Solomon the words in the passage below.

> *My mouth speaks what is true, for my lips detest wickedness. All the words of my mouth are just; none of them is crooked or perverse. To the discerning all of them are right; they are faultless to those who have knowledge.* (Proverbs 8:7-8, NIV)

Controlling Your Fear Response

Fear is a very powerful spiritual force in our lives. In one sense it is a powerful source to influence our learning. This can be effective but more often it is not helpful to be filled with fear. The fear response was given to us to help us survive in a hostile world. In emergency situations fear can motivate and mobilize you to get out of harm's way. That can be effective in that moment, but too often fear works to immobilize people. When fear causes you to freeze up, you may actually be dealing with the spirit of fear. Remember this spirit is not a gift from the Lord but a curse from the enemy. Read aloud and often the words in 2 Timothy 1:7, *"For God has not given us a spirit of fear, but of power and of love and of a sound mind."* Ask yourself: If it doesn't come from God who does it come from? Cast out every remnant of the spirit of fear. Learn the powerful lesson about fear in this passage. If God is on your side, who can be successful against you?

> *When you go out to battle against your enemies, and see horses and chariots and people more numerous than you, do not be afraid of them; for the Lord your God is with you, who brought you up from the land of Egypt.* (Deuteronomy 20:1)

Fear is often a confession of a shortfall in the faith department. Once again, I recommend storing some power statements from the Word of God in your spirit. Then begin to speak them aloud over and over until the power of faith comes to release these promises in your life and work. Confess that you have nothing to fear because the Lord your God is with you. He has delivered you in the past and He will deliver you again. I have listed a few of these power statements for you. Begin to confess them regularly. As you find other similar statements add them to your list and continue to increase your faith that the Lord is consistent and trustworthy. He will do for you what He has promised. Amen?

> *Have I not commanded you? Be strong and of good courage; do not be afraid, nor be dismayed, for the Lord your God is with you wherever you go.* (Joshua 1:9)

> *Do not be afraid of sudden terror, nor of trouble from the wicked when it comes; For the Lord will be your confidence, and will keep your foot from being caught. (Proverbs 3:25-26)*

> *Now the Lord spoke to Paul in the night by a vision, "Do not be afraid, but speak, and do not keep silent; for I am with you, and no one will attack you to hurt you; for I have many people in this city."* (Acts 18:9-10)

> *But even if you should suffer for righteousness' sake, you are blessed. And do not be afraid of their threats, nor be troubled.* (1 Peter 3:14)

Controlling Your Spirit

It is important to know that you can control your own spirit. Some people may not want to know this because they don't want to be responsible for what they are saying and doing. There is an old saying: Ignorance of the law is no excuse. I will assure you that the Lord is not big on excuses. No matter how craftily you may frame one of your excuses, He will immediately see through it and reject it. I urge you to take seriously the message in 1 Corinthians 14:32, *"And the spirits of the prophets are subject to the prophets."* Your spirit is subject to you and can be put under your conscious control by the authority the Lord has already given you.

It is time to take control of your spirit and maintain you authority over it. I often speak to my own spirit. An angel came to me several years ago and taught me what I am now releasing to you. Speaking to my own spirit usually happens when I am releasing commands to it. I recommend this practice for you. Begin by claiming the promise in 1 Corinthians 14:32. Then speak to your spirit. I often command my spirit to open its eyes to see what is happening in the spiritual realm. If you want to begin or expand on your seer anointing, do what the angel taught me to do. Command your spirit to wake up and get to work. This is a powerful way to get the spiritual weapons given by the Holy Spirit to work more powerfully for you. I also speak frequently to my spiritual ears and command them to be open so I can hear the voice of the Lord and obediently follow Him. It works for me, and you can do the same things with His help.

If the world around you is confusing and is challenging you too much and too often, take authority over you spirit and your circumstances. God doesn't bring confusion. Think about it as your read 1 Corinthians 14:33, "*For God is not the author of confusion but of peace, as in all the churches of the saints.*" If things are confusing, remember the Lord didn't do it. Stand on His promises and rebuke every oppressive spirit around you. Confess again the promise of Yeshua in Luke 10:19 "*Behold, I give you the authority to trample on serpents and scorpions, and over all the power of the enemy, and nothing shall by any means hurt you.*" Confess over and over the power and authority of the Lord which has been given to you. Always use the spiritual weapons He has given to you for your work in the Kingdom of God. Amen?

I pray these things will assist you in managing the equipment the Lord has given to you. He gives the gifts and leaves us with the responsibility to maintain, protect and utilize these powerful spiritual weapons in accordance with His Word and under the guidance of the Holy Spirit. The Lord is good all the time. He tells you to do things He has already resourced you to accomplish. He never leaves you without hope or help. He has promised to always be with you even to the end of the age. Trust Him. Put your faith in His promises. He will never let you down. Amen?

PART FOUR
POWER IN RELATIONSHIPS

I encourage you to begin the study of these last three chapters in this book by doing another self-examination. First, ask yourself: Are you part of a courageous band of brothers and sisters united for spiritual warfare in these last days? Before you give your final answer, consider another question: Are you trying to be an army of one fighting alone against impossible odds? The fact is you have already made a decision. Some people are unaware they have made a choice. They may wonder how to determine which choice they have made. If you observe your values and actions, you will soon know which lifestyle you have chosen. You can learn from observing others, but the really important task is to become clear about how you operate in the spiritual realm. As you prepare to deal with the perilous times to come, be honest with yourself and accept responsibility for your choices and actions. Also understand that choosing not to make a choice is in fact a choice.

When warfare breaks out, you do not have a choice to opt out of the battle. You have an enemy who has declared war on you. He has chosen to do his best to "steal, kill and destroy" everything precious to you. He knows where you live and He knows whether you are prepared and ready or vulnerable and easy. The Lord has revealed the plan. The Lord has given many prophetic words describing exactly what is going to happen and

227

what you need to do to get ready and stay ready. In the light of what you have already learned, study the passage below once more and allow the Holy Spirit to guide you into all truth about the last days.

> *But know this, that in the last days perilous times will come: For men will be lovers of themselves, lovers of money, boasters, proud, blasphemers, disobedient to parents, unthankful, unholy, unloving, unforgiving, slanderers, without self-control, brutal, despisers of good, traitors, headstrong, haughty, lovers of pleasure rather than lovers of God, having a form of godliness but denying its power. And from such people turn away! For of this sort are those who creep into households and make captives of gullible women loaded down with sins, led away by various lusts, always learning and never able to come to the knowledge of the truth.* (2 Timothy 3:1-7)

It is foolish to try to achieve a big spiritual victory alone. In spite of the movies you may have seen, no army of one (except Yeshua) has ever succeeded in battle or ended in victory. You need the Lord on your team and you need to unite with other believers to survive these perilous times. This is something the Lord taught over and over. As He taught, He continued to add layers of spiritual wisdom to the kingdom mysteries He came to reveal. We begin with a new commandment released by Yeshua.

> *A new commandment I give to you, that you love one another; as I have loved you, that you also love one another. By this all will know that you are My disciples, if you have love for one another.* (John 13:34-35)

We looked earlier at some force multipliers available to spiritual warriors. In His first letter, the Apostle John gave a powerful spiritual truth in a very brief statement: *"No one has seen God at any time. If we love one another, God abides in us, and His love has been perfected in us."* (1 John 4:12) There it is. Loving one another opens our hearts so the Lord can abide in us. Having the Lord on your side is a powerful force multiplier. The Lord will never lose a battle and you have been invited to join Him in the victory circle in the last days. However, you need to take action right now to open the door for that outcome to manifest in your heart. Rid yourself of everything which hinders you from loving other believers and being in unity with them.

> *Therefore, since we are surrounded by such a great cloud of witnesses, let us throw off everything that hinders and the sin that so easily entangles, and let us run with perseverance the race marked out for us. Let us fix our eyes on Jesus, the author and perfecter of our faith, who for the joy set before him endured the cross, scorning its shame, and sat down at the right hand of the throne of God. Consider him who endured such opposition from sinful men, so that you will not grow weary and lose heart.* (Hebrews 12:1-3, NIV)

Are you surrounded by a great cloud of witnesses? I believe this refers to the heroes of the faith from the past and witnesses who are currently available to surround us and join with us in this great spiritual battle. Many people resist joining the body of believers established by Yeshua. So the Lord gave a promise and put His power and authority behind it to inspire people to partner in their kingdom work. In the passage below, you can see once more that the Lord's math is designed to multiply the power available to believers united by love.

Again I say to you that if two of you agree on earth concerning anything that they ask, it will be done for them by My Father in heaven. For where two or three are gathered together in My name, I am there in the midst of them. (Matthew 18:19-20)

Yeshua made it plain that love is the key to releasing His powerful kingdom force multipliers. Love is the key to making the Temple in your heart ready for the Lord to move in. Love is the evidence of your level of obedience to the Lord. If you love little, you are choosing not to fully obey Him. Without obedience, none of the kingdom authority and power will work for you. You simply need to make a decision to overcome whatever obstacle is blocking you. Do this now so you will be able to demonstrate your love and obedience to the Lord by loving others.

Jesus answered and said to him, "If anyone loves Me, he will keep My word; and My Father will love him, and We will come to him and make Our home with him. He who does not love Me does not keep My words; and the word which you hear is not Mine but the Father's who sent Me." (John 14:23-24)

One of the amazing transformations which occurred in the little band of Yeshua followers is describe in the second chapter of the book of Acts. We are not certain when this transformation took place, but it is clear that something has drastically changed in the lives of those first disciples. They are no longer trying to do things alone. They are no longer competing to see who will be first or who will be in charge. They have fully submitted to the leadership of the Lord and have reached an amazing and wonderful new level in the Unity Glory of the Kingdom. For more information on the power of Unity Glory see my book, "Seven Levels of Glory."

> *When the Day of Pentecost had fully come, they were all with one accord in one place. And suddenly there came a sound from heaven, as of a rushing mighty wind, and it filled the whole house where they were sitting. Then there appeared to them divided tongues, as of fire, and one sat upon each of them. And they were all filled with the Holy Spirit and began to speak with other tongues, as the Spirit gave them utterance.* (Acts 2:1-4)

This new found unity was empowering for the disciples as they began to carry on the mission of Yeshua during times of great persecution and through many different types of hardship. They no longer wavered. They were now totally committed to the cause of Christ. As they continued to live and serve in "one accord" the Lord began to work His special kingdom math in their ministry. Luke says the Lord added to their number, but I believe multiplied is a better interpretation when you consider they went from 200 to 5,000 in a few days.

> *So continuing daily with one accord in the temple, and breaking bread from house to house, they ate their food with gladness and simplicity of heart, praising God and having favor with all the people. And the Lord added to the church daily those who were being saved.* (Acts 2:46-47)

Great spiritual power is released by the Lord for those who choose to be united in love and committed to obedient service. As we go through these perilous times, we need this kind of power and authority to not only survive but to thrive. The fullness of this blessing of spiritual power was released when they prayed to have boldness to proclaim the name of Yeshua in the face of great spiritual warfare. Their new found unity was the environment in which these spiritual gifts could be released. Now it is our turn. Many believers today are too timid to speak the name of Yeshua among their friends. They cower in fear when challenged to speak His name in public. Many people are more afraid of man than they are of the Lord. It is time for a great transformation to be released to the Lord's people. I pray for it daily. I claim the promise released in Romans 12:2, "*And do not be conformed to this world, but be transformed by the renewing of your mind, that you may prove what is that good and acceptable and perfect will of God.*"

How can this kind of power be released to you? The source and power for this transformation of the soul and renewing of the mind is still available from the same source. It is one of the mighty works of the Holy Spirit. It is available to you, and it is necessary for those enduring the perilous times of these last days. All you have to do is ask. All you have to do is claim the promises and remain in love and obedience to the Lord. Claim it again in these last days. Ask the Lord. He is faithful and good. He will give you every spiritual gift you need to become more than a conqueror in Christ Jesus.

> *But when the kindness and the love of God our Savior toward man appeared, not by works of righteousness which we have done, but according to His mercy He saved us, through the washing of regeneration and renewing of the Holy Spirit, whom He poured out on us abundantly through Jesus Christ our Savior, that having been justified by His grace we should become heirs according to the hope of eternal life.* (Titus 3:4-7)

CHAPTER TWELVE
POSITIONING FOR THE PRESENCE

Keep me as the apple of Your eye; hide me under the shadow of Your wings, from the wicked who oppress me, from my deadly enemies who surround me. (Psalm 17:8-9)

David had a plan for getting into a place of safety when wicked people tried to oppress him. When deadly enemies surrounded Him, he knew exactly where to go. To understand his plan you need to understand the meaning of being under the shadow of the Lord's wings. We know the Lord doesn't have or need wings. So where did David plan to go? He was making reference to the shadow of the wings on the mercy seat of the Ark. David's plan was to take his troubles to the Lord and get into His powerful presence. He could go to the tent where the Ark of the Covenant was being kept and get under the shadow of those wings.

David trusted that no harm could come to Him in God's powerful presence. Where do you plan to go when perilous times come upon you? David prepared in advance so he would have a place to go when he desperately needed or desired the presence of the Lord. Do you have a place like that in your life? Again, I recommend that you prepare in advance for what is certain to come. For your personal protection, you need to know where, when and how to get into the powerful presence of the Lord.

PREPARING FOR THE PRESENCE

My pattern for dealing with every topic the Lord leads me to put into writing is to go to the Word of God first. I study every topic as much as I possibly can before I begin to write. When I went to the Word looking for how the great people of faith in the past had prepared for the Lord's presence, I noticed right away that there was no one physical location where they had all gone to be with the Lord. Each one had found that special place of intimacy in their unique relationship with the Lord. I want to take you along on my enlightening journey of discovery. I selected certain key figures from Biblical history, and examined how they built and maintained their special relationship with the Lord. Then I looked at how their relationship with the Lord became the key to understanding their success in the Kingdom of God. Are you ready to make this journey with me? If so, here we go.

ABRAHAM BUILT ALTARS

Together we will travel back to the beginning of God's special salvation history with the Children of Israel. In the book of Genesis we begin to examine the special places where the Lord met with Abraham. Abraham lived a nomadic style of life. He was constantly on the move. He had to do this for several reasons. He needed to remain ahead of potential enemies who would try to steal, kill and destroy his family and what the Lord was calling him to do. He also had to provide for huge flocks and herds who constantly needed food and water. If you have visited the wilderness of Israel and Jordan, you know how sparse these resources are most of the year. Abraham also moved in obedience to the command of the Lord. He was told that he and his family were to inherit the entire land. As he traveled, he literally walked out a promise given to him by the Lord.

> *All the land that you see I will give to you and your offspring forever. I will make your off-spring like the dust of the earth, so that if anyone could count the dust, then your offspring could be counted. Go, walk through the length and breadth of the land, for I am giving it to you.* (Genesis 13:15-17, NIV)

Abraham didn't stay in any one place very long. He was on the move as he continued to walk out the Lord's promise. He didn't have a consistent physical address where he could built a tabernacle for the Lord. So how did Abraham make it work? He built altars in all the key places where he had encountered the presence of the Lord. He marked the territory given by the Lord to him and his descendants with these altars. They became the places where he called upon the Name of the Lord. In other words, these were his special places of intimacy with the Lord. In the story of his travels, you can feel the joy when he returns to a place where he has previously built one of these altars.

> *And he moved from there to the mountain east of Bethel, and he pitched his tent with Bethel on the west and Ai on the east; there he built an altar to the Lord and called on the name of the Lord.* (Genesis 12:8)

When I was on active duty in the US Army, I made a practice of following Abraham's example. On each assignment, I found a way to build an altar to the Lord. Army leaders frowned on the practice of building physical altars on government property. My practice was to build spiritual altars. Like Abraham, I looked for a place where the Lord had manifested and given me provision, protection, or prosperity. In this place, I made a declaration. I called it by the name Abraham had used. I named each altar "The Lord Will Provide." Each time I visited one of these places, I could still feel the powerful presence of the Lord.

It is very important to remember that circumstances cannot dictate how you connect with the Lord. Joseph stayed in touch with the Lord in prison. Moses stayed in touch with the Lord in the wilderness. Never let your circumstances prevent you from building an altar to the Lord. Never let your circumstances block you from having a place of intimacy with the Lord. When your situation is at its worst, this is the time and place where you need Him most. He is always available reminding you not to get immobilized by fear, but to put your trust in Him.

MOSES BUILT A TENT OF MEETING

Now Moses used to take a tent and pitch it outside the camp some distance away, calling it the "tent of meeting." Anyone inquiring of the Lord would go to the tent of meeting outside the camp. And whenever Moses went out to the tent, all the people rose and stood at the entrances to their tents, watching Moses until he entered the tent. As Moses went into the tent, the pillar of cloud would come down and stay at the entrance, while the Lord spoke with Moses. (Exodus 33:7-9)

Have you ever felt the need to get away from people for a little while and just spend time with the Lord? Have you ever tried to lead a group of people who constantly complain, criticize and blame you for their troubles? This is what Moses had to deal with, but on a much larger scale. Can you imagine having over two million grumblers constantly biting at your heels? Moses learned early in his leadership role that He needed to spend time with the Lord. He faced issues for which he had no solutions. He faced problems, which were too large for any living human being to solve. He had no choice but to spend quality time with the Lord. In these private moments, the Lord revealed what Moses needed to say and do. It always worked.

The Children of Israel did not simply complain about their circumstances they attacked the character and credibility of Moses. It was painful for Moses even when the Lord pointed out that their real rebellion was against Him. Moses took his problems and complaints to the Lord. He always did it in a way that gave honor to the Lord. He had learned long before the others about the importance of having a holy fear (awe) of the Lord. The people never seemed to learn this. They constantly complained and accused the Lord of failing to meet His commitments to them. Instead of getting defensive and attacking the people, Moses took it to the Lord. The Lord was always faithful to give Moses a solution to the challenges he faced. The Lord is still faithful. He will give you the answers you need even if they are not the answers you want.

> *The Lord would speak to Moses face to face, as a man speaks with his friend. Then Moses would return to the camp, but his young aide Joshua son of Nun did not leave the tent.* (Exodus 33:11)

Would you like to have the kind of relationship with the Lord described in the passage above? Most people quickly answer the question with a strong "Yes!" I advise people to wait a moment before agreeing. This worked for Moses, but didn't seem to work for the people. The Children of Israel thought this was a good idea until they saw the fire of His glory, felt the shaking of the ground, heard the powerful blast of the heavenly shofar and heard the power in His voice. They decided to stay back from the presence because they were terrified of the power and authority of the Lord. Moses described their behavior in Exodus 33:9, "*Whenever the people saw the pillar of cloud standing at the entrance to the tent, they all stood and worshiped, each at the entrance to his tent.*"

Imagine the spiritual loss in their lives. The Lord invited them into His presence and they were too afraid to accept the offer. You have something they did not have. You have the blood of Yeshua covering you so that you can enter the holy of holies. If you have accepted Yeshua as your Lord and Savior, you have a covering better than any tent or temple. I release two seemingly conflicting points which are both true in the spiritual realm. Don't be afraid while maintaining an attitude of the fear of the Lord. If this is difficult to understand, ask the Holy Spirit to reveal it to you.

Later, at the command of the Lord, Moses built the tabernacle, which also became a tent of meeting. From this time forward, the Tabernacle became Moses' usual place for meeting with the Lord. It was awesome and wonderful to visit with the Lord in the Tent of Meeting, but sometimes the presence was so strong that even Moses couldn't remain in the Tabernacle. Have you ever experienced this kind of power in His presence? I have on several occasions. One morning at the beginning of last year a cloud of His presence filled our worship room. It was so thick I had difficulty seeing the walls of the room. It was so powerful that I couldn't walk through it to enter the room. I stood near the door looking with amazement at how the Lord was manifesting His presence. Suddenly, I felt something like two hands on my back, and I was shoved through the door into the cloud filled room. I quickly fell face down before the Lord in awe of His holy presence. As this happened, I was able to understood more fully what Moses wrote in the Torah.

> *Then the cloud covered the tabernacle of meeting, and the glory of the Lord filled the tabernacle. And Moses was not able to enter the tabernacle of meeting, because the cloud rested above it, and the glory of the Lord filled the tabernacle.* (Exodus 40:34-35)

DAVID ERECTED A TENT FOR THE ARK

Samuel said to King Saul in 1 Samuel 13:14, *"The Lord has sought for Himself a man after His own heart, and the Lord has commanded him to be commander over His people, because you have not kept what the Lord commanded you."* We learn later that Samuel was speaking about David. I believe there are two ways to understand the phrase *"after His own heart."* On the one hand it can mean the Lord was looking for someone who had a heart similar to His. This is a commonly held interpretation of this passage. On the other hand, it could mean someone who was literally trying passionately to find the heart of the Lord for himself. I suspect there are elements of both interpretations revealed in 2 Chronicles 1:4, *"But David had brought up the ark of God from Kirjath Jearim to the place David had prepared for it, for he had pitched a tent for it at Jerusalem."*

David had a heart which literally hungered and thirsted for the Lord. He wrote about it over and over in the Psalms. In order to bring the presence of the Lord closer to his own residence, David erected a tent for the Ark of the Presence in Jerusalem, his capitol city. He had to go through a painful trial and error period to fully understand the proper way to move the Ark. This reminds us that we may need to go through a similar process to establish a place for the presence of the Lord in our own lives. I am willing to do whatever it takes to be close to and inside the awesome presence of the Lord. How about you?

SOLOMON BUILT A TEMPLE

David wanted to build a temple for the Lord, but it was not in the Lord's plan for His life. He did make the plans for the building, provided vast amounts of building supplies and gave his entire fortune to the project. The Lord didn't give David this desire of his heart, but He gave him a promise. David honored the Lord by submitting to His plan. It was up to David's son, Solomon, to build the Temple.

> *Then King David rose to his feet and said, "Hear me, my brethren and my people: I had it in my heart to build a house of rest for the ark of the covenant of the Lord, and for the foot-stool of our God, and had made preparations to build it. But God said to me, 'You shall not build a house for My name, because you have been a man of war and have shed blood.'"* (1 Chronicles 28:2-3)

Solomon joyfully accepted the challenge of building the most magnificent building on Earth at that time to honor the Lord. He spent many years overseeing the project and eagerly awaited its completion. During the dedication ceremony, the Lord gave an awesome sign of His approval for what the people had prepared. The cloud of His presence appeared for the first time in over four hundred years. The people present at the dedication ceremony experienced the same power in His presence, which manifested when Moses dedicated the

Tabernacle. It was so strong that no one could stand in the Presence.

> *And it came to pass, when the priests came out of the holy place, that the cloud filled the house of the Lord, so that the priests could not continue ministering because of the cloud; for the glory of the Lord filled the house of the Lord. Then Solomon spoke: "The Lord said He would dwell in the dark cloud. I have surely built You an exalted house, and a place for You to dwell in forever."* (1 Kings 8:10-13)

Have you experienced this kind of power in the presence of the Lord? Do you hunger and thirst for the presence of the Lord to manifest like this in your life? I don't know about you, but I am constantly pressing in for the presence. I want to establish a place of His presence so that I can get under the shadow of His wings when enemies attack or when the perilous times manifest. How about you? Do you believe it is possible to establish this kind of relationship with the Lord? I believe it is not only possible, but it is possible for you and me to experience it. I thought about how the prophet Ezekiel was given this experience in a vision. *"The Spirit lifted me up and brought me into the inner court; and behold, the glory of the Lord filled the temple."* (Ezekiel 43:5) Before the overwhelming times of tribulation come, build a place where you can go to escape the wrath and spend time with the Lord. Amen?

YESHUA GAVE A NEW LOCATION

When I think about the coming days of tribulation, I always return to the teachings of Yeshua to find comfort and see what we should do in this generation. During His ministry on Earth, Yeshua was constantly asked about the kingdom of God. People were looking for security and hope during a painful occupation of their land by the Roman military. At that time, they still had the temple, but most were not looking at it the way the Lord desired for them to see it. Many of them looked at the Temple as if it were some kind of powerful good luck charm.

After the Temple was destroyed by the Roman army, their situation became much worse. They had no idea where to turn. They didn't know where to go to experience the presence of God. Tragically, they had not listened to the teachings of Yeshua nor had they accepted His prophecy of the loss of their Temple. If they had listened and accepted what He taught, they would have known what to do in their generation. The key to this is found in the passage below.

> *Now when He was asked by the Pharisees when the kingdom of God would come, He answered them and said, "The kingdom of God does not come with observation; nor will they say, 'See here!' or 'See there!' For indeed, the kingdom of God is within you."* (Luke 17:20-21)

Yeshua said the Kingdom of God is within us. We don't have to go looking for it. We just need to embrace it where the Lord has decided to let it manifest. It has always been difficult for a religious spirit to understand that the Lord is always in the process of changing. Consider Revelation 21:5, *"Then He who sat on the throne said, "Behold, I make all things new." And He said to me, "Write, for these words are true and faithful."* I'm not looking for a way to get back into an old manifestation of the Lord's presence. I am living in expectancy that He is about to show us a whole new way. Are you ready for it?

PETER WAS BUILDING A SPIRITUAL HOUSE

Peter wrote about something like the Lord had taught. He phrased it in a little different way, but it was the same basic idea. He urged people to build themselves into a spiritual house. Solomon received all he needed from his father. We have been given all the needed building materials from our Father. Actually we have received more than precious metals and high quality stones. We have been given the "living stone" as the foundation for our spiritual house. We have been called to be a "holy priesthood' and to offer new kinds of spiritual sacrifices which are more acceptable to the Lord.

Coming to Him as to a living stone, rejected indeed by men, but chosen by God and precious, you also, as living stones, are being built up a spiritual house, a holy priesthood, to offer up spiritual sacrifices acceptable to God through Jesus Christ. (1 Peter 2:4-5)

Are you in the process of being built up as a spiritual house? Have you learned the new ways of the Lord? Are you offering up the new spiritual sacrifices? The key to all these processes is revealed in the Word of God. At times I feel like a modern day Indiana Jones searching for the Holy Grail. To make this search you don't have to travel around the world. You don't have to dig up the earth or move huge stones. You just need to accept what the Lord is willing to do for all those who are open to His leadership. Are you ready to be built up into a spiritual house as you obediently follow Him?

PAUL: THE TEMPLE IS INSIDE YOU

Paul takes these same teachings and then expresses them in a manner revealed to him by the Lord. He says something which was much more controversial than the things taught by either Yeshua or Peter. He declared that the Temple of God still exists. He stated that it is located in the hearts of those who have accepted Yeshua as Lord and Savior. He boldly declared that you as a believer are the Temple of God. This is for you. Believe it and receive it. Then begin to give thanks to the Lord for cleansing your heart so that you can host His presence.

> *Do you not know that you are the temple of*
> *God and that the Spirit of God dwells in you?*
> (1 Corinthians 3:16)

This teaching has guided the body of Christ for centuries. It is as relevant and powerful today as when Paul first wrote it. It is as powerful today as when the Lord established it. The place of the Presence is not far away. It is not inaccessible. It is not too distant for you to take hold of it. Think about it. It is already at hand. It has already manifested. It is time for us to fully accept it and live it out in our own spiritual walk with the Lord. Amen?

A WORSHIP ROOM IN OUR HOUSE

When we obeyed the Lord and moved to South Carolina, the Lord led us to a house with several bedrooms. He ruled over our plan to downsize saying we needed more room to do His work. For several years the Lord sent people to us for healing, deliverance and restoration. This house became the place the Lord had chosen for us to do this ministry. In addition to having several bedrooms, there was a large room over the garage, which only needed a closet to officially be called a bedroom. A space was already built in the room, which only needed a door to make the transition and become that closet. We could have done this simple addition to add another bedroom to our house, however the Lord had a different plan for this room.

We converted this room into a worship room. Over the years we have seen the Lord do many amazing things for people in this place. We have seen people healed, restored and anointed in this room. It is the place where I have experienced most of my Third Heaven visits. We have also seen many people make similar visits while they worshipped with us in this place of His presence. As we have gotten older the Lord has allowed us to do much less of this because of the physical challenges of keeping the room clean (physically and spiritually) and organized for ministering to others.

Think about this. Everything the Lord does has a purpose. As the Lord allowed us to transition to other ways of ministering, He revealed one reason for this change. People began to think that there was something special about this room, which they could not replicate where they were located. The Lord wants you to know that you don't need the room in my house. You need the room in your house, which you dedicate to His Presence. You need to build your own spiritual house and practice the presence in your space. Amen?

WHAT AND WHERE WILL YOU BUILD?

Where is your place of intimacy with the Lord? Perhaps you don't have an extra room to convert into a worship room. What can you do with the space you are given? I am reminded of the mother of the great spiritual leader and revivalist John Wesley. She gave birth to nineteen children and was extremely busy caring for them. How could she have a place of intimacy with the Lord? She found her place and taught her children to never disturb her when she was in the presence of the Lord. She simply threw her apron over her head and experienced her special time with the Lord. Anyone can do something like this. Don't make excuses. Make it happen. Ask the Lord to guide you through the process so it will be pleasing to Him.

Where do you go to position yourself to experience the presence of the Lord? Don't make excuses based on your circumstances. Pray and ask the Holy Spirit to reveal it to you. You don't need to imitate another person and do what they did. Find your own way with the Lord. Remember that you serve a creative God who never ceases to change and make all things new. Let Him guide you to the place where you can experience special times of intimacy with Him. This is a good time to ask. Pray a prayer like David when you need the Lord's presence.

> *Hear my cry, O God; attend to my prayer. From the end of the earth I will cry to You, when my heart is overwhelmed; lead me to the rock that is higher than I. For You have been a shelter for me, a strong tower from the enemy. I will abide in Your tabernacle forever; I will trust in the shelter of Your wings.* (Psalm 61:1-4)

Remember the strong words of the Bible, "The Lord is good. His love and mercy endure forever." You can count on Him. He keeps his promises. Take firm actions to stand on the promise in Psalm 34:17, *"The righteous cry out, and the Lord hears, and delivers them out of all their troubles."* What an awesome God we serve! He is good all the time. Accept His promises. I encourage you to stay in prayer as you seek the Lord's presence. Pray like David prayed as he sought after the heart of the Lord. Another powerful prayer is in the passage below. This is a good time to make it your prayer today.

> *Lord, You have heard the desire of the humble; You will prepare their heart; You will cause Your ear to hear, to do justice to the fatherless and*

the oppressed, that the man of the earth may oppress no more. (Psalm 10:17-18)

PRACTICING THE PRESENCE

For many years I have made it a practice to believe and declare that every promise of the Lord given in the Bible is for me. When I see a promise in the Bible, I stop and pray that prayer in the first person believing it is mine. Then I pause and give thanks for it out of a strong faith that I have already received it. I often encourage people to make this their practice as well. As you read the passage below, claim it for yourself. Don't let your spirit get blocked by the admonition to mourn and weep. The Lord has already prepared a method for you to cleanse your hands and purify your heart. The plan is to get under the blood of Yeshua and let His righteousness cover you.

> *Draw near to God and He will draw near to you. Cleanse your hands, you sinners; and purify your hearts, you double-minded. Lament and mourn and weep! Let your laughter be turned to mourning and your joy to gloom. Humble yourselves in the sight of the Lord, and He will lift you up.* (James 4:8-10)

The Lord never leaves us floundering in a hopeless struggle trying to understand how to put His plans into action. He has given us the written Word, the Holy Spirit and the Living Word (Yeshua ha Messiach). He always makes a way even where we cannot first see it. Sometimes we don't have because we don't ask. At other times we ask and do not receive because we are not asking correctly (See James 4:2-3). Don't get frustrated and give up. Keep asking and add to your prayer a request for the Lord's help in asking for the right thing at the right time.

I have found that the Lord has already given us clear and important instructions about how we can seek His presence. These instructions can be found in the passage below.

> *Make a joyful shout to the Lord, all you lands! Serve the Lord with gladness; Come before His presence with singing. Know that the Lord, He is God; It is He who has made us, and not we ourselves; we are His people and the sheep of His pasture. Enter into His gates with thanksgiving, and into His courts with praise. Be thankful to Him, and bless His name. For the Lord is good; His mercy is everlasting, and His truth endures to all generations.* (Psalm 100)

To get on the right track with the Lord let Him fill you with joy so you can serve Him with gladness. Amen? I always make it a practice to begin my times of intimacy with the Lord exactly as mentioned in Psalm 100:2. I begin to sing songs of praise. It is amazing what the Lord can and will open up for you when you follow His instructions. When my spirit gets really built up through the praise songs, I speak out my desire to enter His gates with thanksgiving. Too many people try to break into the Lord's house filled with complaints and criticism. This never works well for me and I don't believe it will work well for you. Try doing things His way.

As I am allowed through the gates and into His courts, I add words of praise to the words of thanksgiving that continue to come from my heart through my mouth. Yes it is important to say things aloud. Remember Romans 10:17, "*So then faith comes by hearing, and hearing by the word of God.*" Remember we are told in the first verse of Psalm 100 to "*joyfully shout to the Lord.*" It is time to be thankful to Him and bless Him. We are instructed to bless His holy Name. Here is the place of intimacy and these are the Lord's instructions about how to enter into His presence. The only thing left is to put it into practice. Amen?

I leave you at the end of this chapter with another word from the Lord. As the Lord has commanded never stop waiting and watching. Trust that He will provide for you in the time of your need. Have faith that He will keep His promise to return. When He comes, be certain that He finds you in obedience. Don't get caught up in the desires of the flesh while you wait. Continuously seek His presence and remind yourself to do His will. The Lord promises to bless those He finds doing these things when he comes back. Amen?

> *Who then is a faithful and wise servant, whom his master made ruler over his household, to give them food in due season? Blessed is that servant whom his master, when he comes, will find so doing. Assuredly, I say to you that he will make him ruler over all his goods. But if that evil servant says in his heart, 'My master is delaying his coming,' and begins to beat his fellow servants, and to eat and drink with the drunkards, the master of that servant will come on a day when he is not looking for him and at an hour that he is not aware of, and will cut him in two and appoint him his portion with the hypocrites. There shall be weeping and gnashing of teeth.* (Matthew 24:45-51)

CHAPTER THIRTEEN
TEAMING UP FOR SUCCESS

One of the first challenges for new soldiers is to learn the importance of teamwork. This seems simple enough in theory, but is much more difficult to put into practice. One of the great recruiting successes in recent years was a media campaign showing a lone soldier with a full load of equipment running across a desert scene. The slogan of the campaign was "An Army of One." Old soldiers laughed at the ad because it was so far out of alignment with all military doctrine. To their surprise, the ad was a great success. The idea of facing a huge military force alone appealed to that generation of young men and women. They had grown up with movies and TV shows depicting lone individuals who went into the jungle and rescued prisoners of war, sabotaged large enemy forces and came out with the Medal of Honor. They had grown up with video games, which were often played alone giving all the credit to the lone player.

The truth is lone soldiers are quickly defeated, captured, killed, or all three. It is impossible for one individual to succeed alone. Every effective military force has learned to use teamwork for success. Those engaged in spiritual warfare need to learn the same lessons about the value of teamwork. Many warriors in epic spiritual battles have become casualties of war. It is important for all of us to know that loners will not survive long, fight well, or complete their assigned missions in the perilous times to come. There is an old military maxim: "Teamwork is a force multiplier." As you increase the number of skilled team members, you are doing more than adding to your base of strength. You are multiplying the impact of the team. Think about this principle as you study the passage below.

> *You will chase your enemies, and they shall fall*
> *by the sword before you. Five of you shall chase*
> *a hundred, and a hundred of you shall put ten*
> *thousand to flight; your enemies shall fall by the*
> *sword before you.* (Leviticus 26:7-8)

Perhaps this is the reason why the Lord sent His disciples out in teams of two. The principle He established is recorded in Mark 6:7, "*And He called the twelve to Himself, and began to send them out two by two, and gave them power over unclean spirits.*" Yeshua used this same principle in more than one instance. Later, He put another seventy disciples in teams before sending them into the harvest fields. Luke 10:1, "*After these things the Lord appointed seventy others also, and sent them two by two before His face into every city and place where He Himself was about to go.*" On this occasion, He added to His instructions a concern about the need for more team members. Look at Luke 10:2, "*Then He said to them, 'The harvest truly is great, but the laborers are few; therefore pray the Lord of the harvest to send out laborers into His harvest.'*" Yeshua knew the importance of having additional team members as force multipliers.

We see in Luke's gospel that Yeshua practiced these principles of teamwork, but He went much further than that. He began to teach openly about these powerful force multiplication principles. As you study the gospels you will see that He

251

did this on numerous occasions. Over time, He began to add an important element to His basic teachings. He revealed a great mystery, which had been hidden from His generation. The Lord had taught these key concepts to the Children of Israel long ago, but the people in Yeshua's time had seemingly forgotten their training. Look back at what the Lord promised to Joshua, *"One man of you shall chase a thousand: for the Lord your God, he it is that fighteth for you, as he hath promised you."* (Joshua 23:10, KJV) Did you catch it when you read this verse? When you add the Lord to your team, the result is a huge multiplication of the power and effectiveness you need to accomplish your mission. Conversely, if you leave the Lord out of the mix, you seriously reduce your potential for success. In the passage below, consider the judgment placed on Israel when they abandoned the Lord.

> *For they are a nation void of counsel, nor is there any understanding in them. Oh, that they were wise, that they understood this, that they would consider their latter end! How could one chase a thousand, and two put ten thousand to flight, unless their Rock had sold them, and the Lord had surrendered them?* (Deuteronomy 32:28-30)

Now is the time to increase your spiritual strength and mental toughness in order to be effective in the perilous times to come. This is the time to practice. It will be too late for those who wait until their troubles multiply and the difficulties of their circumstances go beyond their control. Prepare now by learning the Lord's principles for effective teamwork. Then begin to build up the unity and cohesiveness of your fighting force. This is the time to prepare, practice and activate team building skills. Remember how Yeshua trained and equipped His followers for the perilous times they would face after His death and ascension. They were ready when those times came upon the entire body of believers. This outcome didn't seem possible on that last night Yeshua spent with His disciples. They were quickly routed and appeared to be on the losing end of the battle. Then the risen Lord opened their minds to understand what he had taught and imparted to them. A few days later, power came from Heaven and a new team of spiritual heroes was unleashed on the enemy. I love the way it is summed up in the second chapter of Acts.

> *So continuing daily with one accord in the temple, and breaking bread from house to house, they ate their food with gladness and simplicity of heart, praising God and having favor with all the people. And the Lord added to the church daily those who were being saved.*
> (Acts 2:46-47)

TEAM BUILDING SKILLS

> *How good and pleasant it is when brothers live together in unity! It is like precious oil poured on the head, running down on the beard, running down on Aaron's beard, down upon the collar of his robes. It is as if the dew of Hermon were falling on Mount Zion. For there the Lord bestows his blessing, even life forevermore.*
> (Psalm 133:1-3, NIV)

Psalm 133 is filled with beautiful imagery of the impact a unified group can have on the world around them. In the calm before the storm, it is time to learn some of these powerful lessons on teamwork given to us through the Word of God. These are timeless principles, which are as important today as they were to the generation in which they were first released.

In this section, I will reveal the lessons the Lord shared with me as I worked on this book. I always pray that He will reveal even more of these principles to you as you study them. What I want to do here is to lay the foundation upon which you can build up your spiritual house.

SELFLESS SERVICE

To the natural mind equipped only with the wisdom of the world, these principles are often misunderstood and rejected. How can a culture based on looking out for number one understand a commandment to love your neighbor as you love yourself? Yet this is exactly what the Lord told the Children of Israel to do. *"You shall not take vengeance, nor bear any grudge against the children of your people, but you shall love your neighbor as yourself: I am the Lord."* (Leviticus 19:18) Some people today have a difficult time accepting these powerful principles given by the Lord in the Old Testament. So the Lord gave the command again through Yeshua ha Messiach. After stating that the most important command is to Love the Lord your God, Yeshua said, *"And the second, like it, is this: 'You shall love your neighbor as yourself.'"* Paul continued to release this teaching in Galatians 5:14, (ONMB) *"For the whole Torah (Teaching) has found its full expression in one saying, in this 'You will love your neighbor as yourself.'"*

How can people living in a culture of individualism understand the principles of selfless service? Consider what Yeshua declared in Mark 9:35, *"And He sat down, called the twelve, and said to them, 'If anyone desires to be first, he shall be last of all and servant of all.'"* Trust me, it was as difficult for people to understand this principle in ancient times as it is today. Throughout history, people have asked the same question. How can this love principle possibly be true? How can we understand that the one who wants to be first must be the servant of all? To the natural mind this is nonsense. Yeshua didn't let up because it was difficult for them to understand. He kept making the point over and over in a variety of settings. When the disciples were arguing over who would be the greatest and who would be the next leader of their group, Yeshua explained this Kingdom Principle once more in the passage below.

> *And after He summoned them Y'shua said to them, "You know that those who are considered to lead the heathens are lording over them, and that the great ones of them tyrannize them. But it is not so among you, but whoever would wish to become great among you will be your servant. And whoever among you would wish to be first will be servant of all: for also the Son of Man did not come to be served but to serve and to give His life as a ransom in exchange for many." (Mark 10:42-45, ONMB)*

HONESTY

The principle of "honesty" sounds right and most people would agree to its importance, and yet so many people appear to struggle with putting it into practice. This is one of those places where many parents and leaders say: Do what I say rather than what I do. This is exactly what the leaders in the time of Yeshua were doing and saying. In the passage below, see how Yeshua pointed this out with razor sharp clarity.

> *Then Jesus spoke to the multitudes and to His disciples, saying: "The scribes and the Pharisees sit in Moses' seat. Therefore whatever they tell you to observe, that observe and*

*do, but do not do according to their works; for
they say, and do not do."* (Matthew 23:1-3)

Do you know people who fit Yeshua's description? The
more challenging question is for you to consider your own
life and ask yourself: In what ways do I fail to practice what
I teach? If we are to follow the Lord's commands, we must
always look at ourselves first. During my time in Seminary,
I served several churches, which were set up as "student
charges." In one church I was challenged by some of the
members because I was not preaching what they called "hell
fire and brimstone" sermons. I was young and inexperienced
so I decided to give them what they wanted. I worked very
hard on that sermon and delivered it with all the fire I had.
Afterward, people expressed their pleasure because I gave
them what they wanted. The most common thing I heard was:
"Way to tell them, pastor!" No one said, "I felt convicted and
want to change my life to please the Lord. Then I understood
they wanted me to bring down fire on others so they could
feel more right and more righteous. Then as now people resist
self-examination, repentance and corrective actions.

This was also true in the days of Isaiah the prophet. The
Lord asked him to release a prophetic word of judgment to
His people. One of his summary statements was: *"So justice is
driven back, and righteousness stands at a distance; truth has
stumbled in the streets, honesty cannot enter."* (Isaiah 59:14,
NIV) We also live in a day and among a people who have shut
the door to honesty. It is not allowed in many businesses or
in some of our churches. It is a sad day for the church went it
has gone so ethically low as to refuse to allow honest things to
be spoken. Isaiah didn't receive accolades for releasing these
words to the people, but he obeyed the Lord and released them
anyway. Jeremiah was treated in an even worse way when
he obediently gave similar words of judgment to the people.
Yeshua says we are not to be like the leaders of the world.

Paul taught some new principles to Timothy and gave him a charge to keep.

> *I exhort therefore, that, first of all, supplications, prayers, intercessions, and giving of thanks, be made for all men; For kings, and for all that are in authority; that we may lead a quiet and peaceable life in all godliness and honesty. For this is good and acceptable in the sight of God our Saviour;* (1 Timothy 2:1-3, NIV)

In spite of how people react, we must teach and model honesty. With the same words Paul used to exhort Timothy, his message echoes through the centuries and falls afresh on you and me. We simply cannot have effective teamwork unless we all practice the principle of honesty. Without trust, we can never bond into a cohesive and effective team. Since groups seem to resist this teaching, it falls on us as individuals to choose to live and teach in accordance with the Word of God. Honesty is still, "*good and acceptable in the sight of God our Savior.*" Amen?

LOYALTY

> *...experienced soldiers prepared for battle with every type of weapon, to help David with undivided loyalty...* (1 Chronicles 12:33, NIV)

How would you like for this to be said of the team where you serve the Lord? How would you like this to be a description of you personally as a disciple of Yeshua ha Messiach? I like the way this is summed up in The Message Bible. Sometimes it is very helpful for words of correction to be stated in the common language of the people. It is a powerful principle for us to take hold of when love and loyalty are linked together in this passage. When these two attributes are present in the followers of Yeshua it catches the eyes of unsaved people and draws them into moments of repentance and salvation. May your love and loyalty draw many to the Lord!

> *Don't lose your grip on Love and Loyalty. Tie them around your neck; carve their initials on your heart. Earn a reputation for living well in God's eyes and the eyes of the people.* (Proverbs 3:3-4, TMSG)

I encourage you to pause for a moment and ask yourself what kind of reputation you have. If we asked the people who know you best, what would they say about your life and work? As you honestly evaluate yourself, where do you stand in the eyes of the Lord? After all, your relationship with the Lord is what really matters most. Are you pleasing the Lord by the way you love others? Are you demonstrating loyalty to your leaders, your peers and those who have chosen to follow you? Now is the time to ask the questions and make the needed corrections. Don't wait until you hear a word of judgment or receive admonishment from the Lord. Amen?

RESPECT

In an atmosphere void of mutual respect, teamwork will never thrive. As we have traveled around the world in ministry, we have observed the inner workings of many churches. Sometimes this is a refreshing and encouraging experience because we see them in unity of spirit, mind and ministry. On the other hand we also see the practices which block rather than facilitate teamwork. We have seen leaders who demand respect, but demonstrate none toward those who follow them. People will not stay connected with this kind of leadership for very long. There is an old saying: If you want to be respected, you must show respect for others at all times.

> *Now we ask you, brothers, to respect those who work hard among you, who are over you in the Lord and who admonish you. Hold them in the highest regard in love because of their work. Live in peace with each other.* (1 Thessalonians 5:12-13, NIV)

It is important to respect those who are in leadership positions. I like the way Paul summed it up in the passage above. We do this so that we can: "*Live in peace with each other.*" Does your attitude of respect release the Shalom of the Lord? Do you show respect for your leaders even when they "*admonish you.*" Actually this is the place where respect is often cast off by people. They get offended by the admonishment they receive and then become angry, disrespectful, disruptive and rebellious. Don't allow these things to happen to you. In the perilous times to come, you must resist every temptation to be offended. Don't let the enemy take control of your emotions and lead you into disrespecting other people.

In 1 Peter 2:17 (NIV), Peter sums up the call for respect as follows: "*Show proper respect to everyone: Love the brotherhood of believers, fear God, honor the king.*" When Peter wrote this, there were no truly honorable kings ruling over them. You may not like the person who serves as president or prime minister in your nation. This doesn't excuse you from obeying the Lord's admonition to show respect and to give honor. We don't see much of this in our world today. Politicians, pundits and angry mobs demonstrate a total absence of honor and respect. Leaders are expected to make good decision and serve effectively in a hail storm of accusations and words of condemnation. The Lord has called us to live in a different way. We do not serve the Accuser. We serve the Lord who suffered and died to release people from bondage to sin and death. We are called and commanded to show honor and respect.

> *You must teach what is in accord with sound doctrine. Teach the older men to be temperate, worthy of respect, self–controlled, and sound in faith, in love and in endurance.* (Titus 2:1-2, NIV)

In the second chapter of His letter to Titus, Paul gives a list of people who need to demonstrate the values of the body of Christ and maintain the attributes of our God as they work and minister in the Kingdom. Paul challenges the old and the young, husbands and wives, servants and masters to demonstrate this lifestyle of love and respect. Without mutual respect we will never become the team which overcomes all adversity in the perilous times, which will manifest before the Lord returns. Study the teaching of Peter in the passage below and make a sound and firm decision to do it the Lord's way rather than the way of the world. Amen?

> *But in your hearts set apart Christ as Lord. Always be prepared to give an answer to everyone who asks you to give the reason for the hope that you have. But do this with gentleness and respect, keeping a clear conscience, so that those who speak maliciously against your good behavior in Christ may be ashamed of their slander. It is better, if it is God's will, to suffer for doing good than for doing evil.* (1 Peter 3:15-17, NIV)

HONOR

Husbands, likewise, dwell with them with understanding, giving honor to the wife, as to the weaker vessel, and as being heirs together of the grace of life, that your prayers may not be hindered. (1 Peter 3:7)

Have you ever considered that a failure to honor others will hinder your prayers? Many people ask me why their prayers do not get answered. Of course there are many reasons for this, but it is important to understand that a failure to establish and maintain a culture of honoring will block the blessing flow in your life. At times some people feel compelled to withhold honor toward others because of a personal belief that they do not deserve it. If you sometimes feel this way, consider the fact that none of us deserves the forgiveness and grace of the Lord. If God withheld all your blessings because you didn't deserve them, where would you be today? We would all be lost without the undeserved grace and unmerited mercy of the Lord. Can we do less for His other children?

For this is the will of God, that by doing good you may put to silence the ignorance of foolish men—as free, yet not using liberty as a cloak for vice, but as bondservants of God. Honor all people. Love the brotherhood. Fear God. Honor the king. (1 Peter 2:15-17)

Please notice what Peter did not say. He did not say the will of God is for us to accuse, blame and condemn every sinner we see. He did not tell us to honor only those who deserve it. He clearly stated, "Honor all people." Remember who created them and who cares for them still. It is this lifestyle of honoring which will silence ignorant and foolish critics. It is a lifestyle of showing honor and respect which will open the door for the establishment of the Kingdom of God. This is *"the will of God."*

In the two passages below, Paul gives Timothy what I call the acid test of whether or not people have accepted the lifestyle of honoring others. Some say that these teachings were easier for an earlier generation. I don't think so. I believe people had as much trouble accepting a life of servitude and slavery then as they do today. If you are offended by these things, you can be certain they were too. It was a bitter pill to swallow when they were told to show honor to those who kept them under the yoke of servitude. It was as difficult for people in those days to give honor to the elders who ruled over them in the church as it is today. If you doubt this, study again what the Torah says about what Moses had to endure. As you reflect on these two passages, think about this: It isn't about what others do. It is about what you do. You will not be judged by the actions of others, but by your level of obedience to the Lord. Give honor whether it is deserved or not. Amen?

> *Let as many bondservants as are under the yoke count their own masters worthy of all honor, so that the name of God and His doctrine may not be blasphemed.* (1 Timothy 6:1)

> *Let the elders who rule well be counted worthy of double honor, especially those who labor in the word and doctrine.* (1 Timothy 5:17)

INTEGRITY

For a team to be strong and effective, all its members must have and practice integrity. Whether the team members are young or old, male or female, rich or poor; leaders or followers all must have integrity to build the trust and cohesion needed to survive and thrive in the perilous times to come. People always tend to make excuses for their own failure to practice the key principles of teamwork. On the other hand, most tend to be judgmental and critical of the integrity of others. The Lord will not accept either of these behaviors. Solomon knew this well from his own experiences as a son, brother and later a leader of the people. In Proverbs 20:7, he declared, *"The righteous man walks in his integrity; his children are blessed after him."* Paul also placed a strong emphasis on integrity in his letter to Titus.

> *Likewise, exhort the young men to be sober-minded, in all things showing yourself to be a pattern of good works; in doctrine showing <u>integrity</u>, reverence, incorruptibility, sound speech that cannot be condemned, that one who is an opponent may be ashamed, having nothing evil to say of you.* (Titus 2:6-8)

You have doubtless experienced leaders and people who show a lack of integrity. How does that make you feel? Does it inspire you to join the group and follow these leaders? More likely it inspires you to stay very far away from such people. If we want to bring the lost to the Lord in this great end-time harvest, we need to be people of integrity. We need to display the attributes of our Lord and show love, respect and honor for all people. We need to practice what we preach so that the integrity of our ministries will draw people back to the Father. If our call to repentance is to be effective we must live as Yeshua taught us and as His apostles admonished us. Amen?

PERSONAL COURAGE

One of the cornerstone doctrines of military teamwork is for every member to have personal courage. This is also an age old principle for teamwork among the Lord's people. When the majority of your people fail to have personal courage, it opens the door for trouble to come in and disrupt the entire group. Moses had to lead something like a mob of around two million people who did not willingly choose to fight when they needed to fight or stand when they needed to stand. Many times he had to admonish them as in the passage below:

> *And Moses said to the children of Gad and to the children of Reuben: "Shall your brethren go to war while you sit here? Now why will you discourage the heart of the children of Israel from going over into the land which the LORD has given them?"* (Numbers 32:6-7)

Do you know people who constantly look for other people to fight their battles for them? Do you know people who sound courageous as they talk a good game, but cower and hide when confronted by threats from others? Do you know people who are better at discouraging others than standing with them? In my military experience I met many people like this. I can remember times when I suggested that some people be discharged earlier than their enlistment period. I was often challenged by some of the leaders who wanted to hold them to the letter of the law. On more than one occasion I asked these leaders: If we go to war do you want this person on your team? Are you willing to allow this person to cover your back as you fight? After reflecting on these two questions most leaders made a sudden shift and supported the early release of those who would discourage others with their fear.

> *Now therefore, proclaim in the hearing of the people, saying, "Whoever is fearful and afraid, let him turn and depart at once from Mount Gilead." And twenty-two thousand of*

the people returned, and ten thousand remained.
(Judges 7:3)

Sometimes it is better to let those who cannot cope with their fear go back to the safety and security of their homes. Imagine how Gideon felt when he followed the Lord's command and twenty-two thousand people suddenly left his team. Imagine how he felt as the Lord continued to reduce the size of his force to only three hundred men who were called to fight an army too large to count their numbers. The lesson here is that when the Lord is on your side you don't need a huge number. You do not need people overwhelmed by their fear on the battlefield. In fact just you and the Lord together make an unbeatable team. Remember the promise released in Deuteronomy 31:6 (NIV), *"Be strong and courageous. Do not be afraid or terrified because of them, for the Lord your God goes with you; he will never leave you nor forsake you."* It is better to send the cowardly home than depend on them to carry their weight in a fight.

This is the kind of courage David experienced when he wrote Psalm 3:5-6. *"I lay down and slept; I awoke, for the Lord sustained me. I will not be afraid of ten thousands of people who have set themselves against me all around."* Moses and David stood strong because they had faith in the Lord who was with them and had promised that He would never leave them or forsake them. You have the same promise. You have the same Lord. Now is the time to allow Him to give you the strength and courage to stand against your enemy. Consider that the cowardly are identified as the first people who will be cast into the lake of fire. Revelation 21:8, *"But the cowardly, unbelieving, abominable, murderers, sexually immoral, sorcerers, idolaters, and all liars shall have their part in the lake which burns with fire and brimstone, which is the second death."*

ABOVE ALL
HAVE LOVE FOR ONE ANOTHER

The second most important command of the entire Bible is to love one another. Loving one another is the key to having God abide in us. Consider again what John taught in 1 John 4:12, *"If we love one another, God abides in us, and His love has been perfected in us."* When you stand before the Lord, this will likely be one of His first questions of you, "Have you loved others as you love yourself?" How will you be able to truthfully answer Him? He sees into the depth of your heart and soul and knows the truth about you. You cannot fool Him. My recommendation is that you deal with this question now rather than when you stand before the judgment seat of Messiah. The Apostle John put it this way: *"Beloved, let us love one another, for love is of God; and everyone who loves is born of God and knows God."* (1 John 4:7)

Yeshua took the old command about loving others from the Torah and updated it for the Kingdom of God. A lesson here is that Yeshua expects more of His followers than is required by the Torah. The original command was to love others as we love ourselves. Yeshua added that we need to love others the same way He loves us. Wow! Do you have that kind of love for others? If not, you need to begin to work on it right now before the perilous times come. Notice in the passage below that Yeshua says this kind of love will be our most powerful witness to others in these last days.

> *A new commandment I give to you, that you love one another; as I have loved you, that you also love one another. By this all will know that you are My disciples, if you have love for one another.* (John 13:34-35)

The Apostle Peter was one of the students in what I call the advanced course for the Kingdom of God. Before receiving the Holy Spirit, the disciples were all limited in their ability to understand the deeper mysteries of the Kingdom. After they received the indwelling Holy Spirit, their minds were opened to grasp these deeper truths, which Yeshua taught for forty days between His resurrection and ascension. Have you been filled with the Holy Spirit? Have you been given the Spirit of truth? If not, you need to seek that now so that you can also understand the deeper things of the Kingdom of God. With the help of the Holy Spirit seek to fully embrace Peter's teaching in the passage below:

> *Since you have purified your souls in obeying the truth through the Spirit in sincere love of the brethren, love one another fervently with a pure heart, having been born again, not of corruptible seed but incorruptible, through the word of God which lives and abides forever,* (1 Peter 1:22-23)

All the team building principles listed above are given to us in order to establish strength through unity in our groups and ministries. When we fully embrace these principles and put them into practice, we are better equipped to handle the challenges of the last days. If we will allow the Lord to be our leader and guide, our groups for ministry will be more like the description of the disciples on Shavuot (the day of Pentecost). Are you ready to be in one accord with other believers in order to open the door for a greater outpouring of the Holy Spirit?

> *When the Day of Pentecost had fully come, they were all with one accord in one place. And suddenly there came a sound from heaven, as of a rushing mighty wind, and it filled the whole house where they were sitting. Then there appeared to*

them divided tongues, as of fire, and one sat upon each of them. And they were all filled with the Holy Spirit and began to speak with other tongues, as the Spirit gave them utterance. (Acts 2:1-4)

A UNITY PRAYER FOR YOU

May the God who gives endurance and encouragement give you a spirit of unity among yourselves as you follow Christ Jesus, so that with one heart and mouth you may glorify the God and Father of our Lord Jesus Christ. (Romans 15:5-6, NIV)

POWER IN NUMBERS

For thousands of years, it has been known that teamwork is essential for success. Yet people have to learn these lessons over and over in each new generation. Now is the time for the people in our generation to learn, embrace and live by these principles. Solomon declares in the passage below, "*Woe to him who is alone when he falls.*" Are you alone as you face the approaching perilous times? Don't let this happen to you.

Two are better than one, because they have a good reward for their labor. For if they fall, one will lift up his companion. But woe to him who is alone when he falls, for he has no one to help him up. (Ecclesiastes 4:9-10, NIV)

Even one additional person can make a huge difference in how you are able to handle troubles and tribulations. Remember that people are one of your force multipliers. As you add more and more to your team, your strength multiplies. Solomon often used repetition to help anchor his teachings. Compare the admonition of Solomon in Ecclesiastes 4:12 (NIV) with the passage above: *"Though one may be overpowered, two can defend themselves. A cord of three strands is not quickly broken."*

POWER IN AGREEMENT

Yeshua taught these principles in a slightly different but much more powerful way. He connected these principles to a promise. He challenged people to get into unity and agree with one another to strengthen them for the perilous times, which would soon begin to manifest. Then He gave them an amazing promise that their authority and effectiveness would soon be increased exponentially. He declared that whatever they asked in unity of mind and purpose, the Father would do it for them. The way we can understand how this works is actually based in another promise. Yeshua promised that when two or three of us get into unity, He will be right there with us. Now we have our dream team. A couple of you with Yeshua can overcome all the power of the enemy and accomplish your purpose and destiny for the Kingdom.

> *Again I say to you that if two of you agree on earth concerning anything that they ask, it will be done for them by My Father in heaven. For where two or three are gathered together in My name, I am there in the midst of them.* (Matthew 18:19-20)

The Apostle Paul embraced this teaching and expanded on it for his readers. This is a good time to answer the apostle's appeal and get into agreement with other believers. When we are able to do this, we will have no more divisions in the Body of Christ. The ultimate goal is to reach a state of agreement where we are *"perfectly united in mind and thought."* Impossible you say? Remember nothing is impossible with the Lord. May you be committed to strive for the level of unity described in the passage below! Amen?

I appeal to you, brothers, in the name of our Lord Jesus Christ, that all of you agree with one another so that there may be no divisions among you and that you may be perfectly united in mind and thought. (1 Corinthians 1:10, NIV)

AGREEMENT WITH THE WORD

The most important of all the force multipliers is to have God on your team. This means that the most powerful expression of unity is reached when we fully accept the teachings and admonition of Yeshua. When we learn to operate at this level of unity, we will release a world changing witness to those who do not know the Lord. The Lord makes another huge promise. When we reach this stage of unity, we will see that the Father loves us as He loves His own Son, Yeshua ha Messiach. Would you like to receive this level of love from the Father? I know this is my heart's desire. How about you?

I united with them and you with me, so that they may be completely one, and the world thus realize that you sent me and that you have loved them just as you have loved me. (John 17:23, CJB)

Failure to follow the Lord's teaching and commands will produce a much different outcome. If we begin to teach false things and encourage others to abandon the Lord, we will experience a life, which comes to nothing. We will find that all our wisdom and counsel to others will come to nothing. We will find that the outcome of our entire life and work will be worth nothing. Who could possibly desire this outcome? Yet we still find people who are making these same old mistakes. They are making the same worthless decisions as a previous unwise generation. The tragic result is that they are ruining their God given purpose and failing to reach their destiny for the Kingdom.

If anyone teaches false doctrines and does not agree to the sound instruction of our Lord Jesus Christ and to godly teaching, he is conceited and understands nothing. He has an unhealthy interest in controversies and quarrels about words that result in envy, strife, malicious talk, evil suspicions and constant friction between men of corrupt mind, who have been robbed of the truth and who think that godliness is a means to financial gain. (1 Timothy 6:3-5, NIV)

Remember and hold on to the teachings and promises of the Lord. When you hold to the true and righteous ways of the Lord, you will receive all the promised benefits and blessings of the Kingdom. You will be doing your part in fulfilling His purposes for the world. You will be standing ready to experience the glorious restoration of the tabernacle of David. It fell down, but the Lord is raising it up again so that you and I can join those who worship the Lord in Spirit and truth. You and I will stand firm in perilous times and enter the winner's circle at the end of the race. Amen?

And with this the words of the prophets agree, just as it is written: "After this I will return and will rebuild the tabernacle of David, which has fallen down; I will rebuild its ruins, and I will set it up; so that the rest of mankind may seek the Lord, even all the Gentiles who are called by My name, says the Lord who does all these things." (Acts 15:15-17)

CHAPTER FOURTEEN

LEARNING FROM THE BEST
YESHUA: THE ULTIMATE PREPPER

Let no one on the roof of his house go down to take anything out of the house. Let no one in the field go back to get his cloak. How dreadful it will be in those days for pregnant women and nursing mothers! Pray that your flight will not take place in winter or on the Sabbath. For then there will be great distress, unequaled from the beginning of the world until now—and never to be equaled again. If those days had not been cut short, no one would survive, but for the sake of the elect those days will be shortened.
(Matthew 24:17-22)

Countless numbers of books have been written about Jesus and the various aspects of His ministry on Earth. One of the first of these was written by the Apostle John. He concluded his gospel book with an interesting statement: "*And there are also many other things that Jesus did, which if they were written one by one, I suppose that even the world itself could not contain the books that would be written. Amen.*" (John 21:25) The extensive number of books on the life and ministry of Jesus bear witness to the truth of John's statement. This is especially true considering that all these books were written based on the select few stories made known to us by the Biblical authors. How many more books would have been written if we were given knowledge of all those other amazing works and teachings, which John and others chose not to include?

Early in my walk with the Lord, I noticed that the "main line churches" which I attended in my youth almost never mentioned the vast number of teachings Jesus gave on the end times. Entire chapters in the gospels contain the teachings of Jesus about the coming "Day of the Lord." Many religious leaders have almost totally ignored all these teachings of Jesus as if they were in the Bible by accident. I am one who believes that every part of the Word of God was inspired by Him and that He intended each part to be handed down to us for a purpose. Consider what Paul wrote in 2 Timothy 3:16-17, "*All Scripture is given by inspiration of God, and is profitable for doctrine, for reproof, for correction, for instruction in righteousness, that the man of God may be complete, thoroughly equipped for every good work.*" In my understanding, Paul is saying that if we ignore any part of Scripture we will not be "*complete*" or "*thoroughly equipped.*" Now is the time for us to be certain that we are indeed thoroughly equipped. The Lord is coming soon and I want to be ready. How about you?

Jesus used a very interesting passage from Isaiah for His first recorded public sermon. He chose a passage in which Isaiah spoke of the spiritual gifts and strengths of the coming Messiah. To the surprise of His audience, Jesus asserted that this was written about Him. This upset many of the people who listened to Jesus that day. It is still upsetting and unnerving for many people today especially when they are confronted by His declaration that one of His primary missions was and is, "*To proclaim the acceptable year of the Lord.*" How comfortable are you with this word from Jesus himself? Study the passage below and consider all the things included in His mission statement given centuries before by the Father.

> *And He was handed the book of the prophet Isaiah. And when He had opened the book, He found the place where it was written: "The Spirit of the Lord is upon Me, because He has anointed Me to preach the gospel to the poor; He has sent Me to heal the brokenhearted, to proclaim liberty to the captives and recovery of sight to the blind, to set at liberty those who are oppressed; To proclaim the acceptable year of the Lord." Then He closed the book, and gave it back to the attendant and sat down. And the eyes of all who were in the synagogue were fixed on Him. And He began to say to them, "Today this Scripture is fulfilled in your hearing."* (Luke 4:17-21)

Interestingly, Jesus only quoted the first part of verse two in this passage from Isaiah chapter 61, *"To proclaim the acceptable year of the Lord..."* Think about it! In his first sermon, Jesus chose to comfort the people rather than challenge them. The remainder of His mission written in this passage was to be revealed to them and us at a later time. In reality, He was alluding to it when He read the first part of verse two, but not everyone understood it. You can see a more complete picture when you read the next few words, *"And the day of vengeance of our God;"*

The people who began to believe that He was the promised Messiah started to realize that there was more to the completed work of Messiah than they first thought. They started to wonder if He would usher in the "wrath of the Lord" which they believed would come at the end of the age. They began to bring up the subject of what we might call the "last days."

Many of His later discourses were in response to these questions. The disciples also wanted to know the answers to these questions. Perhaps His disciples in this generation also want to know about these things. We see this in Mark 13:4, *"Tell us, when will these things be? And what will be the sign when all these things will be fulfilled?"* To get a more complete understanding we must look at His teachings recorded in all the gospel accounts. Consider the passage below from the Gospel of Matthew.

> *Immediately after the tribulation of those days the sun will be darkened, and the moon will not give its light; the stars will fall from heaven, and the powers of the heavens will be shaken. Then the sign of the Son of Man will appear in heaven, and then all the tribes of the earth will mourn, and they will see the Son of Man coming on the clouds of heaven with power and great glory. And He will send His angels with a great sound of a trumpet, and they will gather together His elect from the four winds, from one end of heaven to the other.* (Matthew 24:29-31)

Jesus was very straight forward and honest with His disciples. He didn't hold back in His description of the troubles and challenges, which will come at the end of the age. For non-believers this will be an extremely frightening time and most will be totally overwhelmed by what they will see, hear and experience. It will be a challenge for believers as well, but they will have an advantage. Think about this in the first person. You have the Holy Spirit to give you comfort and to guide you through every difficulty and deliver you from every frightening moment. As you consider the pain and suffering non-believers will experience in these perilous times, you should be inspired to become more dedicated to winning the lost. In this season of harvest, we need to become more active in our evangelistic outreach so that many will be saved from destruction.

JESUS' WARNING TO PREPPERS

In Chapter One, I gave an illustration about soldiers on guard duty. I want to expand on these lessons learned from soldiers to bring a greater understanding of what we need to do to get ready and stay ready. As I previously mentioned, one thing we learned in the military was how difficult it is to train people to stay vigilant all the time. We saw this most clearly in the practice of putting soldiers on guard duty. They were able to stay alert and watch for short periods of time, but gradually lost their focus and began to daydream or even fall asleep. When there was no perceived threat, their attention span was much shorter. The sergeant of the guard often served as the threat which would keep them alert. By constantly checking on each guard and chastising those who lost their focus, he/she was able to help them maintain alertness for a little longer. Who will do this task for the soldiers of the Lord in the perilous times to come?

Over time we learned that it helped to rotate guards every two hours, but soon learned that two hours was beyond the capability of most soldiers. Think about this in the following account about Jesus and His disciples: *"Then He came to the disciples and found them sleeping, and said to Peter, 'What! Could you not watch with Me one hour? Watch and pray, lest you enter into temptation. The spirit indeed is willing, but the flesh is weak.'"* (Matthew 26:40-41) Have you experienced something like this: Your heart is willing but your flesh is weak? Have you fallen asleep while praying? Have you drifted off during a sermon? Have you struggled to complete a prayer vigil? If we are honest, most of us would have to admit it has happened. This is why it is so important to heed Jesus' warning to preppers in the following passage:

Be careful, or your hearts will be weighed down with dissipation, drunkenness and the anxieties of life, and that day will close on you unexpectedly like a trap. For it will come upon all those who live on the face of the whole earth. Be always on the watch, and pray that you may be able to escape all that is about to happen, and that you may be able to stand before the Son of Man. (Luke 21:34-36, NIV)

Notice there are no exceptions. These things will come upon each and every one of us. We always face the danger of becoming weighed down by the problems of the world or the weakness of our flesh. It is easy to let worries, fears and anxiety lead us into the same old trap of falling asleep on duty. Do you believe that Jesus will soon return? In the last chapter of the Revelation of John, Yeshua declares three times that He is coming quickly. Think about this as you read the three passages below.

Behold, I am coming quickly! Blessed is he who keeps the words of the prophecy of this book. (Revelation 22:7)

And behold, I am coming quickly, and My reward is with Me, to give to every one according to his work. I am the Alpha and the Omega, the Beginning and the End, the First and the Last. Blessed are those who do His commandments, that they may have the right to the tree of life, and may enter through the gates into the city. But outside are dogs and sorcerers

*and sexually immoral and murderers and idol-
aters, and whoever loves and practices a lie.*
(Revelation 22:12-14)

*He who testifies to these things says, "Surely I
am coming quickly."* (Revelation 22:20)

The Lord has spoken these same words to me over and
over in the past few years. Perhaps you have heard these
same declarations from the Lord. Tragically many people who
have heard His word of warning still find themselves growing
weary, giving up and becoming slack in their assigned duty
of waiting and watching. When this happens, most people
let the focus of their attention turn back to the things of this
world. When the promises of the Lord don't happen on our
time schedule or as soon as we expected, we are tempted to
lose heart and to lose our focus. During these times, we need
to go back to the teachings of the Lord, and hear His wake up
call once again. It is important to understand that when you
first begin to lose your alertness, is the very time when it is
most important for you to be watching and praying. I don't
know about you, but when I stand before the Son of Man on
that day, I don't want to hear about how I let Him down. How
about you?

DATES AND TIMES UNKNOWN

Over the years, I have observed many people who focus a
great deal of time and energy on trying to determine the exact
time of the Lord's return. They examine various teachings in
the Bible and search out minute details of prophetic messages
to make these determinations. Some have declared the times
and seasons of the Lord only to be greatly disappointed when
the Lord doesn't move as they have predicted. The world is
not filled with grace and forgiveness and will hold people

accountable for what they have taught. Many reputations have been wounded by the failure of prophetic words to manifest on a person's time table. This is especially true of those who teach that the Lord will return on a specific date or that the judgment will come at a specific time.

I remember as a child that people repeatedly gave me tracts or small handbooks by certain groups that declared with certainty that the end times events would happen on the schedule they believed had been revealed to them. I was amused by the excuses made by one particular group each time their numerous predictions failed to manifest. Many of these well-meaning but disobedient people have ignored some of the teachings of Jesus and misrepresented the teachings of other New Testament writers. I consider the teachings of Jesus to be the primary source for all spiritual things and that others have written to agree with or help explain things in greater depth. When it comes to identifying dates and times, I always go back to the teaching of Jesus.

> *No one knows about that day or hour, not even the angels in heaven, nor the Son, but only the Father. Be on guard! Be alert! You do not know when that time will come.* (Mark 13:32-33, NIV)

I ask somewhat in jest, "What part of *"No one knows"* are you having a difficult time understanding?" No one in heaven or on the earth knows these things except the Father. Jesus affirmed that He did not know the "day or hour" when these things would happen. Here is the word of warning: You must not lose your focus by getting caught up in endless debates about things you cannot know. Jesus calls us back into focus in the passage above. What is He asking you to do? *"Be on guard! Be alert! You do not know when that time will come."* Here is the point. There is value in not knowing these things.

It is because we don't know that we are challenged to be more alert and to be fully committed to staying on guard.

Think about it! You must stay alert, because it could happen at any moment. This is the reason that the good soldiers of Messiah have been placed on guard duty. When I was the chaplain for a basic training unit, a drill sergeant told me about an incident he said happened the night before. He shared it because he was caught off guard and didn't know what to do. He had been assigned as the sergeant of the guard and found a soldier sleeping on duty. He was ready to give him a strong rebuke for his failure, but was totally caught short by the soldier's response. The drill sergeant had walked up to him and poked him on the shoulder to awaken him. As soon as he touched the soldier, he heard him say, "Amen!" He then told the drill sergeant that he had been praying. The sergeant knew this wasn't true, but couldn't come up with an answer. The soldier later confessed he had practiced this over and over for several weeks so that he could do it immediately upon being awakened. The sergeant decided not to punish him because of his initiative. Here is the key question. When the Lord checks up on you, will He find you awake and alert? The sleeping prayer excuse will not work with Him

In the three passages below, the Apostle Paul expounds and expands on these teachings of Jesus. I recommend that you go beyond merely reading them. Make them personal so you can learn more. In each of the three passages think about what Paul is teaching you about being awake and alert. I like Paul's words in the passage below from Thessalonians, "*For God did not appoint us to suffer wrath but to receive salvation through our Lord Jesus Christ.*" I also like the simplicity of what I call the "down home" way The Message Bible presents two of these teachings.

> *But you, brothers, are not in darkness so that this day should surprise you like a thief. You are all*

sons of the light and sons of the day. We do not belong to the night or to the darkness. So then, let us not be like others, who are asleep, but let us be alert and self–controlled. For those who sleep, sleep at night, and those who get drunk, get drunk at night. But since we belong to the day, let us be self–controlled, putting on faith and love as a breastplate, and the hope of sal-vation as a helmet. For God did not appoint us to suffer wrath but to receive salvation through our Lord Jesus Christ. He died for us so that, whether we are awake or asleep, we may live together with him. Therefore encourage one another and build each other up, just as in fact you are doing. (1 Thessalonians 5:4-11, NIV)

Don't burn out; keep yourselves fueled and aflame. Be alert servants of the Master, cheer-fully expectant. Don't quit in hard times; pray all the harder. (Romans 12:11-12, TMSG)

So if you're serious about living this new res-urrection life with Christ, act like it. Pursue the things over which Christ presides. Don't shuffle along, eyes to the ground, absorbed with the things right in front of you. Look up, and be alert to what is going on around Christ—that's where the action is. See things from his perspec-tive. (Colossians 3:1-2, TMSG)

KEEP WATCH
(BECOME A KINGDOM PREPPER)

I remember when the books in the "Left Behind" series were first published. These adventure filled books appealed to many people who were not really believers. I had to do a great deal of counseling with people who became extremely shocked and fearful after reading these novels. These were people who had never been exposed to the teachings of the Bible about the last days. For the first time, they were confronted with the idea that they might fall short and be left behind when others are raptured to Heaven. They were afraid, but didn't have enough Biblical understanding to work through it on their own. I was reminded over and over of Paul's teaching in 2 Timothy 1:7, *"For God has not given us a spirit of fear, but of power and of love and of a sound mind."* Think about how frightening these teachings can be to those who are lost – those who have not found Jesus and been born again. They think that God is making them afraid, but that is not true. He doesn't give a spirit of fear, but He does from time to time issue a wakeup call. Think about this as you study the two passages below.

> *Then two men will be in the field: one will be taken and the other left. Two women will be grinding at the mill: one will be taken and the other left. Watch therefore, for you do not know what hour your Lord is coming. But know this, that if the master of the house had known what hour the thief would come, he would have watched and not allowed his house to be broken into. Therefore you also be ready, for the Son of Man is coming at an hour you do not expect.* (Matthew 24:40-44)

> *Watch therefore, for you know neither the day nor the hour in which the Son of Man is coming.* (Matthew 25:13)

Did you catch that: ready or not *"the Son of Man is coming"*? He is coming at an hour you do not expect. I have often asked people when is the hour when they least expect Him to return. Most cannot answer that question. I have a belief that the "hour" is right now. This moment is the time when we expect His return the least. We might admit that it could be tomorrow, next week or next year, but how about right now. Are you ready? If you are not ready what should you do? The answer is found when we ask ourselves about our own understanding of what Jesus said. In both passages, Jesus declares, "Watch therefore, for you do not know."

The disciples learned the hard way that staying alert and watching is not easy. Like the disciples, you may be ready and willing in the spirit, but your physical body will place limitations on your faithfulness. In the passage below, I can almost feel the disappointment in the Lord's voice. He is about to go through a terrible ordeal that will test Him to the limit. He asked His intercessors to pray for Him, but they all fell asleep. He didn't have the support of anyone on Earth at that time. Have you ever felt that way? Does it seem like all your intercessors have fallen asleep? Do you feel completely alone in your hour of greatest need? Take heart. Jesus knows your pain and He will never leave you or fail you in these times

> *And He took with Him Peter and the two sons of Zebedee, and He began to be sorrowful and deeply distressed. Then He said to them, "My soul is exceedingly sorrowful, even to death. Stay here and watch with Me." He went a little farther and fell on His face, and prayed, saying, "O My Father, if it is possible, let this cup pass from Me; nevertheless, not as I will, but as You will." Then He came to the disciples and found them sleeping, and said to Peter, "What! Could you not watch with Me one hour? Watch*

283

*and pray, lest you enter into temptation. The
spirit indeed is willing, but the flesh is weak."*
(Matthew 26:37-41)

The fact is that we are still in the body. We get tired. We get
sleepy. We are no different than the disciples of Jesus. What
can we do to keep from failing the Lord and others when we
have been asked to watch and pray? These are very serious
issues. Consider what Jesus said about these times. Deceivers
will come when you need the truth most. They will tell you
things which may sound good, but they will not be helpful for
you. Some will be like Job's friends who make things worse
with every utterance. These are the times when you most need
to be "spirit led." In the times of deep darkness and deception,
your greatest need is for the Spirit of truth to both guide you
and strengthen you.

> *Now as He sat on the Mount of Olives, the dis-
> ciples came to Him privately, saying, "Tell us,
> when will these things be? And what will be the
> sign of Your coming, and of the end of the age?"
> And Jesus answered and said to them: "Take
> heed that no one deceives you. For many will
> come in My name, saying, 'I am the Christ,' and
> will deceive many. And you will hear of wars
> and rumors of wars. See that you are not trou-
> bled; for all these things must come to pass, but
> the end is not yet."* (Matthew 24:3-6)

Listen to Jesus. Take heed that no one deceives you. It is
likely that you have experienced most if not all these things
already. I cannot count the number of times people have
approached me and warned me to get into fear because we
are hearing of *"wars and rumors of wars."* When this happens,
I turn back to the teachings of Jesus and reclaim His promise:

"See that you are not troubled;" I remind myself as I remind you that the Lord does not give us a spirit of fear. He gives power, love and a sound mind. Receive it now and speak it aloud over and over so that in the hour when you most need it, this promise will flow from your heart. Remember, we used to call these "sword drills." Are you practicing you skills for spiritual warfare? You don't start practicing after the battle begins. That will be too late to do you any good. Practice now and keep doing it always. Amen?

> *But watch out for yourselves, for they will deliver you up to councils, and you will be beaten in the synagogues. You will be brought before rulers and kings for My sake, for a testimony to them. And the gospel must first be preached to all the nations. But when they arrest you and deliver you up, do not worry beforehand, or premeditate what you will speak. But whatever is given you in that hour, speak that; for it is not you who speak, but the Holy Spirit. Now brother will betray brother to death, and a father his child; and children will rise up against parents and cause them to be put to death. And you will be hated by all for My name's sake. But he who endures to the end shall be saved.* (Mark 13:9-13)

Trust the Holy Spirit to take care of you when you need it most. Memorized and practiced answers to challenging question based solely on the wisdom of the world never seem to work well. The enemy sees right through them, but he cannot anticipate what the Holy Spirit will give you to say. You will not always be able to put your trust in family, friends or pastors. You need a real and vibrant relationship with the Holy Spirit. He is the only one you can count on when that hour comes. It is important to remember that you don't want to be found sleeping when the Lord returns.

> *Watch therefore, for you do not know when the master of the house is coming—in the evening, at midnight, at the crowing of the rooster, or in the morning—lest, coming suddenly, he find you sleeping. And what I say to you, I say to all: Watch!* (Mark 13:35-37)

WATCHERS WILL BE BLESSED

I always take note when the Lord says something twice. Biblically it means that something has been established by the Lord and will soon manifest. In the passage below from the Gospel of Luke, Jesus states twice that those who watch will be blessed. He makes a truly astounding comment that the master will have those servants sitting down at the table and He will serve them. Take it to heart. Those who stay alert and watch will be blessed by the Lord. You can count on it.

> *Let your waist be girded and your lamps burning; and you yourselves be like men who wait for their master, when he will return from the wedding, that when he comes and knocks they may open to him immediately. Blessed are those servants whom the master, when he comes, will find watching. Assuredly, I say to you that he will gird himself and have them sit down to eat, and will come and serve them. And if he should come in the second watch, or come in the third watch, and find them so, blessed are those servants.* (Luke 12:35-38)

For those who have difficulty staying alert while watching, the Lord gave a very serious warning. He will return at an hour when they do not expect Him. You simply cannot put off your assignment of watching and count on being able to get ready at the last moment. I remember a time when I could get ready for a physical readiness test in a few days. Then the time came when I had to train every day to remain strong enough to succeed. In Luke 12:40, Jesus said, *"Therefore you also be ready, for the Son of Man is coming at an hour you do not expect."* Are you ready? Don't wait until it is too late. The time you spend watching will not be wasted. You will be blessed for your obedience to the Lord. He will take care of you and protect you from what is to come. Watching demonstrates to the Lord that you are worthy of something very special. You will be counted worthy of escaping the troubles and hardships, which will manifest in the last days. Some people refuse to believe that you can become worthy, but I am trusting what Yeshua taught. How about you?

> *Watch therefore, and pray always that you may be counted worthy to escape all these things that will come to pass, and to stand before the Son of Man."* (Luke 21:36)

FINAL WARNING

We understand now that watching brings a double blessing, but what happens when we lose our focus and stop watching? People who stop obeying the Lord and get caught up in the things of the flesh will be caught in a snare. Each time this happens it also impacts the lives of others. People you care about may come under attack because you grew weary and failed to watch for them. You must constantly resist the temptation to get weighed down with the things of the world. There will be no escape from the hardships, troubles and tribulation of the last days for those who are not following the Lord. Review again the teaching of the Lord given in Luke 21:34-36.

Paul supports these teachings of Jesus. In the passage below from Acts chapter twenty he warns that the enemy will send other people to tempt you to depart from the safety of the Lord's sheepfold. Like savage wolves who come to steal, kill and destroy, these agents of the enemy are seeking those they can draw away. They will appear to be righteous people with great prophetic gifts, but their purpose is to bring great harm to the Body of Christ. Remember His warning in 2 Corinthians 11:14-15, "*And no wonder! For Satan himself transforms himself into an angel of light. Therefore it is no great thing if his ministers also transform themselves into ministers of righteousness, whose end will be according to their works.*" Think about all these things as you study the passage below. Paul warned the people for three years and yet they were not ready and willing to keep standing watch.

> *For I know this, that after my departure savage wolves will come in among you, not sparing the flock. Also from among yourselves men will rise up, speaking perverse things, to draw away the disciples after themselves. Therefore watch, and remember that for three years I did not cease to warn everyone night and day with tears.* (Acts 20:29-31)

WHILE YOU WAIT

As you wait for the return of the Lord, what should you be doing? Always be alert realizing how short the remaining time is for you to complete your purpose for the Kingdom? Jesus made it clear in the passage below. There is much to do as we prepare for His return. We are to be working in the fields of harvest bringing lost souls to the Lord. We should also be taking care of all kinds of people in need. If you want to be blessed by the Lord and have a place in His eternal kingdom, you must be about His business right now. Don't lose hope. Don't give up. Now is the time to press in more than ever.

When the Son of Man comes in His glory, and all the holy angels with Him, then He will sit on the throne of His glory. All the nations will be gathered before Him, and He will separate them one from another, as a shepherd divides his sheep from the goats. And He will set the sheep on His right hand, but the goats on the left. Then the King will say to those on His right hand, 'Come, you blessed of My Father, inherit the kingdom prepared for you from the foundation of the world: for I was hungry and you gave Me food; I was thirsty and you gave Me drink; I was a stranger and you took Me in; I was naked and you clothed Me; I was sick and you visited Me; I was in prison and you came to Me.' (Matthew 25:31-36)

A BRIEF SUMMARY

Continue to ask yourself some important questions about the perilous times to come. First, how are you handling your preparations for these times, which we know are coming very soon? Are you spiritually ready as we draw nearer to the return of the Lord? Are you committed to being spiritually alert as you obey the Lord's command to watch and wait for Him to appear? I see many people today who are still using up too much time and energy trying to learn the exact day and hour of the end. As I write this another person has gained attention by declaring that the world will end next Tuesday. If I believed that prediction, I would not have spent my last few hours writing a book no one would ever read. I am trusting in the words of Yeshua in Mark 13:32, *"But of that day and hour no one knows, not even the angels in heaven, nor the Son, but only the Father."*

My personal goal is to follow the commands of the Lord. He did not tell us to ignore the trouble and tribulation, which will manifest in these last days. These things will not simply go away if we ignore them. The Lord has promised that this time will come. The Lord did not tell us to hide from the reality of the coming perilous times. He told us: *"Take heed, watch and pray; for you do not know when the time is."* (Mark 13:33) I remind you that not knowing the day or the hour is actually a gift from the Lord. It is unknown because it is meant to inspire us to constantly watch and pray. It is left unclear to motivate us to prepare ourselves in spirit, soul and body. Luke 12:43, *"Blessed is that servant whom his master will find so doing when he comes."* We have not been left in the dark by our Lord. I remind you once more that Yeshua has already told us how a faithful disciple is expected to prepare for what is to come. Read it again with greater revelation than before.

> *Let your waist be girded and your lamps burning; and you yourselves be like men who wait for their master, when he will return from the wedding, that when he comes and knocks they may open to him immediately. Blessed are those servants whom the master, when he comes, will find watching. Assuredly, I say to you that he will gird himself and have them sit down to eat, and will come and serve them. And if he should come in the second watch, or come in the third watch, and find them so, blessed are those servants.* (Luke 12:35-38)

Through various parables and lengthy lessons recorded in the Gospel accounts, Yeshua worked diligently to inspire you and me to be prepared for what is to come. In one of his parables, Yeshua tells a simple story about a man who is departing on a long trip. He gives ten servants money to be utilized properly during his absence. Of course we know this is more than a cute story to get the attention of the people. Yeshua is teaching them what they should be doing between His ascension and His second appearance. In the King James Version of the Bible, it is recorded that Yeshua made a very interesting comment in Luke 19:13, *"And he called his ten servants, and delivered them ten pounds, and said unto them, Occupy till I come."*

More recent translations have avoided this occupation terminology. It sounds too militaristic, and many people want to avoid this imagery. People still falsely believe that if you ignore these things they will never happen. Notice the difference in the translation in the New King James Version. It records that Yeshua said, "Do business till I come." This version takes it from terminology similar to a military order and softens it with words related to the business world. Do you think that Yeshua was actually talking about making good business investments or was He referring to spiritual warfare? The New International Version softens the meaning even further in this way: "Put this money to work, he said, until I come back." Are people today being lead back into sleep as they do business as usual? The big question now is: How do you interpret these instructions?

I find this parable of Yeshua to be so fascinating and mysterious that I cannot reduce it to mere business terms. What do you think? I will ask again. Are you doing business as usual or have you been told to occupy (militarily) until He returns? We are at war with a determined and destructive enemy. In the last hour before the Lord's return, we cannot afford to simply be doing business as usual. We are not called to build a financial empire, but to establish the kingdom of God in the middle of enemy territory. Like it or not we are at war with the most evil enemy in human history. You cannot afford to let down your guard for even one moment. Stay alert and watch for the attacks you know are coming. Stay alert and watch for the coming of Messiah.

The purpose of this book has been to help you prepare to occupy enemy territory as the army of the Lord until He returns. The truth is not hidden. These things will not be easy to accomplish. The enemy has not rolled over and given up. He knows the final outcome, and is still determined to do as much damage as possible until he is cast into the lake of fire. You cannot ignore an enemy like this. He will not go away if you try to appease him or compromise with him. He will invite you to make a covenant of peace with him, which he intends to break at the worst time for you.

Most people do not understand that when they make a covenant with the enemy they have actually made a "covenant with death." The Lord will never allow a covenant with the enemy to stand. Consider His words in Isaiah 28:18, "*Your covenant with death will be annulled, and your agreement with Sheol will not stand; when the overflowing scourge passes through, then you will be trampled down by it.*" This covenant has never worked in the past and it will not work for you. Many people will only realize this after they have given away all their spiritual authority and all the wonderful benefits coming from the Father. Don't be like most people. Listen to the Lord and take appropriate action now.

Remember James 1:16-17, "*Do not be deceived, my beloved brethren. Every good gift and every perfect gift is from above, and comes down from the Father of lights, with whom there is no variation or shadow of turning.*" You can be certain that the enemy does not have any good or perfect gifts for you. If he did have these good things, he would intentionally withhold them from you. Always understand that he only has cheap counterfeits, which will fail as soon as you attempt to use them. Don't fall for his deceptions. Don't give in to fear. Don't give up. Remain faithful and obedient to the end so that you will receive the prize the Lord has promised – eternal life in Christ Jesus.

> *And do this, knowing the time, that now it is high time to awake out of sleep; for now our salvation is nearer than when we first believed. The night is far spent, the day is at hand. Therefore let us cast off the works of darkness, and let us put on the armor of light. Let us walk properly, as in the day, not in revelry and drunkenness, not in lewdness and lust, not in strife*

and envy. But put on the Lord Jesus Christ, and
make no provision for the flesh, to fulfill its lusts.
(Romans 13:11-14)

Are you ready to occupy until He returns? As you remain faithful with your assignments to occupy, wait and watch what else should you be doing? Remember the Lord is the same yesterday, today and forever. He does not constantly change the rules of the game. He is consistent throughout the Bible. Only deeply deceived people talk about the inconsistencies of the Bible. Have you ever noticed that when asked they cannot actually articulate any of these so called inconsistencies? Don't get caught up in useless arguments. Take Paul's sound advice given to Timothy.

If anyone teaches differently and does not agree
to the sound precepts of our Lord Yeshua the
Messiah and to the doctrine that is in keeping
with godliness, he is swollen with conceit and
understands nothing. Instead, he has a morbid
desire for controversies and word-battles, out
of which come jealousy, dissension, insults,
evil suspicions, and constant wrangling among
people whose minds no longer function properly
and who have been deprived of the truth, so that
they imagine that religion is a road to riches. (1
Timothy 6:3-5, CJB)

Have you gotten caught up in some of these controversies? If you have, do not despair. You can repent and return to faithful obedience to the Lord. Ask yourself again if you are faithfully and obediently waiting and watching? Remember Yeshua's warning in John 9:4-5 (NIV), "*As long as it is day, we must do the work of him who sent me. Night is coming, when no one can work. While I am in the world, I am the light of the world.*" The day is far spent and the darkness of night is at hand. Now is a good time to ask the Lord what else He would like for you to be doing as you wait. The answer is close at hand. When "*the light of the world*" ascended to heaven, He did not allow the world to go into darkness. He left another kind of light to reveal His truth and plans for this generation. Remember how He said:

> *You are the light of the world. A city that is set on a hill cannot be hidden. Nor do they light a lamp and put it under a basket, but on a lampstand, and it gives light to all who are in the house. Let your light so shine before men, that they may see your good works and glorify your Father in heaven.* (Matthew 5:14-16)

Yeshua's light is now shining through His faithful followers. Are you one of them? Are you ready and willing to be Yeshua's light shining into the darkness of this world so that people will be led to the salvation of the Lord? Do you know what to do as you watch and wait for His return? Now is the time to understand and prepare for His second coming. I believe the Lord has already summed up what He expects of you. He spoke it beautifully through the prophet Micah. What Yeshua and others taught is still in agreement with the earliest prophetic words. Consider this as you embrace the message in this final passage of scripture released in this teaching. Trust the Holy Spirit to guide you and teach you how to occupy until He comes.

> *He has shown you, O man, what is good; and what does the Lord require of you but to do justly, to love mercy, and to walk humbly with your God?* (Micah 6:8)

OTHER BOOKS BY THIS AUTHOR

"A Warrior's Guide to the Seven Spirits of God" - Part 1: Basic Training, by James A. Durham, Copyright © James A Durham, printed by Xulon Press, August 2011.

"A Warrior's Guide to the Seven Spirits of God" - Part 2: Advanced Individual Training, by James A. Durham, Copyright © James A. Durham, printed by Xulon Press, August 2011.

"Beyond the Ancient Door" – Free to Move About the Heavens, by James A. Durham, Copyright © James A. Durham, printed by Xulon Press, April 2012.

"Restoring Foundations for Intercessor Warriors" by James A. Durham, Copyright © James A. Durham, printed by Xulon Press, May 2012.

"Gatekeepers Arise!" by James A. Durham, Copyright © James A. Durham, printed by Xulon Press, February 2013

"Seven Levels of Glory" by James A. Durham, Copyright © James A. Durham, printed by Xulon Press, June 2013

"100 Days in Heaven" by James A. Durham, Copyright © James A. Durham, printed by Xulon Press, August 2013

"Keys to Open Heaven" by James A. Durham, Copyright © James A. Durham, printed by Xulon Press, November 2014

"Appointed Times" – The Signs and Seasons of Yeshua, by James A. Durham, Copyright © James A. Durham, printed by Xulon Press, December 2014

"A Fire Falls" – Moving into Holy Spirit Fire, by James A Durham, Copyright © James A. Durham, printed by Xulon Press, February 2015

"Seeing the Unseen Realm" – Destinies Revealed, by James A. Durham, Copyright © James A. Durham, printed by Xulon Press, December 2016

"7 Hidden Keys" – Unlocking Your Supernatural Mind, by James A. Durham, Copyright © James A. Durham, printed by Xulon Press, May 2017

These Books plus teaching CDs and DVDs
are available online at:
www.highercallingministriesintl.com